Since Stanislavski and Vakhtangov

THE METHOD AS A SYSTEM FOR <u>TODAY'S</u> ACTOR

by LAWRENCE PARKE

*A System of Acting Role Preparation
for Contemporary Theatre, Film and Television Actors
Combining the Many Elements of
THE STANISLAVSKI SYSTEM,
VAKHTANGOV'S IMPORTANT CONTRIBUTIONS
And Later Developments Contributed
by Others Into
A COMPLETE SYSTEMATIC APPROACH
For Actors!*

ACTING WORLD BOOKS
Hollywood

Published by **Acting World Books**
Post Office Box 3044
Hollywood, California 90078

Manufactured in the United States of America

First Printing 1986

Library of Congress Cataloging in Publication Data

Parke, Lawrence, 1922-
    Since Stanislavski and Vakhtangov.

    "A system of acting role preparation for contemporary theatre, film, and television actors combining the many elements of the Stanislavski system, Vakhtangov's important contributions, and later developments contributed by others to a complete systematic approach for actors."

    1. Stanislavski method. 2. Stanislavsky, Konstantin, 1863-1938. 3. Vakhtangov, Evgenii Bogrationovich, 1883-1922. I. Title.
PN2062.P37   1986   792'.028   85-26685

ISBN 0-9615288-8-5 (pbk.)

Acknowledgements

The author wishes to express his deepest gratitude for important contributions to his life work and to this book, first, to the late Miriam Goldina, student of Stanislavski and Vakhtangov, and translator and adaptor of *Stanislavski Directs* and *Stanislavski's Protege: Vakhtangov,* whose inspiration, loving friendship and encouragement fed the fires of my own continuing search; also to those special members of my acting classes whose belief, loyalty and talents enabled me to discover the additional steps, one after another, in the evolving of the System described in this book; to the many dedicated teachers of the Stanislavski System who remained steadfastly committed to the Stanislavski System and to those who have used that System as springboard and framework for continuing research and adaptations of their own while still keeping the original System as their touchstone and inspiration; to those noted acting teachers who so clearly elucidated the differences between the System of Stanislavski and the "medicine show" school of acting called "Method" which, emerging in America in the early 1930's, had laid guilt through association upon the Stanislavski System itself which it was for a time thought to represent; to the *Tulane Drama Review* and

iii

other publications for affording voice to those wishing to call attention to those differences; and, last but far from least, to Konstantin Stanislavski, whose System and writings have been the most important inspiration for intensive study and development of the processes of the actor that the world has ever known; and to the historically less known and less documented Eugene Vakhtangov, who was first Stanislavski's most trusted student, later was the head of the Third Studio of the Moscow Art Theatre, was the one with whom both Stanislavski and Michael Chekhov consulted for coaching in preparing their own roles, and who, until his so early death in 1922, was the one who, in coaching Stanislavski on his roles, inspired developmental contributions of his own toward the final correlation and systematizing of the different approach items of the Stanislavski System.

LAWRENCE PARKE

Contents

Section II
THE DIRECTED SUBTEXT

Section III
THE CREATIVE SUBTEXT

Foreword

The acting art did not begin with Stanislavski. There were actors, and acting art, long before he burst like a flaming rocket over the world of acting, leaving a trail of animated controversy which still, as this book is written, daily and nightly sets actors against actors on a giant battlefield, defending "this method" against "that method", "method" against "non-method", method of the early Stanislavski form against the later Stanislavski System and, more recently, the last published versions of Stanislavski's approaches vs. any further refinements even though they have been based on those approaches by teachers who have gone forward with the research.

Acting is an individual art. It can be an art more surely when the actor knows what he or she is doing. What Stanislavski did— and he laid claim to no more—was to separate a multitude of elements of good acting for individual study so that through making them conscious and thereby turning them into a technique the actor could find a deeper, more secure approach to roles, a clearer understanding of them, a more cohesive preparation of their subtexts, and in the end a more creative form for their final performances—while, along the way, learning to use his or her instrument more fully and effectively.

Stanislavski distinguished himself through the depth of his perception; the dedication of his life to little else but acting; his indefatigable notemaking; the conviction that his search could be meaningful for all actors; his continued use of his discoveries in the daily rehearsals at the Moscow Art Theatre and in the preparation of other productions of his associates and himself elsewhere in the world; and his eventual courting of editors and translators so that his discoveries and theories might be promulgated to the optimum degree to future artists.

There are, and always have been, other teachers perhaps equally dedicated in searching out the elements of good acting, but none has so consistently employed the many activities which Stanislavski included along the way to his immortality, or so painstakingly documented them, so that they might prove helpful to those pursuing the same studies later.

To this day, no other codifier of acting principles is so widely discussed or the subject of so much controversy. The elements which he brought into so brilliant focus made actors tingle with added excitement from the very start. Where those elements may have been half-conscious or intuitive before, they became lucidly conscious and more exciting when planned in depth for their specific results and successfully used through the employing of conscious approaches.

Where individual facets of roles had been overlooked before, they became catalogued and methodically checklisted as the result of his extrapolations. One by one, they were discovered by him and added to the excitements upon which an actor might call when they could be used to bring those "extras", as well as more depth and conviction, to the role. One by one, they became part of the System of Stanislavski or were tested and later discarded as they were displaced by other tools and exercises.

What most American students of acting fail to note is that (1) Stanislavski died in 1938—still modifying his System and still searching; (2) the discoveries he had made *prior to 1920* (when Richard Boleslavsky left Russia and came to America) *and 1924* (when Maria Ouspenskaya and others remained here after a tour)

ix

were what those noted acting coaches taught here in America—the pre-1924 tools, the pre-1924 exercises and analytic approaches, and the *pre-1924* "system" (which was the early form of Stanislavski's "system" but not yet even his "Method of Physical Actions" up to that time)! Also, those members of the Moscow Art Theatre who had studied with and worked under Stanislavski in Moscow, then later remained in the United States and began teaching American actors after their early 1930's tours and appearances here were teaching the *pre-1930's* approaches with some amount of variations of their own, such as Michael Chekhov's innovations and exercises which became his more emphasized manner of teaching after disagreements with Stanislavski and his leaving Russia in 1928.

Most American coaches never worked directly with Stanislavski or with his most loyal and trusted protege, Vakhtangov. Those who immigrated from Russia and later taught here, such as Boleslavsky, Maria Ouspenskaya, Germanova, Vera Soloviova and her husband Andrius Jilinsky, Leo and Barbara Bulgakov and Tamara Daykarhanova, had worked with Stanislavski and other teachers and directors at the Moscow Art Theatre for varying periods only in *the early stages* of his development of a System which progressed in his later years to far beyond what was brought to America in 1920, 1924 and in the early 30's. Those who had worked with not only Stanislavski but also with Vakhtangov, Chekhov and other directors of the Moscow Art Theatre brought to their teachings here certain colors of persuasions and System adaptations instilled in them by those other directors.

When Stella Adler, one of our leading American coaches and one of Boleslavsky's early students here in America, obtained a period of private coaching by Stanislavski in 1934 and returned to America with a graph of the then still changing System approach, including Stanislavski's abandoning of the "affective memory" approach, her news caused a tremendous furor among the then "method" coaches here (mostly at the Group Theatre) with the changes she brought from a still discovering, still searching Stanislavski. The seeds of lasting confusions and controversies were the predictable result.

It's regrettable that Stanislavski, in spite of his voluminous notes on individual experiments and discoveries, did not during his lifetime see in publication, in any of his writings, *a recommended sequence of use, with interrelationships clearly spelled out,* for the many things he handed on to actors for their use. Fortunately, an *approximate* sequence has been made available much more recently from one of his diary notations. It appears on page 253 and following pages of *Creating A Role.*

It should be noted, however, that even that "Plan of Work" does not reflect the increased emphasis he had begun placing on what he called *Inner Objects* and various other similar character motivation sources as the *cause of and stimuli for* all desired action.

The book in your hand as you read this attempts less to explain the processes of the Stanislavski System as they were originally postulated (there are many, many books that are available, both by Stanislavski and by others, which do that excellently) than to describe further developments and proposed adaptations toward modifying and finally sequentializing the use of those processes more productively for the demands of contemporary acting. First and foremost among those proposed adaptations and further contributions must stand those of Eugene Vakhtangov, but there have been many, many others as well.

It has seemed to me for many years that a putting down of *a sequential and interrelated use* of the many excitements available in the system begun by Stanislavski and to some degree adapted and built upon by Vakhtangov and others since is very urgently needed.

Many of the readers of this book will be familiar with many of the aspects to be discussed, whether they call those items by the same names or by different ones as a result of studying with different teachers. Acting tools and exercises are of course subject to the terminology preferences and vocabulary nuances of their teachers. The problem has been that so many tools are taught in *isolated* form; often taken as complete acting system approaches by themselves; and not taught in terms of *how they may be fitted together* into an overall, sequential approach which may be applied to all roles.

Like any other system, the Method comprises many elements and, like any other system, it is impossible for the machinery to function ideally as a whole when a wheel which should function here is placed there or vice versa. The misunderstanding or lack of understanding of how the various approach items can fit together is widespread among actors. They know that they should be able to find a way in which *everything can fit together* so that the separate elements will not be confusing but will instead serve the over-all approach in an exciting manner, just as Stanislavski intended that they should when he called his approach a "System" first and a "Method" later.

There would be no possible justification for yet another book about the *separate* approach items of the Method as they were originally postulated by Stanislavski. Such books fill library shelves already, and some of them are excellent. On the other hand, there is a desperate need, I feel, for a book that directs the actor's attention to one after another of the items with which he may or may not be already acquainted—most of them having their origin in Stanislavski's System even if not their form or manner of use as described herein, and doing so in a sequence and recommending a manner in which most if not all of the parts can be used *in a combined manner* to bring depth and creative subtexts to acting roles.

There have also been those, including Vakhtangov and later others of us, who have felt that the desired actions of characters should be more conditioned, in their early deciding moments, by the inner justifications which Stanislavski, placing "action" first, had to seek so laboriously, later in role preparation, throughout his creative life.

It should be stated here, in the early pages of this book, that, although the Stanislavski System approach items are for the most part included in the System recommended herein, there are changes in some of their manners of functioning and even in their form in some cases. Where this is true the reader will find the justifications for such changes and adaptations clearly set forth.

Perhaps the most evident of the changes will strike some as the most debatable, but the writer has made it, and has taught it with deepest conviction for many years—that of emphasizing the importance of the Object of Attention (or Object of Concentration) over the Actions produced by it. In my earliest research, and increasingly through experimentation, I became convinced that the Actions of a role could more effectively derive from previously analyzed and psychologically motivated Objects of Attention of other than purely physical form. So many notes from the diaries and recorded lectures of Stanislavski, Vakhtangov, I. Rapoport and others seemed to hint at this variation from the "Action first" postulation of Stanislavski, and it seemed the not only more expedient but also more sound order for the actor's preparation. I observed the many, many separate steps which were necessary in the Moscow Art Theatre's postponement of the "justification" step and the seemingly circuitious and self-duplicating explorations which that later work on inner motivation required as a result of its postponement.

Stanislavski, Vakhtangov and others involved at the MAT constantly referred to "objects", only on occasion referring to them as "inner thought objects" rather than physical ones. It would have been a short step to replace those many later explorations made necessary by the postponement discussed here—which Stanislavski called "objects of attention", "objects of concentration", "justifications", "motive power", "inner rhythms", "problems", etc.—with a much earlier concern with, simply, "Objects" of the kind the reader will find punctuating the pages of this book. Vakhtangov was apparently aware of the desirability of this step. His writings do not say so, but I. Rapoport, a documentarian of Vakhtangov's work, has been quoted as saying that the only correct course is (1) justification, (2) attitude to a fiction as though it is real, and (3) finally action. And Vakhtangov himself, in his diary, said "At first, a desire arises that becomes the will," also that the actor "must think first of all about what he wants to obtain". In other diary notes he states that "desire is the motive for action".

I believe that Vakhtangov had discovered that actions which were determined intellectually too early, as a first step, were more subject to miscalculations and shallow experiencing levels than were inner stimuli, justifications and desires emanating from a psychological core. I have become convinced also, from Stanislavski's own writings, that, having adopted and promulgated the label "Method of Physical Actions" and having advocated for so long and so articulately the "action first" precepts, he himself simply felt it important, in his later years, to maintain that postulation to avoid confusing those who had come to believe so totally in that approach, rather than at that late time advocate the first and primary application of the "inner objects" of which he increasingly wrote and lectured.

Aside from the "object" vs. "action" first step advocated in this book, the reader will note an adaptation of the "Vague Super Objective" and the "Through Line Of Action" functions, designating the former as the clear and urgently desired action of *the entire life* and the latter as the clear and urgently desired action in the different *major units* of the role.

As to the "Vague Super Objective" and "Super Objective", the form in which this book recommends this basic System step is strictly as an urgently desired *action* willed as a result of a life problem (as Stanislavski recommended it on occasion), rather than as a desired goal (as he recommended it on other occasions). All the other "objectives" recommended by him were in action form—physical, psychological and creative, all of them, so to finally determine that it should be of similar form has represented no major presumption. The ever present need of the actor to take the desired action, and the impossibility of its being successful at any point during the character's life, makes it even more affecting in an experience very similar to its alternate "desired goal" manner of use.

Stanislavski called the Super Objective "one of the most important tools" for the bringing of the inner essence and motive forces of the character. In its strictly action-worded form, in combination with the "Life Object" recommended in this book, it is still precisely that.

Also, I advocate herein the use of "Objects", rather than the actions they cause, as the means of bringing more focus and dimension, as well as the need for action, to separate *beats* of roles. This, too, may appear controversial to some readers. I shall try to justify this option in the section devoted to the Creative Subtext.

The foregoing represent the major adaptations which I recommend for exploration by those who currently use the Stanislavski System in other manners. If the actor can benefit from a new understanding of how the parts of the Stanislavski System, or this derivative system's parts, can be used in a combined and sequentialized manner for the preparing of roles, this sharing will have served the end toward which the author is addressing himself in this book.

Another reason for my being moved to write this book had its origin in the early 1960's. Until that time I had of course known of, and to an extent known about Eugene Vakhtangov. But, like most American actors and teachers, when I spoke of the Stanislavski System the name of Vakhtangov only faintly if at all crossed my mind and usually was not mentioned. But in 1962 this was to change.

My closest friend, Miriam Goldina, who studied with both Stanislavski and Vakhtangov and later translated and adapted for American publication both *Stanislavsky Directs* by Nicholai Gorchakov and *Stanislavsky's Protege: Eugene Vakhtangov* by Ruben Simonov, became intrigued with my manner of furthering the use of what Stanislavski called "objects of attention" and I had come to call simply "objects"; encouraged me to teach my classes at her small Hollywood studio on Cassil Place (where Michael Chekhov had taught previously); observed my teaching regularly and observed my direction of a number of productions; finally worked under my direction in Ibsen's *"Rosmersholm"* there.

In that early period her constant comment that she considered me to be the reincarnation of the spirit of Vakhtangov—the man whom she so greatly admired—was merely taken as a compliment and an expression of her respect for my own developing approaches. It was considerably later, after this comment was repeated to another person and reported to me, that I learned in conversations with her that she did indeed firmly believe in what is commonly called reincarnation and that she did truly believe that I had inherited the spirit of that brilliant man who had died just a few days before my birth.

Mostly out of curiosity as to why she believed what she assertedly did, I began searching out all the printed references I could find regarding Vakhtangov and listening even more closely as she constantly spoke of him with deepest respect alongside Stanislavski. Increasingly, I came to believe as she did that, as Stanislavski himself reportedly said, Vakhtangov did understand most clearly how the separate Stanislavski System preparation items could be formed into one sequence of use—as they were in his private coaching of Stanislavski's own role preparations as well as in his own teachings at the Moscow Art Theatre and elsewhere.

Like many others, I'm sure, I had read in several books but hardly noticed the comment by Stanislavski, "You, Eugene, teach my Method better than I."

My many years of research in later years have convinced me that my dear friend Miriam was at least correct with respect to Vakhtangov's importance, and that one of the saddest things in the evolving of the Stanislavski System was and still is the fact that Vakhtangov's so valuable life and his contributions to the acting art through that System were to be ended so early and that he had not, prior to his death, been as published or as publicly recognized as Stanislavski and Michael Chekhov.

Undoubtedly it was first my dear friend Miriam's firm conviction that fed the flames of my dedication to a continuing search for an increasingly clear combining of the Stanislavski System's many parts. Perhaps it would simply have happened at some point without my recognizing its becoming such an obsession in my life. Which is more true, I shall never know. What I do know, deep in my heart, is that whenever the Stanislavski System is spoken of or written of it might with equal appropriateness be called "The Stanislavski/Vakhtangov System", finally and so belatedly acknowledging the immense contributions of Vakhtangov in the evolving of the form in which it was eventually passed on by Stanislavski.

Throughout this book are so many references to "The Stanislavski System"—because that's what it's always, even by Vakhtangov, been called. However, I hope that as you read that label you'll add, even if only in passing thought, the name of Eugene Vakhtangov, in whose memory—I think as much as in memory of Stanislavski—this book has been written.

LAWRENCE PARKE

Chapter One

A History of Confusions and Contradictions

I assume that, reading this book, you are an actor or actress or intent upon becoming one. If you're serious enough to read this book, then I can assume that you're also serious enough to have read a lot of other books on acting as well. After you've read them all; remembered the multitudes of theories they contain; become familiar enough with the terminologies (they're all different!) to understand them, correlate interpretations and misinterpretations and follow the progress through adaptations and diminutions or exclusions of some points...if you're a genius to begin with, you'll come out with a method. However, it will probably be your own, not Stanislavski's or anyone's else. Stanislavski, for one, would have approved. He should, because he knew he hadn't finalized the system which he felt was his crowning achievement until he was 73 years old—and he died at 75, two years later, still working on his system!

As to his books: It was during the early years following his evolving of the major portions of his System and its official adoption by the Moscow Art Theatre, eventually coming to be called the *Method of Physical Action* in 1927—the system which was to revolutionize all his previous work—that he had written

1

the notes which appear in *An Actor Prepares*—published in the United States in 1936—documenting chiefly those earliest interesting but wandering experiments which reflected only some of the System so swiftly evolving when this very first book reached bookstores here in America many years later. That book could now be called "first year class work", as it literally was when he made so many of the notes it contains. That first book was simply where things stood during those early years of his Moscow Art Theatre work.

Then his notes resulted in the second book to reach America, *Building A Character*, which at least detailed *a partial system* for approaching and preparing roles, but its edited notes were from the period when he was spending six to eight months preparing a single production, and he himself found later that the approaches in that book would not be simple or rapid enough for the standard commercial theatre preparation period. That book was finally published and distributed in America in 1949—nearly thirty years after much of his actual System had been formed! Like his earlier *An Actor Prepares*, this second book, *Building A Character*, was already close to thirty years behind time insofar as reflecting his own progress! It had been Stanislavski's plan to combine the internal truth-seeking and the subsequent external characterization work in one large book, but this was not to be.

Moreover, it wasn't until 1961 that Elizabeth Reynolds Hapgood, his American translator and editor, working from notes he furnished her just a short time before his death, finally—after years of collating so many of his later notes (and without his consultation because he had died twenty-three years prior to that)—got *Creating A Role*, the third book of the trilogy, onto American bookstands! In other words, *twenty-three years after his death* what is so broadly thought to be his "final system" (which he himself felt wasn't really final at all and which he was still modifying in 1937 and 1938) reached American actors!

No wonder the confusions and contradictory interpretations. What was already history and already changed by Stanislavski himself was always being "caught up with" some twenty to twenty-three years behind time!

Also, under the very roof of the theatre he founded and headed

2

there were other teachers who had been taught by him who had begun teaching and had themselves begun modifying and adapting his teachings with their own innovations and concepts, while still accepted by their students as teaching "the system of Stanislavski".

The director-teacher most often referred to as his real heir, Eugene Vakhtangov, was perhaps the most faithful to his master's teachings in his own presentation of and use of the system. It was to Vakhtangov that Stanislavski and Michael Chekhov regularly turned for coaching on their own roles. Vakhtangov it was who, in those private coaching sessions, is said to have attempted to persuade Stanislavski to recognize the importance of establishing the *needs*, *stimuli* and *causes* behind physical actions in seeking the actions themselves. (It is said by some that Stanislavski, while recognizing at once the value of this alternate approach, had so postulated the "physical action" theory by that time that he felt he should not change. However, his own bringing what he came to refer to as "Inner Objects" into more and more prominence, over later years, is reflected in the ongoing record of his work and writings.)

The actor-teacher Stanislavski had once called the one who most epitomized the results of his teaching, Michael Chekhov, was also already teaching his own innovative approach, attributing it in the main to Stanislavski and certainly at least identifying it with Stanislavski in spite of its vast differences.

Vsevolod Meyerhold, recognized as a leading pupil of Stanislavski, had broken away even earlier and founded his own acting and production style which, involving what at the time was called "the grotesque", was closer to Bertolt Brecht's "Living Newspaper" teachings than to Stanislavski's.

Stanislavski himself began with studying the great actors of his day; then migrated to Freudian precepts which were new and strikingly revolutionary at the time; then, much later, became interested in the Pavlovian theory of "conditioned response"—and the possible earlier involving of the motivating personality forces—which modification he hadn't yet made to his appproach at the time of his death. His *Method of Physical Actions* was of course quite a distance along the way, involving his "psycho-physical" concept that action eventually and logically involved

3

feelings and emotions. That concept was simply missing the important preparation item which had been earlier pointed out by Vakhtangov as being needed and which was to be further suggested by the publications of Pavlov's "conditioned response" findings. In the end it was perhaps Pavlov's exhaustive examinations of personality and response which persuaded Stanislavski to observe that more consistent and more meaningful result *could* be obtained by an actor if conditioned by a stimulus of a more tangible form, incorporated early among other given circumstances, than could be produced by a simple action.

It can be observed from his writings and notes to his actors that during the later years of his life Stanislavski was constantly seeking manners in which actors could create their own "stimuli" and apply them to their own responses to bring deeper and more truly emotional experiences than actions alone could evoke. He continued to call them "rhythms", "motive forces" and other identifying labels, but more and more often referred to them simply as "objects". He never felt he had quite completed this task of ideally incorporating Vakhtangov's ideas or Pavlov's theories into his System, but he was well on the way and had laid the ground for an important new development in the perception of how much more depth experiencing could be produced by a *thought Object* (really just an adaptation of his previously written of *Object of Concentration* turned into a new, feeling-worded form).

Returning to the confusion which spread to and throughout America about his System:

Several of Stanislavski's own pupils emigrated from Russia to America in the 1920's and early 1930's. Boleslavsky (who wrote *Acting—The First Six Lessons*) was a member of the Moscow Art Theatre from 1906 to 1920. He had not taught there, however, prior to leaving Russia for political reasons and coming to the United States. Although he had directed the first production of the First Studio of the MAT, Boleslavsky did not work with Stanislavski after 1920—a time when Vakhtangov's influence on Stanislavski was occasioning much reexamination of the System. When Boleslavsky's own book was published here much later, it gave a pocketful of desired results inspired by his work with

4

Stanislavski but no "how to do it" information at all.... and little or no specific insight into the Stanislavski System.

Maria Ouspenskaya, after three years of private training with Sulerzhitsky, one of Stanislavski's trusted associates, joined the MAT in 1911 and went through those same earliest explorations. When she toured America in 1923-24 with the MAT she decided to remain here when the tour ended and joined Boleslavsky and Germanova to teach at the American Lab Theatre, later establishing her own studio in New York for some years and in 1936, summoned to Hollywood for a role, relocated her teaching there. There followed many years in which the early Russian teachers continued to teach in the same manner while Stanislavski and his system went forward with continuing developments about which they are reported to have been unaware. It has been a fairly accepted fact among historians that these two teachers apparently fossilized the early experiments and explorations into being thought of in America as the final Stanislavski System itself, while 1924 to 1938 represent some fourteen years of continuous, fanatic developments in Stanislavski's own work which these two teachers failed to incorporate in their "Stanislavski System" teachings.

Others who remained in America after touring here included Michael Chekhov, Tamara Daykarhanova, Vera Soloviova and her husband Andrius Jilinsky, Leo and Barbara Bulgakov and the previously mentioned Germanova. They established their own classes and taught the Stanislavski System as they had learned it, either from Stanislavski or from one of his trusted associates in the main.

When three of their students did later visit Stanislavski and observed his developments they brought back those advances which they felt to be highly desirable, but they could not reverse the tide of supposedly authoritative teaching approaches of the American Actors Lab and the others who had migrated from Russia who, as they added adaptations and modifications of their own devising, widened the gap between the original source material and the many offshoot techniques existing today which claim the Stanislavski System as their source or in some cases their totalities.

Lee Strasberg, who was a student at the American Lab briefly (1924-1925), also began teaching in New York, first downtown and later at the Group Theatre, employing his own understanding of the early Stanislavski approaches which he had learned at the Lab. It is common knowledge that in later years his teaching approaches veered farther and farther away from Stanislavski—and from Vakhtangov, to whom he often referred—into exercises and approaches of his own devising for more specifically conditioning the instrument of the actor, rather than the teaching of the Stanislavski System for which he received so much publicity and recognition during his lifetime.

When Stella Adler returned from her visit with Stanislavski in 1934 and told Mr. Strasberg and others at the Group Theatre (which was at the time considered the "Mecca" of "the Method") that Stanislavski had abandoned his extensive work theretofore with *emotional memory* (later to be called *affective memory* and *emotional recall* by some), Mr. Strasberg is reported to have said "I never will!" And he didn't. Others, following Stanislavski's lead, did not involve affective memory in their work, at least as a tool, and criticized its use for that purpose. This is of course only one example of the many controversies aroused and perpetuated in America about the method and the Stanislavski System from whence came its label. Out of the Group Theatre experience where the then current understanding of the Method was used went Mr. Strasberg, Miss Adler, Robert Lewis, Sanford Meisner, Harold Clurman and several others, all teaching their own individual understanding of the approaches and their own adaptations of them—all with equal fiery conviction that their way was right.

A more recent attempt to teach "the Method" side by side started in 1947, when Robert Lewis, Elia Kazan and Cheryl Crawford founded the Actors Studio in New York. Mr. Lewis, after teaching there for a time, left following a reported disagreement with Mr. Kazan. At that point Mr. Strasberg was brought in as teaching head, with his own approaches—some say as a last resort long resisted by Kazan, who disagreed with much of Mr. Strasberg's teaching concepts—and the passing of some time proved that they too were so far apart in approach concepts that the bridge to working together could apparently not be crossed. Mr. Kazan's association with the Studio became less and less over a period and Mr. Strasberg's name became synonymous with the Studio and any mention of it.

6

With acceptance at the Studio and lifetime membership in it being available free of any charge to many already well trained and some very gifted actors, as well as some already well established professionals, and the Studio's growth and prestige fostered impressively by the fact of such established professionals and others working together under its aegis, it is easy to understand why it continued to attract so many theatre and film luminaries and thereby continue to build the reputation of Mr. Strasberg, its head, as the almost exclusive interpreter and teacher of "the Method" in the public's eye. He didn't proclaim it publicly; it was simply assumed by many actors and other professionals and, eventually, by the public at large. The truth is, of course, that not only he but most other teachers—those mentioned previously and a score of others—continued to drift farther and farther away into their own systems, their own approaches and their own terminologies. That drift continues to this day, with the people taught by those early teachers and, later, the people they taught, as they too turned to teaching, still drifting ever outward along separate networks and tributaries of widening differences. In many cases they claim to teach "the Method". Most are certainly of "method" persuasion, but most are different. It's been so very confusing to actors for so very long!

In the end, however, there is that important central "spine" to all those networks at least. With so many branches and offshoot fronds on the "tree" it's fortunate that the "trunk" has been so strong. The reference point begins with Stanislavski and Vakhtangov still, but it ends at just plain good acting principles and no one will be that far off as long as he or she keeps that touchstone at the beginning and that goal at the end.

After all, what is a "method actor?" Any actor or actress whose work is respectable in all probability has some approach and continues to look for a bettering of it. It is perfectly logical that, because of different acting study backgrounds and their subsequent adapting of what has been learned both in classes and in professional experience, most other actors will be found to be using altogether different techniques, adaptations and preparation terminologies from our own. Stanislavski and Vakhtangov would have approved!

7

However, returning to Stanislavski: During his own lifetime he himself passed through several stages of development. First came the early *truth-seeking explorations* (with as yet no finally articulated means for creating the truth itself); then came his early codifications of role analysis and approach items, which led to the System which was officially adopted by the Muscow Art Theatre in 1911 and in 1927 became known as the *Method of Physical Action*; and, finally, there were those later years of intensified exploration toward some means of incorporating the use of *Objects* (about which he had written earlier, calling the earlier versions *Objects of Attention* and *Objects of Concentration* and other things on different occasions). The last years of his life were more involved with psychologically conditioned "inner objects", "thought-feeling objects", and searching for the forms which would enhance their use, than is easily detected in the available public records. But this aspect of his continuing search is certainly there if you seek it—in *Building A Character*, in *Collected Works, Vol. II*, in *My Life In Art*, in *Stanislavski's Legacy* and elsewhere.

If one closely examines the Chart of The Stanislavski System which he handed to Stella Adler in that 1934 consulting visit she had with him, it should be noted that, while still calling "Action" Item 1 of his entire system, Steps 8, 9 and 10 of the chart, labeled "Mind, Will and Feeling" (in that order!), by that time he had obviously come to accept Vakhtangov's postulation that what lay in the mind of the character should ideally be considered before the action provoked by it!

Many teachers have apparently not researched more deeply those later years of modification of the System by Stanislavski himself or discerned the direction of Vakhtangov's conceptual thinking, and have failed to find in their own independent teachings the area of which Stanislavski himself had always been aware but hadn't codified sufficiently as to the best manners of integrating it in his notemaking and the resulting printed versions of his work—the importance of *an underlying, defined stimulus which causes, particularizes and intensifies* the multiple actions, moods, feelings, emotions and responses which result from this so much richer source than could possibly result from the Action itself, alone.

8

Of course "action" does remain a central and integral part of the system. It is primarily when actors fail to understand that action ensues, or is intensely desired, when there is a need, an aversion, a "light at the end of the tunnel" goal or something else which *creates the need to take* action. Stanislavski came to recognize this and, upon doing so, could have relegated the "action" more to the *Through Line of Action* for use in the longer periods and larger divisions of roles. In the application of actions to the separate short "beats" of roles the results in too many cases accentuated almost exclusively *outgoing* action and left other aspects of the character's (and the actor's) experience to some degree unfulfilled and needing to be searched out in endless improvisation and other time-consuming activities and discussions. Stanislavski often asked "What is it that disturbs you?," "What is in your mind?" and "What are you thinking about?"—questions obviously not soliciting "action" responses. They can quite clearly be seen as inviting his actors to consciously define what this book and some coaches—these many years after Vakhtangov's and Stanislavski's original concepts of them—call "Objects".

Action without its stimulus can be a shallow-feeling experience. Many actors have found this out after they have failed to find this one item—what is now called "the Object"—sufficiently developed in any thus far published version of the Stanislavski System as a motivating tool to attract, hold and excite their attention, their imagination and, yes, definitely, their will to take action. Too often the impression was received that "objects" referred to simply physical things rather than being *inner, thought-feeling, worded* objects. The latter understanding is more easily drawn from excerpts from Stanislavski's own recorded directions to the cast members of the opera "*Werther*", in which he admonished his cast to create visual images of their characters' inner lives, explaining that such *Objects of Attention* demand much more stability than external ones. In his own words, in those recordings, he stated that if the attention of the actor is constantly moving from one *Object* to another, then the constant changing of the *Objects* of his attention creates the unbroken line of the character's experience!

9

I believe this argument between "Action" as the main "involve-ment" tool and "the Object" replacing it as the focus of concen-tration in separate beats and their moments as well as being planned and used in the preparation process to act as the *cause for and conditioner of* the action is one of the main differences between teachers' basic beliefs within the large, many-roomed house called "the Stanislavski System". I believe the majority of those teaching the System or derivative systems recommend the "action" as the means and the end in the actor's involvement, while many others of us (myself included) believe, as Stanislavski's last years seem to have finally concluded long ago, that the closest approximation to the Pavlovian theory of "conditioned response" that an actor can experience through preparation approach can best be achieved through the use of "the Object", whether one chooses to call it that or call it by one of the several labels used on different occasions by Stanislavski. In our estimation, there is just no comparison!

Sprinkled throughout this book you'll find examples of *Objects* aplenty. You'll find them recommended to focus the *life* concern of characters toward the planning of *Super Objectives*; they appear as the first choice for larger *units* of roles toward planning of the units' *Through Lines of Action*; and they are extensively dealt with and recommended as the "tool" for use by the actor in each *Beat* of the role. Having never observed this wonderful tool to be described in sufficient detail in any of the other books dealing with the Stanislavski System and its more recent developments, I feel the emphasis placed on *Objects* in this book to be one of the main contributions which can be made by this work.

Of course it is impossible to just read a book, be exposed to a number of new ideas (a number of which may even be in direct contradiction to what you have known before), and instantly be able to assimilate the entirety of something so complex and multi-faceted as *any* system through reading about it, no matter how clearly it may be put into words. However, I'll be attempting to help each reader understand *how the many parts can function* and how to *put the pieces together* into a very effective approach for the preparation of most if not indeed all roles.

For those oriented toward graphic presentation, on page 13

there is a Chart advocating a sequence of use and interrelationship of all the tools. Despite the obvious adaptations which are described herein, much of that chart is based on Stanislavski's system itself. What method isn't? To varying degrees, most work in acting classes is also, unless the teacher is violently opposed to the use of *any* method.

You'll note that my chart says "As of 1985" In all probability it will develop further, but this is the moment of bravery in putting it down for a book and handing it out for scrutiny, with the inevitable possibility that some things have been overlooked, and with the foreknowledge that ten years from now it too will have been subject to additions and subtractions as all other systems are and have been, including Stanislavski's.

The chart is divided into four major parts— *The Analytic Subtext, The Directed Subtext, The Creative Subtext* and *The Rehearsal Period.* This manner of titling the several basic steps involved in preparation of a role seems the best way to point out the different things you can do along the way while still keeping a logical sequence through which all parts can be fitted together productively.

The first part of the Chart just ahead, *The Analytic Subtext,* is the phase of role preparation which is most clearly discussed in so much of Stanislavski's published writing, however I believe that some of the preliminary study which must be done prior to finally defining this part of the subtext—the initial choices of *personality type* and manners of relating the character to the events put down by the writer—has remained somewhat random and unsequentialized in those works. I have been told by one former student of Stanislavski that his own manner of teaching this phase of preparation was much more clear than is reflected in the books. One must remember that Mrs. Hapgood, the editor and translator to whom he passed on his notes, was not a student of his at any time and may have simply not been able to clearly establish from his notes exactly how all the pieces might be fitted together. Certainly a productive sequence of preparing *The Analytic Subtext* has to be the first step in attempting to better clarify this phase. That's why it's included here.

It's an old adage that "Everything begins with the word!" An actor certainly can't ignore the facts, the nuances, the characterization signpoints, the subtleties or the "given circumstances" supplied by the writer. The serious actor who wants to serve the writer's work and bring additional insight and any brilliance to the ultimate performance must base all subsequent preparation on what is gleaned from an in-depth, clear and appropriate preparation analysis ahead of time. All the rest of the role preparation depends upon this first step and how thoroughly it's attended to.

Again, how to read the role many times to discover facts, how to appraise and particularize them in terms of early impressions of personality type, etc., have been lengthily described in Stanislavski's and others' works, but I feel what contribution this book should make is in terms of establishing *a sequence for the taking of the steps* which can lead more definitively to the choices which can best serve the writer's work and produce the many extras which can be brought by the actor. Whether you choose to experiment with such sequence and attempt to find out whether it can be effective for you or not, you'll at least find *a* sequence in these pages that works excellently and is uniquely adapted for the use of actors in this later day's professional mediums, whether in four or five week professional theatre production preparations, or the hopscotch mosaic of the shooting schedules of motion pictures or the always hurried, logistics conscious television works.

If after considering the systematized approach herein you feel you already have a better one, of course use it.

So.... to discussion of Section I!

THE LAWRENCE PARK SYSTEM - AS OF 1985

1. Readings of the Role

2. Listing the Facts

3. Appraising the Facts

4. The Six Questions

THE ANALYTIC SUBTEXT

5. Life Object

6. Vague Super Objective

THE DIRECTED SUBTEXT

7. Neurosis-Provoking Moment (Optional) and
8. The Super Objective It Produces, If Used

9. Consider Use of Character Image, Motive Center
or Imaginary Surroundings Characters for External Colors

10. Units Breakdown

11. Plan Unit Object and Through Line of Action for Each Unit

12. Consider Use of Obstacle in One or More Units

13. Individual Beats Breakdown

14. Plan Beat Object for Each Beat

THE CREATIVE SUBTEXT

15. If Desired, Plan Creative Psychological Objective
or Other Creative Tool for Separate Beats Suggesting Them

16. Improvisations—Using Planned Characterization Tools

17. Line Study—One Beat at a Time, Using Tools' Subtext
to Form Body Participation Habits and Involvement Specifics

18. Throwing Away the Tools; Experiencing the Character's
Moments in their True and Real Form as They Are Conditioned by
the Preparation Tools Which Will Still Be Working Without Any
Concentration Upon Them. Certain Creative Tools May Be Still
Used Consciously for Creative Result in any Moments
Where Desired.

13

Section I

The Analytic Subtext

'Highway signposts are dull and uninteresting to many a traveler, but beside them lie the wreckages and lost dreams of those who failed to observe them. It is the eager tourist who stops a moment at each one and simply looks around a bit who discovers the majestic mountains, the sparkling streams and all the wonders of the universe."

—**Lawrence Parke**

Chapter Two

First Impressions— How to Make Use of Them

While the written word of the author conveys meanings and arouses the imagination of the reader, it is only a part of what the actor must seek to later convey to the spectator. As the actor reads a role initially, he is denied—except through his creative imagination—the opportunity of watching a living human being going through moment after moment of a meaningful situation, surrounded by living conflicts, tangibly present obstacles in the way of goals, the staccato surprises of sudden door slams and sudden shouted words which take place when the written word is eventually brought to life. The audience's first impression— which comes after the actor has done his work—is a fuller one. But even in the printed black and white words there are impressions, images, revelations, uncoverings of new facts and stimuli to emotional reactions in the actor during the first reading of the role.

When an actor first reads the role such impressions are available and merely to be actively sought out page after page. The actor should bear in mind always that the same impressions and responses presented by the cold print before him must later be conveyed to the audience in an even more vivid form. With a little practice it is possible to note each significant moment in passing, even in the first reading. But so many of those moments can be passed by unnoticed if the actor doesn't remain alert for the bits and pieces of cumulative information and facts provided by the author.

Reading can be either a dull or an exciting experience. In the observation of the author, a dedicated actor, keenly tuned to the observing of *parallel behavior patterns* and the twistings and turnings of interpersonal relationships and their conflicts, can find great pleasure in exercising intelligent insight and a lot of attention to each fact and action of each character's experience in a script as they are divulged one after another by the writer. The amount of pleasure and zeal with which analytic powers are employed in first readings usually parallels the amount of depth of the final analysis of the character and the depth of the later performance of it.

Parallel behavior patterns cannot be too strongly stressed for their importance. They are without equal in the defining of the emotional core and personality type of the character. They are sure signposts to its inner goals, its manner of experiencing different circumstances and events, its positive or negative mindset and its focal concentrations as they differ from how others would experience similar things and their true motive actions as they pursue their ends. Those same parallel behavior patterns are indeed the "golden keys to the inner life of the character", and the actor is limited only by the sensibility of his own mind as to the depth with which such behavior patterns can be initially perceived, then successfully analyzed for their significances, then incorporated into the creating of the appropriate personality type for the role. Stanislavski realized that some actors' perceptions and powers to analyze may be less developed than others'. Coaches in the process of teaching actors observe the same thing, as do directors in the later preparation of their actors' performances. However, even those actors who are less able to stimulate their subconscious selves and draw them into their creative processes to help them reduce the study of inner lives for their characters to any scientific technique should at least try their best to go as far with it as they can.

18

Of course you will read the play or film role many times; not just once or twice and feel that its totality is sufficiently understood. The very first reading will usually arouse many feelings and emotional responses in the reader (you, the actor). That they seem to diminish and have less impact in subsequent readings is inevitable, since those subsequent readings are for the purpose of gaining keener insight and familiarity with the material. There is more thought and study demanded—more "work" —in place of the initial "audience" reactions.

In those later readings certain behavior patterns are observed to recur more frequently than have initially been perceived. Relationships with other characters become more clear. The reasons for this or that scene being included by the author at all become more apparent. The imagination of the reader can be kindled further and further into the sensory surroundings with each trip through them.

Psychologists, analysts and psychotherapists go over the same ground time and time again in attempting to study their patients. Actors should do no less with their characters. Except in the case of small or hurriedly prepared film roles, there is normally time for this analytic process, and it is neglectful of the actor to dismiss it as "tiresome work" which he has no inclination to do, hoping the director will later supply all the illumination needed.

First impressions can be allowed to remain shallow and one-dimensional or can lead to more intensive examination and result in a performance of greater insight and far greater depth. The dedication with which the actor examines and analyzes the behavior patterns of the character will most often be *the scale on which the entire preparation and performance of the actor will later be weighed!*

The problem for the lazy actor, unwilling to do this important preliminary work, is that those first impressions which have been allowed to remain shallowly perceived and less deeply studied usually suggest only one overall experience of a quite general nature. Such an actor forms the habit of surface performing of characters and is prone to allow his characters to wander through the situations of roles without the distinctive guidelines and experiencing parameters of conditioned personalities.

19

For example, suppose a script contains this situation in which several characters appear: Two small boys are trapped in an old mine shaft. There has been a cave-in. Now two volunteers dig frantically to extricate them, while two mothers wait in different states of agitation at the mine entrance as television news cameras try to capture all the details. Without reference to the personality types of the participants it might in first impressions be concluded that both small boys are frightened; that the men digging to rescue them are frantic; and that the two mothers are desperate and in states of anguish for their two sons.

On the other hand, it might be true that one boy is trapped and, yes, frightened because of his personality type while the other boy, with a different personality, may be simply excited at the dangerous adventure and may be feeling no fear at all. Waiting outside the shaft entrance while the workers dig to free their sons, one mother might indeed be wringing her hands in desperate fear for her son's safety as it appears, but the other may be pacing out of fury at her son for disobeying her order to stay away from the old mine. Because of her unique personality, she feels perhaps no fear at all, or little at best and only to the extent that her domineering personality can experience those feelings.

The digging volunteers, too, might be perceiving the event with very different viewpoints from what first impressions could provide. One might be digging feverishly because the television camera is directly behind his back and he's excited by the drama and his own personal moment in the spotlight (because he seldom has any) while the other may be digging so feverishly and taking out his wrath on his shovel because he came to work at the used car lot next to the mine entrance that day at all, thereby becoming involved unexpectedly in this backbreaking work instead of begging off sick as he had planned in order to go to the ball game.

The surface fact of the mine cave-in and two trapped boys being rescued is what the television audience will see on the evening news, and the flash-on, flash-off story will satisfy the viewers' craving for drama. They have not paid admission to view a meaningful drama involving characters about which they care

20

because of skillfully written earlier scenes in which they've become acquainted with those characters.

But wait. There are still more possibilities, if the actor looks more closely and exercises some analytical powers. The boy who does actually feel trapped and frightened may not feel any mine-shaft danger at all but instead may know that becoming trapped there will gain him a beating for disobeying his mother, and that's why he appears so frightened. The other trapped boy, recognizing the adventure more than the danger, may be enjoying the knowledge that he's finally afforded an opportunity to gain the attention of a lot of people—the attention which he's always been denied in his own home.

Further, if other scenes of the diggers are closely scrutinized by the actors preparing to play them it may be found that the digger enjoying his moment in the limelight may have deep-seated identity problems that reach far beyond this one gratifying moment of recognition and will need to dig even more feverishly because of the recognition he'll achieve if he's the one who in the end finally accomplishes the rescue. The other digger, taking out his wrath on his shovel as he digs, may actually be venting his wrath on his own usual clumsiness and misfortune for being in the vicinity when the cave-in rumble was heard, for volunteering rather than standing back and watching, for missing the ballgame, etc. If the actor has observed the parallel behavior patterns and apparent mindset of the character closely enough in previous scenes he may recognize that this digger should be focused more on his eternal clumsiness and stupidity than on the desperate situation.

And, as to the two mothers, insight into clues presented earlier by the writer could perhaps indicate that the first mother, apparently frightened for her son's safety, is actually frightened that if anything happens to him her husband will beat her in a drunken rage again because she has again, and characteristically, displayed her usual inadequacy as a human being, while the second mother may have previously been divulged by the writer to be a personality who always feels used and abused and therefore should be focused on the fact that she let herself be talked into having this unwanted son in the first place!

21

What should be perceived from the foregoing is the multitude of truths which may always lie awaiting the actor's recognition at different depths behind the mere surface impressions about characters, their personalities and the manners in which situations may be other than what they appear at first glance.

Lajos Egri, author of the popular book for playwrights, *The Art Of Dramatic Writing*, provided the answer: "It is the dramatic character who creates the dramatic situation; not the other way around." Each of the two boys in the above situation, each of the two mothers and each of the diggers is doing precisely what Mr. Egri proposes!

Now, let's sneak quietly into the back row of one of the many small theatre production rehearsals conducted nightly in any major theatrical community. We have come in just as the scene described in the foregoing paragraphs is being rehearsed. There are the two mothers attempting to cry, wringing their hands in anguish as they wait in the manner accepted for all mothers in such situations. There are the two diggers, digging feverishly and huffing and puffing from the represented effort and urgency of saving the two trapped boys' lives. And there are the two boys, hugging each other close, wideeyed in manifested fear, completing the perfect surface tableau just as the television news would stage its reporting.

Suddenly the two digging men let out a joyous shout and a moment later two gasping boys stumble across the stage past the collapsing diggers into the arms of their hysterically relieved mothers. There is a moment of a perfect tabueau much like the tableaux at the end of Victorian melodramas of the early 1900's. Then the stage lights are faded and the house lights come up on the watching director, stage manager and a nail-biting producer who knows something is wrong as well as all the others know it. We note the skeptical frowns on the faces of the three as the stage lights are brought up again and the two actresses and four actors take seats in the bright light looking out toward the throat-clearing director, awaiting notes on their performances.

The director and stage manager leave their seats and climb to the stage. The director takes out his notes. One after another the cast members are given surface admonitions and new suggestions with regard to better realizing the drama of the event. Little or nothing is said about any character's own inner experience. Most of the discussion in each case is about the actors' inadequate involvement with the event itself.

The two mothers are distraught—quite believably now—because they know they were only *indicating* emotions. The two diggers are criticized by the director for *playing results* and *representing*. Both are shamefaced because they are both aware that at least in that respect the director is right. They receive from the director a brief mumbo-jumbo about *playing the situation* with more conviction and disciplining their concentration more effectively. The two younger boys, now appearing older and disillusioned with their profession, are given one of the recipes for the re-evoking of an appropriate childhood memory, which recipe probably appeared in a 1930's or 1940's book on acting.

At the end of the critique all six slink morosely toward the restrooms wondering whether wrist-slashing may be more painful than cyanide-swallowing later that night when they get home to suffer their latest failure to achieve a truthful acting experience.

Perhaps these six actors will never come to realize that they have all failed—at least in this one example case—to simply look more deeply past the many facts of the author into the behavior patterns and there find *the core personalities* which could bring specific and unique experiences of far more truthful kinds for all the moments they failed to experience with any true feeling. They failed because there is no such thing as an "anguished mother", a "desperate digger" or a "trapped boy" without the inner core of a personality which determines that individual's partiular kind of anguish, desperation or trapped feelings and its particular cause at a particular point in time. Actors who trust surface impressions and leap headlong into the studying of the dialogue of their roles before searching more deeply for the true characters involved are destined for failure.

Such failures result most often from acting study backgrounds involving almost no attention to *character analysis and emotional personality construction* and too much repeated practice in simple "situation-playing". In some acting class environments the class members are simply given situations or asked to plan them, then are encouraged to concentrate on the situation itself and any other actors involved with them. In such classes the words "action", "intention" or "problem" are stressed heavily. If this aspect is being stressed in an individual's development to *cure a work habit problem* or to *free an instrument*, well and good. If not, many of us agree that it may develop a surface manner of perceiving and playing roles. Of course a certain amount of attitude becomes involved in the deciding and use of an action or intention, but the truth of such experiencing is elusive and ephemeral at best if there has been no personality constructed to enrich the total experience.

THE POWER OF PERSONALITY

Before progressing to the next step on the Chart—*Listing The Facts; Appraising Them*, I want to express my own deep biases about the most desirable end result of the entire *Analytic Subtext* preparation. These biases are of course amply documented in upcoming chapters, but it may help your understanding of why, with the next step of listing the facts and appraising them stressing some facts more than others, the *negative* aspects are considered more important by me.

Behavior patterns of parallel and fairly consistent types have in the preceding chapter been called by me "the golden keys to the inner life." What the actor can hope to unlock for his use with such golden keys are the emotional experiences at the cores of all behavior of his character.

In direct contrast to the "situation-player" is that actor who prepares characters which in performed works can be recognized and identified with from their first entrances because of their consistent behavior patterns and their always evident and uniquely engrossing concerns with their own lives. The actor who habitually prepares such characters knows that different personality types have different feeling, emotional and mood experiences, as well as different basic responses, in situations which would be experienced in very different manners by other personality types.

Emotionally constructed characters are usually given more importance in or near the core of important stories than less definitive personalities. There would be little or no story without such a

24

character's experience as its focus. That experience is what rivets the attention of the viewer; not the situations which will bring it moments of frustration, outrage, pain, satisfaction, joy or sorrow. It is the experience of such a character which gives meaning to everything that happens, moment after moment.

By the time most contemporary theatre, film and television scripts approach production they offer and in fact demand an emotional clarity in at least the central characters, if not also in the lesser ones of the supporting casts. The actor or actress who is not prepared to equal and perhaps exceed the writer's contribution in this respect will personally fail and disappoint through substantially lessening the entire work. The actor who is not concerned with the preparing of a personality of depth and substance for his character will not add to the written text those human colors and experiential excitements which cannot be put onto paper and can only be brought by the actor's experiencing of the character's feelings and emotions. The actor who doesn't understand the importance of preparing a living and feeling character base which may even surpass the writer's concept will touch few if any of the sleeping edges of possibilities hidden behind the text. The character's own personality and experience simply cannot be there to excite both the mind and body of the actor's instrument.

The character's own experience, rather than the situations it must confront and deal with, will in moment after moment create illuminating depth, unique and fascinating impulses which could not emerge from mere "situation-playing". *It* creates those myriad inner responses which involve the body interestingly and divulge the spirit's processes to the spectator without any need for intellectualizing of actions or intentions or objectives out of classroom terminology. Each character which has been prepared emotionally, with a definite core, will determine for itself easily—without the need for labored thinking out—its own appropriate behavioral responses and all the foregoing aspects which should be integrated with those emotionally based patterns and mindsets.

It does of course matter that the personality to be prepared must be one which in every single moment presented by the author accommodates and illuminates with its own inner truths, the character's needs, its attitudes and its feelings.

The mistake so often made by a more shallow actor or actress is to prepare a character who seems to have been born to live only the short moments in the script rather than *an entire lifetime—not only during but also before and after the events in the script.* So often we see performances of characters which have missed the inner experiences which would cause their behaviors. In the performances of some actors their characters' behavior patterns reflect only the carrying out of single, momentary and rather inconsistent actions.

A mother who fights for her child because the writer has determined that she will fight for her child must have some more important psychological need creating her behavior. If the story involves a divorce story, for instance, and the child is very much desired by the mother, a closer look into her behavior patterns might uncover the fact that her personality would consider the child simply one of her possessions and that she is simply guarding her property more than feeling any need for the child otherwise. Another possibility easily missed in first observations might be that she requires badges of assurance of her womanhood or worth as a human being, and the child in such a case would represent such a badge to her. In still another case a different core personality might determine that she is using the child as an instrument of revenge for the imagined wrongs of its father, simply because she goes through life avenging imagined wrongs of all kinds. Or, if a matriarchially dominated woman all her life, she might be so under the dominating influence of her mother still that she is sure she will suffer her mother's wrath if a grandchild is taken away from the family.

There are so many, many personalities which lie behind the simple shells of behavior which can be missed by so many players who don't look for them or, having found them, later don't prepare their characterizations with those patterns in mind.

It is devastating to the serious actor to read a critic's review of his performance and see the word "adequate" describing the result of all those long rehearsals and headaches they produced because a director was continually asking for deeper and more emotional work while the actor didn't know how to achieve it.

The fact which should be clear to the actor, but alas often isn't, is that his concept of the character was in fact *prepared* to be only "adequate" to the demands made of him by scripted events and no more. He unfortunately did not realize the importance of *exceeding* simple adequacy in his preparation, so later during rehearsals and on into performance could not feel any depth of need or frustration, any sense of denial or deprivation, any sense of loss or rejection or any of the other experiences which, with a stronger and more definitive feeling base in characterization, would have been experienceable by his character and himself together throughout the work. It is probable that in moments of performing the role those which required anger had to be either "represented with result-playing" (a poor substitute always) or manufactured laboriously through attempting to use some acting class fiction having nothing to do with the character's experience or his own resources, therefore destined to fail.

It cannot be too strongly stated that *a clearly defined personality is the first and most important consideration as an actor approaches a role.* Nothing else can later define so impressively the character's experience itself or deepen the actor's own experience throughout all moments of the role!

Chapter Three

Listing the Facts; Appraising Them

There is a difference between what the author presents as *facts* and what the reader must realize are *assumptions* easily drawn from those facts. Facts are easy to overlook. Assumptions are often made too hastily. A composite fact, drawn from the printed page, creates an instantaneous over-all assumption of a total fact, but the broader the impression the shallower the information gleaned from it. A composite fact produces one facet, one revelation of behavior, one nuance—one simple fact. A composite fact might initially produce a *feeling* impression in the reader, but upon more examination the composite fact is made up of several small facts which would probably chalk up another occurrence of one or more of the behavior patterns which run consistently throughout the role.

In the very beginning of a script, the author, in an attempt to set the scene as clearly as possible for the events which are to ensue, frequently presents something like "The outskirts of Toledo, Ohio, on a Sunday morning in June, 1922." Many readers might be tempted to accept the image of a fairly large city on a day, practically any day, in the summer of almost any year. But each item examined on its own can produce so much more. Each item is important and leads to more facts in the hands of a thorough and conscientious actor. Facts run the gamut of descriptions, events that take place (both large and small), circumstances that exist, characters' behavior patterns and actions which are taken because of those patterns. In his own writings Stanislavski frequently referred to facts as "given circumstances"; at other times as "facts". Quite often an important fact is presented a little sneakily by the author in brief parenthetical words or phrases such as "(shyly)", "(grudgingly)", "(shaken)", etc. Those tiny one-word signposts must be observed and studied just as alertly as the more obvious fact-producing phrases such as "(glowering at him for once more observing her eternal inadequacy)".

Too many actors are anxious to get to line study and are often tempted to skip such preliminaries, allow intuitive judgment to creep in too quickly, and overlook available facts which if ignored early will surely trip them up later.

The only way to avoid the missing of individually important facts, and I think the best way to successfully (and still individually) glean their nuances toward analyzing the character's personality, is to first *list the facts* down a page (or probably several pages, since there are so many facts, both large and small, which should fall under the actor's microscope). All assumption and all appraisal should be put off until the simple job of listing has been completed. Then, and only then, go back and give close scrutiny to fact after fact after fact, squeezing every drop of nuance and suggestion from each in turn. Sir Laurence Olivier is reported to have said "Acting is thinking until you get a headache—*before* you start to act."

Some of the analysis processes can certainly be intuitive and instinctive, but *most* of it should at least pass through the conditioning sieve of the mind at some point to make any lasting impression.

In one or two readings of a role there should in all probability be one or two or perhaps at most three behavior patterns and response categories which are most frequently observed. After a moment of recalling similar behavior patterns detected most frequently it is fairly simple to divide them into general, first-impression categories. Actors who begin the listing of their characters' facts in this manner have found that this first-step categorizing into separate columns affords them a more accelerated perception of the apparently dominating pattern, since one column of facts will grow swiftly while one or more of the other columns will grow slowly and in the end have fewer entries. That the patterns in the shorter columns must be considered in preparing the character is of course obvious, but the larger list of facts in the longer column commands the greater emphasis. As its facts are separately appraised with respect to their *raison d'etre* it's not uncommon for the actor to find that certain entries in the other categories' columns are simply result actions or reactions used by the character to implement the dominating pattern's behavior or survival techniques. Often the shorter columns' items are one after another transferred to the longer column as their relationships to it are established.

Following is an example of a three-categoried list of entries which might occur as an actor culls through the facts presented by a writer.

Note that many facts seem so obviously repetitious that the temptation might be indulged to simply pass them because they're so similar to other facts already noted and jotted down. This is a common temptation, and unfortunately it's too often indulged by actors too impatient to get to the "appraisal" step.

The actors who put down all such items, repetitious though they may seem at first, may later be surprised to discover that instead of belonging under the first-impression category they in fact are more applicable in another column and by being moved there in fact establish more importance for the other column of facts!

To illustrate more clearly how this columnar listing process can be used to clarify and speed the analysis of the "facts" as presented by the writer, here's a possible columnar listing of facts as one actor might put them down initially:

FEELS CAGED AND NEEDS FREEDOM
Often leafs through travel magazines.... Often leans against the window looking out.... Grabs the telephone as soon as it rings usually.... Tells his mother he hates home-cooking.... Tells Sara

their affair means less to him than to her.... Refuses to discuss marriage with her.... His mother says he drives too fast.... Tells his mother he can't come see her on Sunday; that he's too busy when he really isn't.... Sara says he's always a bundle of nerves; can't settle anywhere.... He sometimes stays out, walking around all night, without coming back to the apartment.... After Sara tells him she's pregnant he stays away two days.... Hates the shirt Sara buys him; says it makes him look like a "family man".... His mother says he stole a car when he was 16.... He tried LSD and other drugs; still smokes pot quite often.... Ran away from home, Mom says, when he was 12; again when he was 17....

(This list might continue to fill two or three pages.)

STATUS-STARVED
He's jealous of his boss and others.... Buys the convertible rather than the Volkswagen.... Always overdrawn at the bank because of over-spending for expensive things.... Carries the briefcase, even when there's nothing in it.... The car he stole as a boy belonged to rich Lon.... Loses his job at the ad agency because of irritating one-upsmanship ploys reported by his coworkers.... Tries to get the bank loan to start his own agency immediately after being fired.... Doesn't like to visit Mom in the old family home in the low cost housing district....

(This category might have fewer facts, but it is still evident as another recurring pattern.)

PUTS OTHER PEOPLE DOWN
Is sarcastic about Sara's friends and their men.... Refuses to visit her friends with her.... Says his brother Don is a nobody and Don's wife is a baby factory.... Sarcastic about the people at the agency party.... Tells his mother she dresses like somebody's maid.... Always puts his long dead Dad down with apparent hatred....

(This category might have fewer or more than the middle column, but it indicates another recurring behavior pattern.)

Having completed the listing of available facts, the actor facing the next step of appraising and analyzing the role will have found the largest number of facts involve a caged feeling and a strong need for freedom. That there are the two other categories of facts, each now containing a shorter list of items, would probably reinforce the first conviction that the caged feeling appears the dominating experience of the character. The actor might therefore stop at that point, feeling his work is finished, and prepare a character based on that one single facet with a label such as "caged," "suffocated" or even "adventure-seeking" or "adventure-starved". The wiser actor, though, will know that the facts in the other two columns, seeming nonsequiturs though they remain up to that point, must not be ignored. That they exist in the writer's text signals the need to find their relativity within the character's basic neurotic framework.

The appraisal of the first column's facts will almost invariably produce the same or similar notations as those which a first impression of them would evoke. "Hates feeling caged" or "Wants freedom", depending on the actor's feelings as to which focus— the positive or the negative—brings the most for the character, might be the single outstanding reason for all that column's entries. But an actor determined to integrate the other columns' entries to better serve the author and the character would find them bringing slightly different colors from the simple caged or freedom-needing feelings.

Immediately upon rechecking and analyzing one after another of the second column's facts the actor would begin to see how important *status* apparently is to the man. Everything in that column, rather than pointing to freedom, points more to recognition of status and identity in other people's eyes. The originally difficult to relate jealousy of his boss points to status-*jealousy*; the convertible suggests status-*flaunting* as much as it relates to freedom; being overdrawn at the bank and buying expensive things indicates a need for possessions that are special and status-*projecting* far more explicitly than a need for freedom; carrying the briefcase with little or nothing in it indicates status costuming for a desired role; stealing rich Lon's car when he was young (rather than a different one) confirms even more surely the desire for wealth and the jealousy of it in others; constant one-upsman ploys being the reason for his dismissal from the ad agency leaves little doubt that he would step on anyone and everyone to advance himself; seeking a loan to immediately start his own agency pins down the need to be "top dog"—and upon study even implies a certain revenge motive (something not encountered in any other fact!); not liking to visit his childhood home stands as a reminder of his low beginnings and could as well be listed under his third column items of putting others down, but applies equally in this column.

At the end of analyzing the second column the actor willing to suffer the momentary bother of now having *status drive* to consider, in addition to the *caged* aspect, might hate to proceed to studying the third column, but knows he must.

Sarcasm about Sara's friends and their men suggests dissatisfaction with their circle of acquaintances; refusing to visit them shows again a lack of concern for either her feelings or for maintaining any social life which is currently available; calling his brother Don a nobody and his wife a baby factory might suggest disgust with all nobodies and the obstacles presented to advancement by having children (and the actor would probably note in this fact a parallel to staying away two days when Sara tells him she's pregnant); sarcasm about the people at the office party allows the impression that he will never be satisfied with the people currently around him; telling Mom she dresses like somebody's maid displays possible embarrassment at the taste in clothes which represents a less prominent social milieu than he wants; putting his father down with apparent hatred could upon examination indicate hatred for where he came from and the deprived childhood he suffered because of his father's humble lifestyle.

For the actor willing to go through this deep and searching scrutiny of *all* the facts provided it is indeed a tougher self-imposed task. It takes time and thought. And by now this actor has the apparently dominant *caged, status-driven* and *primary circle deriding* elements obviously needing to be blended together into one neurotic-patterned, "conditioned response" whole!

The last step of combining the major aspects and patterns into one choice of personality type is actually easier than is at first apparent:

Still holding the dominant *caged* feeling foremost in this last

34

step, the actor must consider with some insight how *status-driven* and *primary circle deriding* shall alter or qualify it without losing its dominance. Perhaps "mediocrity-caged" (provoking the status drive and causing the current environment to be always derided out of embarrassment or frustration) would suffice. Note that the *negative* (the things and people caging the character, not the more one-dimensional "positive goal" freedom need) is chosen. A positive goal choice could of course be made, but to achieve those special experiential qualities that negatives of any kind can produce in terms of more many-dimensioned emotional experience, the negative would be my own first choice always.

Other negative possibilities as labels for the character's personality, before setting forth into preparing its "tools", might be equally appealing adjective phrases such as *slum-suffocated, gutter-smelling, Thompson Street*, etc. The imagination of the actor can easily evoke the most urgent and aggravated core feelings for its character if the thinking is allowed to wander through the negative environment already recognized as affecting the character and fixating its personality and behavior to find the most evocative negative label which the actor can come up with to affect his character and his own responses as he goes forward with his preparation.

Any one of the foregoing labels could create a strong enough basis for beginning the preparation of the characterization "tools". What is important is that each is based on *all* the facts provided by the writer and gathered together through the interrelating of *all* of them into one central core. It is then improbable that any director could later point out to the actor something important about the character which might have been overlooked. The actor would be able to justify every moment of the role and the character's experiencing of it to a quickly convincing degree!

So.... now the personality type is chosen. Some actors would at this point decide to proceed immediately into the preparing of the "tools". Other actors, however, might prefer to set aside their preparation up to that point and apply themselves to the next step this particular teacher recommends. The "analyzing" brain may be tired and welcome a respite, but that's not the main reason for going to this seeming side trip which could be but

35

often isn't unrelated to the emotional core.

The next step I propose is called "The Six Questions". And one reason, an important one, for going to this step next is that on occasion it produces sentiments, social milieu, mood colorations or other modifying influences which should be blended into the character's "inner language".... and the "tools" to create and bring that "inner language", if found prior to exploring the "Six Questions", might require much tools-changing later to bring the character more into focus with its environment, its location, its social role, its style and, again, its appropriate "inner language" or "inner vocabulary" as it conditions the thoughts and actions of the chararacter.

Journalism students certainly know the "six questions" by heart, but actors may not and, not knowing them and how they can be used in role preparing, may miss out on so much of the excitement available through their use at this point.

So.... for those who will take the time to find this exciting "side trip's" results, they must be explained.

Chapter Four

Who, What, When, Where, Why and How?

The *Six Questions* apply to acting in two different ways. The first application of them could well be as an omnibus description of a role's entirety much as its brief story might be written up in the first paragraph of a news story as prescribed in Journalism classes and publicity courses: *Who* (the character) does *What* (the overall scripted event), *When* (in what period of history, at what time of year, month, day and hour), *Where* (in what country, state or province, region, town, physical location where scenes are to be played), *Why* (the apparent reasons for doing what is done) and *How* (the manner of doing).

More important for the actor, however, is the role which the same questions can play in terms of *research reminders, authenticity enrichers and reality gatherers.* The role-enriching inspirations which can be found through the application of the "six questions" at this particular point in preparation are absolutely staggering! I believe that, once tried, the actor will never thereafter neglect this important step.

Commencing with the *Who*, the actor might take some amount of time to list any research required and—what is even more exciting—jot down the inspirations which come to mind regarding obviously appropriate props, wardrobe, makeup, hairstyle, activities not mention by the writer, etc. In using the *Who* to produce these, any written character might be divided up into a "pie" consisting of a number of "pieces" to be considered separately. Imagine the many inspirations which might be gleaned from a character who is composed of these different "pieces":

He might be a *father*, a *president of the school board*, a *farmer*, a *football or baseball enthusiast* and still, throughout the script's timeframe be a *tourist* on vacation for sightseeing in New York. Think of all the things which can be thought of and explored for integrating into the role if each "piece" of this character's "pie" is studied separately on its own merits!

Similarly, the role of a doctor, for another example—even though the emotional life of this doctor will have been fairly well thought out earlier—still requires researching of the kinds of activities, props, schedules, commonly used terms, practical wardrobe, preoccupations, daily "automatic role behavior" items, and so forth which complete the understanding of what a doctor is on the outside, as opposed to his emotional life. And any one or several of these items, considered separately, will probably trigger important inspirations as to other externals for the characterization, if not perhaps some "inner language" which should also be thought of.

Once the actor has completed this kind of application for just the one question, the *Who*, there will be excited anticipation of what lies ahead in applying the other five questions. And they won't disappoint, if the actor has the patience and conscientiousness to proceed with them.

In listing the *What* research and inspiration items for attention, the actions provided by the writer supply, one after another, so many possibilities. If the character is one who grovels for food out of trashcans, sleeps in alleyways, spends meaningless daytimes walking the slum district streets, etc., there are so many tiny details involved which can inspire ideas to enrich and excite the preparation of the role as well as trigger any needed or desirable research.

By the time that the *When* "pieces" are listed and considered the actor will have already found the excitement of the role

38

becoming more immediate, more enjoyable and more engrossing.

Since now a timeframe is to be considered, perhaps the first thing to examine is whether the character is really of the time and place with which the overall work is concerned or whether it is in fact living in a past time and holding onto an earlier era's lifestyle by choice or habit. Whichever is true, the time and place of the actual events of the role must also be served. If there is living in the past to be added (for the old spinster aunt, a grandparent, a hermit or whatever), it simply adds more color and a whole gardenful of more inspirations.

When must of course, and firstly, suggest researching anything not known about a specific period in history. Most actors recognize the necessity of this aspect of research and inspirations even if they customarily overlook the other "six questions" items. Actual history sources should be investigated to learn more surely the religious beliefs of the time and their influences on society; social climates and mores; government; customs of the day; fads; costumes; interesting hand props of the time long forgotten or not known of by present-day actors; etc. Library picture plates, old newspapers and magazines of the time, any illustrated books and of course history books will help. A heightened identification with the role will certainly occur as all this research and the many inspirations produced by it are gathered.

Next, the specific year is important to pinpoint the wardrobe more specifically, to suggest presidential campaign posters or lapel buttons or other easily overlooked items of wardrobe, props or even set dressing which the actor can suggest to the director (who may be too busy to do as much research, being preoccupied with so many other elements of production preparation).

Don't overlook the month or season. Among winter, spring, summer and fall there are substantive differences in wardrobe and props, activities the author may have overlooked, etc. The director and set designer, and of course the costume designer, will have supplied the major details, usually, but the ingenuity of the actor and actress can supply so many fascinating smaller touches which make the standard wardrobe and props spring to life more dynamically and supply an endless array of small but valuable involvements which the director might not think of.

Beyond the year, the season and the month, the week of the month might be of little importance usually, but when we come to considering the day of the week changes and differences again occur more interestingly. Many times authors simply don't specify the day of the week, but a director should, for the details which can be added thereby (at least in terms of appropriate activities which may seem unrelated to the action of the play but which can add so much interesting and enriching activity to the overall).

In listing the *Where* items, don't overlook the country. It may require researching of a language, a dialect, a social influence, its government and how individual lives are affected by it, its customs, its unique dress, dominating hairstyles and usual props. Consult a good geography book or a travel guide for the appropriate period and find out how exciting the discovery of so many unique differences from your own environment can be.

Also, in any country there will be regional variations of language, climate, politics, customs, dress, dialects, family life, props, etc., as well. Don't overlook these.

Next, don't overlook the differences among urban, suburban, village, farm or ranch existences and lifestyles. Each has its distinctive habits and activities which may have been overlooked by the author preoccupied with the unfolding of a dramatic event. There may also be a common life pace or rhythm suggested, an education level, accepted norms, etc., which could be missed if not considered for a moment.

Even the exact place in which scenes are to take place can affect wardrobe, props, atmosphere and manner, etc. The kitchen or the bedroom has its atmosphere and affects us. The country club lounge does also. The barnyard is not the twenty-third floor executive office with its thick carpeting and quiet voices—whether your character should be quiet too or not.

The *Why* items will often seem to have been covered in the "Listing The Facts and Appraising Them" stage. However, even if the "Why" of a role is psychological in the main then the particular psychology should be investigated clinically as well as recognized intuitively from the actor's past observations. In examining the "Why" items, moreover, it might come as a surprise that suddenly religion or government-imposed lifestyle becomes a theretofore undetected dominant influence and cause of much of the character's action. Imagine John Proctor, for example, in Arthur Miller's "*The Crucible*", being prepared by an actor without inclusion of the so dominating religious influence on his "inner language" or "inner vocabulary" to truly place him in the appropriate timeframe. (This character is one example of why the "Six Questions" investigation should be conducted before finally forming the "tools" for the characterization!)

The *How* items are more or less the "wrap-up" items. We should not consider only the actor's "tools" and the personality type behavior they produce as the end. We must consider that how things are to be done by the character should be done by the character as they were done by such characters in that time, in that place, etc. A doctor of a certain time, for instance, may have to do things a little differently from the manner in which they would be done today, regardless of his or her personality. Although a character may kill with a gun, and the actor will certainly have considered finding out how to use a gun, it it's not a present-day model it may need to be prepared, used and handled in a quite different and unique way. Performing an operation on a patient or pleading a case at court may seem simple at first, but in a particular time and place could vary vastly from what would be first thought.

I suggest, in the end, that you do as much of the research and inspiration-gathering which can be provided by the "Six Questions" as you have time to do. You'll be amazed at how much more excitingly the role will have now sprung to life for you when this admittedly time-consuming work is finished and you're preparing to get into "tools" for the inner life of the role. I always encourage my cast members to do this role-enriching homework because of what can be produced from the many cast members' thinking in terms of setting refinements, wardrobe and props to be added and used, activities to be integrated, etc. The latter item, in fact, is what's commonly called "Organic Blocking".

Organic blocking, as a phrase, certainly shouldn't be new to most actors. It has been used, heard and misunderstood or only partially and halfheartedly employed for centuries. At its base it means that the character contributes much of its own blocking out of its own preparation, rather than receiving movement and activity directions exclusively from the director in rehearsals.

Actors who have used the Six Questions for research and inspiration sources are ideally prepared to contribute all manner of suggestions of the foregoing kinds. Following are some examples of the tremendously contributive and authenticity-enriching items brought by four of my cast members into two one act plays presented in a bill of my own original works approximately a year prior to the finishing of this book. Rather than reprint the entire text of each play, brief synopses are provided of each to provide the bases for the "Six Questions" research and organic blocking inspirations contributed by the actors in two pre-rehearsal meetings.

(I recommend that such ideas be brought by the cast members to pre-rehearsal meetings with the director so that they can be immediately, before rehearsals, integrated into the overall planning as they affect action, setting, props, wardrobe, etc. If not presented to the director ahead of time, much of what the actor is prepared to contribute will not have the opportunity to be integrated into the director's own pre-planning once rehearsals are commenced.)

Here are the two plays and what the cast members in each contributed:

"I CAN'T HEAR YOU WHEN I'M CRYING"
One Act Play by Lawrence Parke

Synopsis:
LOU, a factory worker, and his wife GRIZ, a non-working housewife, sit in their usual places in their suburban living room on this warm summer night. She, hearing their neighbors' party across the street, complains about their not being invited; about her husband's inability to ask for a raise so they can afford more; about the comparative squalor and nowhere direction of their life because he can't talk to people. Her husband hides behind the sport pages of the newspaper and his pipe, unable to offer more than perfunctory, inadequate responses even to his own wife. Eventually her nagging out of her own desperation gets to him and causes him to explode with anger and his own desperation.

42

Unable to even present his own self defense, he pleads with her to simply come to bed in the belief that that will avoid further conflict. His wife, however, knows that his boss is at the neighbor's, a co-worker's, party. She has found out in her husband's outcry that they were in fact invited but that he had declined, and she decides she will dress up and go across to the party alone and accost his boss to better their situation. He is unable to bring himself to go or to keep her from going alone. She finally goes, leaving him alone in the house in a state of emotional despair with himself.

The actress who originated the role of GRIZ arrived at our pre-rehearsal meeting with the following "six questions" and "organic blocking" contributions. While some are seemingly unimportant of and by themselves, when gratefully incorporated into the work by me they brought so many interesting and colorful touches and fine organic blocking suggestions for her role.... and for the performance of the overall:

The *Who* of *Factory Worker's Housewife* suggested doilies on the used and dirty arms of the old sofa; embroidery to which she would periodically be returning during the play (because she could not afford to buy pretty things); supermarket grocery ads open on the coffee table (for her necessary daily efforts to save what could be saved); almost empty TV dinners beside both of them (because LOU's homecoming time from the factory was never predictable enough for organized dinners); a sewing bag (paper, not an expensive wooden one) beside her with a mended sock hanging out of it; plastic flowers in two places in the room (to lend the room what attractiveness could be afforded); a cheap wraparound housedress to wear, and her shoes off (because this, like all other nights, would obviously have no going out in store for them); the front door open (because they wouldn't be able to afford air-conditioning); her hair hanging uncoiffed; since she had to dress quickly to go to the party, the dress she finally considered wearing was to be a flashy one (so long hung in the closet unworn that she would have to quickly iron its wrinkles out with a wetted finger); a simple, pinned up hairstyle was to be quickly arranged at the mirror (because she wouldn't be able to afford an attractive hairstyle at other times); her going-out shoes would have to be dusted and wet-polished (because she seldom had occasion to wear them). There were still more suggestions brought by the actress. Many more.

The *What* brought organic blocking suggestions ahead of time including the housewifely taking of the TV dinners to the kitchen even when preparing to go out; slamming her embroidery into the sewing bag and depositing it under an end table; standing in the open doorway looking across the street from whence the party music and laughter were to come; returning to the door occasionally to more pointedly express her own dissatisfaction without words; elongating her time before the mirror in preparation for leaving because of planning how to use feminine wiles to persuade LOU's boss, since a line in the script indicated that she knew him to be a womanizer; closing the front door before raising her voice at LOU, and more things.

Where, while not indicated as to exact location of their small factory town in a particular part of the country or region, caused her to suggest going to the door for the listening to the music and laughter and peering at a definite spot, supposedly across the street, because in a small town she would know where the other worker giving the party lived. This is only one example of the many brought.

Why brought her some surprises, and some revelations which were typical of those magic little touches these "Six Questions" can provide. In this role's instance, the Why suggested the establishing of some justification for her staying with LOU in spite of her deprivations and frustrations. She suggested a crucifix around her neck on a chain and a Catholic Madonna on the endtable to explain her not having divorced LOU long ago. And this suggestion led to a nice organic blocking item later in the play.... just before going to the party, knowing what she would have to do there, she suggested that she remove the crucifix and lay it next to the Madonna. She suggested that because of a personality centered around frustrations and deprivations, combined with a Catholic upbringing which to her would only aggravate such core problems, the dress usually left in the closet should be a bright,

44

flashy color. Again for this *Why* use there were many more things brought.

The *How* suggested to her that hating to have to embroider and not just buy beautiful things might irritate her with the needle and the stitches while talking; it suggested that she should sit in leg positions that were more appropriate for the life she was denied than for a factory worker's wife; it suggested that she should not even spend much time actually looking at LOU to remind herself of her problems; etc.

The "six questions" were equally productive in triggering the imagination and inspiration of the actor playing LOU. He brought the following suggestions, among others, in that pre-rehearsal meeting, and they were all gratefully used:

The *Who* of the *factory worker* brought the work clothes not taken off when he got home, with just one workboot removed and the foot being flexed from time to time (to suggest an overworked and aching foot); the sports pages indicated by the author were to be only vaguely scanned (not avidly read, since they were more an accepted pastime for his factory level man than a consuming interest). A beer was to sit beside him (rather than an after-dinner drink as suggested by the writer). His lunch pail should sit beside his big old easy chair (since his personality would probably seek his customary refuge—the chair—every night upon returning home from work, also because he would probably have slumped into the chair immediately from the day's work and its resulting fatigue).

The *Who* of *a man unable to relate to people around him* suggested a pipe (an excuse for silence) and a more obvious hiding position behind the sports pages; finding excuses occasionally to get up and go out to the kitchen (to avoid GRIZ's questioning) and come back with a fresh beer. In organic blocking terms, his outburst later in the play would be best served in the center of the room, he felt, away from not only GRIZ but also away from furniture and any connection with his surroundings.

The *Who* of *a husband in his wife's living room* suggested dumping the ashes from his pipe very carefully (to avoid another complaint by her); moving his stockinged foot farther under his chair when she came closer (because of sweaty odor which would

45

probably be smelled otherwise); the pile of sports pages under his chair endtable, his pipe stand and ashtray, his beers and his factory worker things clustered close around him (to suggest an island of refuge appropriate for his psychology in very graphic form).

Many of his suggestions from the *What* and the *When* and *Where* examining paralleled GRIZ's, which is fairly usual when there are two or more participants in a cast.

The *Why* in his case, however, being almost exclusively psychological as determined by the subject matter of the play, the book "*Man Alone*" was to lie under his chair stand with inserted markers; his work shirt was to be buttoned up (rather than unbuttoned a bit as other personalities might have preferred); he suggested he wear fairly thick glasses (for further protection from seeing and relating to others); and his workshirt was to be wrinkled and sweaty (from several days of having no concern with social neatness).

The *How* thinking had simply confirmed much of the previous list of items and others suggested, and simply enforced the character's feelings, and use of those feelings in organic blocking, that he was more a guest in his own home than its head of household.

A large number of the suggestions from the "six questions" brought by these two cast members might not have occurred to the director or the set designer or the costume designer. Also, many of the organic blocking suggestions brought by the actors were easily and effectively incorporated into the action as it was later developed, allowing them to bring more personal experiencing to their moments than they might have if movements were left to being imposed by the director's own conceptual mind and the many things which that one mind could have overlooked.

Also, some of the scenic and environmental elements suggested by both cast members contributed to the atmospherizing of *each other's* subsequent preparations through talking together about them in that pre-rehearsal discussion.

As the playwright and director, I was pleased to have reviewers praise "my attention to so many small details", "my having given my actors totality of character" and "my creating a so balanced and pulsating organism", but both the actors and I recognized, as I have so many other times as well, how much they had individually contributed to the partially undeserved credit bestowed upon the director. If the actors had not been equally praised I would have protested. I wonder how many directors would do that. But at least the actors would know.

Another one act play and another set of "six questions" results comes to mind, and follows as an added example of what can be accomplished by conscientious actors ahead of time:

"HAPPY HOUR"
One Act Play by Lawrence Parke

Synopsis:
HE and SHE, both nearing midlife, have obviously just finished sexual intercourse on the living room sofa of her home. She is in her slip, sitting on the edge of the sofa. He is finishing putting on his trousers. It becomes apparent that this has been another afternoon tryst of two very lonely people, both married to others, who for their own individual reasons are unfulfilled in their marital situations. Each is lost and is trying to fill the void by having these relations sometimes twice a week. Each is guilt-consumed about their unfaithfulness but both feel they need their times together. It becomes apparent that sex has little to do with what they seek from these stolen afternoons. During the play She wistfully inquires about his daughter and speaks with respect about his wife. We guess that she has been unable to bear children and is in a marital situation which would not encourage them even if they were possible. He is obviously uncomfortable discussing his wife and daughter with Her at such a moment. Obviously She knows his family quite well. He also knew Her husband in the Army years ago. Discussing her husband with him at such a moment is equally uncomfortable for her. After He is fully dressed and it is time for him to leave She pleads that he come again on Friday. He is not sure, but we have the impression that he will. They at least partially fulfill a certain need for each other.

The actress playing the lonely woman, in considering the *Who*

47

of this *unfulfilled and lonely wife*, suggested that there should be some flowers and little carnival prize statuettes in the living room (to brighten the empty feeling of her home and herself), a "*True Romances*" magazine on the coffee table, and a few other dullness-relieving items around the room. As *the wife of an ex-Army man* she suggested two Army pictures of her husband on the wall next to his easy chair (to indicate a hanging onto the past on his part to the point of suffocating the present of both their lives).

The *What* thinking, involving what she was doing with the visiting husband, prompted the suggestion that a towel and pillow from the bedroom be on the sofa; that the towel and pillow be taken to the bedroom in the early moments of the play; that the door be locked (to prevent a neighbor's dropping in without any warning); that the window shade be drawn throughout the play and that the radio be playing softly; and that, the tryst being only one of many with the man, her skirt and shoes be neatly arranged where she has taken them off earlier (rather than giving an impression of having been dropped hurriedly as if in an unplanned one-time encounter).

The *When*, being fairly late in the afternoon according to the author, suggested going to the kitchen twice during the last moments of the play (to check the dinner being prepared for her husband); putting the "*True Romances*" away behind other books and magazines on the bookshelf during the scene (so her husband would not see it later and to vividly establish the impression that she reads that magazine in secret to experience vicarious love and romance feelings lacking in her marriage). The *When* also suggested the turning on of a lamp and flicking on of the outside front house light near the end of the play, then setting the day's newspaper and some house slippers beside her husband's easy chair for his return from work.

The *Where* suggested only some small touches, such as a direction of looking for her toward where the man's home and family were waiting for him as she talked about them. This established the same direction for the man's looking off and thinking about them in similar moments. She also suggested looking right and left outside the door before letting the man out to go to his home (implying nearby homes and neighbors who might otherwise see him leave).

The *Why* was already so rooted in her mind as psychology that, other than a mannerism of rubbing her child-barren stomach from time to time, little else was suggested. Even that small item was a vivid inspiration in performances, however. Perhaps the only other item was her choice of a sombre-hued wraparound skirt to put on after the sofa encounter (which she felt to be appropriate for some instinctive self-suppressing or self-criticism need in her character).

The *How* thinking confirmed for her the need for both of them to drink before each time together. It also suggested a laconic, slow manner of dressing (because of the more important mental processes being experienced); the manner of cautiously letting the man out; and, with her facts already appraised and her character firmly in mind prior to the "six questions" investigation, her withdrawn positions in the room while talking with the man after their tryst.

The man's preliminary thinking produced the following:

The *Who* of the *businessman* determined his wardrobe.... a neat suit outfit mostly lying on a chair near the sofa at the beginning; determined that he would have his briefcase from the office waiting on a table nearby; and required that he should become his very neat businessman self before leaving the house (to go home as if coming directly from work). His being a married man and father suggested a small package he might have picked up at a store to take home to his wife or daughter, which he touched softly when speaking of them.

When suggestions included his wristwatch lying on the coffee table next to the sofa (for checking of the hour when he should be getting home). The time being after work, the "*Wall Street Journal*" (which his businessman role had already suggested in the *Who* thinking) should lie with his briefcase for reading at home that night; the keys for his car would lie on top of his papers where he would have left them upon coming into the house.

The *Why* for his character's scripted actions and dialogue brought little more than what his listing of facts and appraisal of them might have, but after discussing them with the director in the pre-rehearsal meeting there was joint attention to what became very impressive moments of immense and tragic lost feelings at the end of the play while the woman urged him to return on Friday.

The *How* thinking, exploring the psychological despair and lack of fulfillment of his character, suggested a slow, unhappy winding up of the encounter. To his listless putting on of his clothes that slow, unhappy pace for the scene afforded the addition of more vivid fogginess in retrieving his car keys, his watch, his tie tying and his briefcase as symbols of emptiness and things alien and not connected to him spiritually, with each bringing its moment of cold detachment from all realities around him. Also, standing for long moments knowing he didn't belong there any more than he belonged anywhere else was suggested by his exploring the psychological overtones more deeply.

These are just two examples of what actors themselves can think to bring. Imagine, on the other hand, the research and reminder inspirations which would obviously be forthcoming for an actor preparing a centuries-ago role, or a work based in a rural section of Italy, a crowded hillside of Hong Kong or a scientific outpost in Alaska!

It should be obvious that, left undone, the lack of some process such as this one I'm calling the "Six Questions" would limit the actor in making any contribution to authentic and creative aspects for his or her role and in addition limit the truth and conviction which could otherwise have been frameworked and experienced as a result of the foregoing kind of pre-thinking. Those who are willing to do this kind of admittedly time-consuming exploration on just one occasion will recognize its value and always thereafter repeat such exploration before getting into the emotional defining of their character's subtext tools.

Now, let's suppose that we're one of those actors who has gone through the "Six Questions" and that all that hard work of preliminarily "listing and appraising the facts" is also behind us. We're ready now for the next step I recommend. We're ready to form the most evocative and truth-deepening subtext tools we can for the experiencing of the character's inner personality.

The reader will perhaps encounter a number of approaches, terms and methodology items which differ from those he or she has studied and, to whatever degree, perfected. It's my hope that if, upon exploring these new approaches, they're not found to bring more exciting results than the actor has previously experienced, those which are new and somewhat different will at least contribute in some way to the actor's continuing search for the bettering of his preparation approaches.

Even if the actor should find the rest of this book helpful in no other way, I think in the previously unpublished *sequential, step by step manner of incorporating the steps of preparation* it should be found to be of some amount of clarification and aid. The prime goal of this book is just that, more than revising the basic concepts of the Stanislavski or any other system.... *putting the many pieces together* so they can all more surely contribute their individual results to the actor's overall preparation.

Section II

The Directed Subtext

"Our own personality is the inhabitant of but one sunlit room in the haunted house of our experience where we have chosen to spend the hours of our life. If the actor would conjure other spirits for roles, he must rediscover the doors behind which they lurk in our memory, find the long-lost keys to enter their dark domains without fear and, entering, learn the magic words to call them forth from their dark and musty corners."

—Lawrence Parke

Chapter Five

Every Role is a Character Role!

At this point, since we're at the point of "getting into the character" and also "getting the character into us" (both being necessary in the end), and since we're at the exact point where the *"I don't want to do anything consciously"* (intuitive approach) people usually begin to run into big, big problems I'm reminded of a little gem of wisdom that appears in that important final section of *Creating A Role* (in Stanislavski's notes about the improvisations on *"Othello"*) following the Plan of Work being described, in which he hypothesized that the right course of creativeness operates from the *text* to the *mind* (those first readings of the role and the absorbing of what the author presents); from the *mind* to the *proposed circumstances* (the gleaning of the facts and what they imply to us about the character); and from the *proposed circumstances* to the *subtext.* (That's where we stand right now— at the door to the defining of the subtext.... at least the *Directed Subtext.*)

Stanislavski continued his steps, recommending continuing from the *subtext* to *feeling (emotions)*, from *emotions* to the *objective, desire (will)* and from the *desire* to *action.* It's the clearest, most concise step-by-step laying out of procedure as he recommended it that appears anywhere. At least it outlined his own method and how it functioned as an integrated system up to the time of putting down his notes which were contained in that last book of the trilogy which was published so long after that outline was codified. With few changes—those being mostly in the last steps and their implementing of their "Object" content, it has remained as the general concept of his overall system.

You can't persuade me (or any other acting teacher who is confident that a conscious system of some kind is far better than none) that those who want to "just let it happen" know *what* is going to happen or will have any control over it if it does.

Observing and studying actors' work I've come to the conclusion that if there is no plan or directed approach beforehand *little* will happen except self-consciousness, embarrassing fumbling for re-alities which causes ridiculous accidents and distractions, uncomfortable desperation for the actor, exasperating delays for productions and, of course, early and quite justified consideration of replacing the actor or actress!

I, and all the others who believe as I do, propose that you *direct yourself consciously* toward more surely justifying the author's intentions for your character through some systematic approach. If you don't, the director assuredly will, unless he or she feels it wiser to fire you at the end of the first rehearsal week and get someone else.

What follows in this chapter is a description of how certain "tools" for preparing characters which have been passed down through the last few decades (some of them improved along the way) can be formed toward creating enhanced experiencing for the actor playing a role and certainly more vivid emotional life for the character being played.

To begin with, the character's life didn't begin as the curtain went up or as the television commercial faded into the start of the story. At least the leading characters will be living on after the closing credits or curtain calls and should enter for the first time with some uniquely individual personality quite different from the other characters. Isn't it desirable that an audience or viewer be able to recognize intuitively what makes the character do what it does in this short period of observing its life under the dramatic microscope? Most assuredly it is! So now we must lay aside the cold pencil and paper of the analyst and take up the instruments (the "tools") of the actor.

Webster's definition of an actor is "One who does a thing." With few exceptions, to do things requires *tools* if those things to be done are done with maximum effectiveness and with the desired results. Again, Webster: the definition of a "thing" is "a tangible *object*."

We'll start with the most important "thing" we must strive to bring—a human life. Obviously we should first of all find a "life thing". I recommend that it be called the *Life Object*.

Remember, as we start forming this first "tool", that all the author's facts as given to us, all the appraisal of those facts which we've done thus far, all the research we've done in the "six questions" phase…. that's a lot of analysis and acquaintance-gathering all seething around in our mind or, more graphically, in the top of a giant funnel. Now it's time for us, the one deciding the "thing" we're to do, to decide which ingredients are to bring the most vibrant and dominating colors among all the rest as they come down through the neck of that big funnel into our inter-pretation of the role. That's where we are right now…. at the neck of the funnel…. the jumping off place. We're about to make the first conscious decision as to the "thing" we're going to do. It is the first moment of *directing* the subtext of our character!

THE LIFE OBJECT

The *Life Object* is, simply, a decided, feeling-evoking, worded "thing"—the most important "thing" that seems to dominate the character's whole consciousness; its central concern from early childhood trauma to the grave as that "thing" determines and affects its actions, its most frustrated goal-pursuits, its behavior and all its experience.

To form a wording for the Life Object, we could use just one or two words, as Stanislavski did when he first recognized the need of, and wrote about, the "thing" that helped find the *Super Objective* of a character. However, I and I'm sure many others who teach have discovered that one or two words aren't enough for the optimum experiencing of feeling degree which can be kindled in this first very important tool of character creating. The moment of deciding our character's direction and forming a tool to activate it internally is too important to leave that tool unwarmed by more feeling words, since we want a feeling character in the end. Therefore, instead of simply picking a single word such as "love", we need *more than the one word* to bring more feeling, and more specifics, into the Life Object.

For instance, if it is a strongly demanding love search or strongly felt love denial experienced by the character, perhaps some wording more like *"The love nobody gives me!"* We can immediately feel the different shading from the single word form of the Object. As another example, perhaps the character wanting love more than anything else is without much hope of ever having it and is too weak-natured to fight for it. *"The love I'll never have!"*, with its forlorn hopelessness, will spell out much more feeling experience direction in the actor's use than, again, any single word might hope to.

Another character could be an obvious power-drive character. The single word "Power" would not be enough to direct the feeling responses of the actor in any specific manner. Other, longer response-defining phrases should be sought for the enhancing of what is to be brought, such as *"How hard I have to fight for things!"* or *"The respect I deserve!"* (not getting that respect is understood), etc. You might notice that these are still worded as "things"—*Objects*; not as complete sentences; not as actions; not as questions.... instead as compactly worded phrases, focussed "things" to use as the source for strong feelings for the core of such inner experiences. An Object is always designed to produce a core experience, a core focus, and strong feelings of some kind. The action which the character might feel compelled to take in order to cope with that experience and its feelings will be discussed in the next upcoming tool.

There are endless lists of possibilities for Objects of the *Life Object* level (as the personality's core concern) for an equally endless list of personality types in humankind.

The personality which seems afraid of not only everybody and everything externally but perhaps also of self might have a Life

58

Object like *"How frightening life is!"* or *"This scary world!"* or *"What they're all trying to do to me!"*. A character who always experiences inner hurt and rejection might be focussed throughout its life (with its Life Object wording) on *"The way they all treat me!"* or *"How mean everybody is!"* or *"How shut out I am!"*

For some actors it might take a bit of trying each Object—whether it is a Life Object, a Unit Object or a Beat Object (the latter two to be discussed later)—to find out how much deep feeling experience it can produce before its manner of wording style can be ultimately adopted to augment or in some cases even replace "actions". However, once the actor has understood and experienced the use of Objects a few times, any Object, at any step of the preparation and later performance experience, can produce a meaningful and truth-deepening experience. What we must always seek in forming any Object is a wording that can move us, whether it be something we (and the character) fear, hate, must fight against or for, must strive to achieve or attempt to remedy. This is just as true of the Life Object which is being considered at this point (to move the character's entire life) as it is of the *Beat Object* which will be described later. The latter is formed to focus a particular feeling concern and experience in a separate "beat" of a role after all the larger framework for the character is completed. We're not there yet. Back to the *Life* Object:

At this point, having decided what is the most important "thing" on which the character's entire personality must focus all its life, and having worded it into a Life Object that captures the shadings involved for that particular character, we can feel how our subtext is now emotionally directed into a core personality focus as we go forward into planning the subsequent tools. It can be a magical moment. We feel like shouting out *"I've got it! I've got my character!"* In all probability we at least have the motivating force at its core. The most difficult of all the choices is now past.

But strong feeling creates in any human being a need to attempt the taking of some definite action. Although Stanislavski in the last years of his life had shifted the main emphasis of his own system from *actions* to *objects* (calling them "thought objects" and "inner objects", as previously explained), he knew that the urgent need to attempt to take action was still an important part of the core of personality.

The next tool discussed—the *Vague Super Objective*—should be formed to define in feeling words the action the character would *like* to take, and at times should *attempt* to take, because of the Life Object.

THE VAGUE SUPER OBJECTIVE

This is easier, this step, after choosing the Life Object. Stanislavski listed this next step as Item 5 in the "Plan of Work" referred to previously. In that description he referred to it as the "temporary, vague or rough" Super Objective. (It was called "temporary, vague or rough" by Stanislavski on the assumption that after lengthy rehearsals of a role it might be changed as the result of later discoveries by an actor. He had not yet codified a tool for creating a Super Objective which was sufficiently moving and emotionally viable that it could remain without any question from its earlier finding forward.)

The actor can of course use an emotionally worded Super Objective which can be chosen logically and worded simply via the intellectual process as being right and having a goodly amount of feeling. At least it does, even in such a rough form, decide the particular action the character wants to take in order to cope with the problem of the Life Object. We might, on the other hand, after reading the upcoming material about the *Neurosis-Provoking Moment*, find it much more productive in emotional result to obtain the final Super Objective in that manner.

As to the Super Objective itself, you may want to read about it in a couple of books which describe its earlier (and in the hands of some teachers still current) form and purpose. In Stanislavski's own writings for *Creating A Role* you can find the early wordings and some description of the tool's manner of working. Remember, however, in referring to these earlier descriptions, that this tool, like others, has been further refined since that time.

Another good reference section is in Chekhov's book *To The Actor*, on pages 166 through 170 of the original edition.

What is not widely realized is that this particular tool—one of the most important of Stanislavski's original system tools which has remained—was originally codified by Nemirovich-Dantchenko, the literary head of the Moscow Art Theatre. Stanislavski recognized its worth as an acting tool too and promptly adapted it into his developing system. It has subsequently become one of the main characterization tools of most of the "tributary" systems emerging from Stanislavski's own. For what it produces, it deserves its enduring place in all such systems.

A simple definition of the *Super Objective*, as originally formed and still used, is: The *desired action*, both psychological and physical (Stanislavski called the process "psycho-physical), which the character feels it must attempt to take throughout all its life as a result of its Life Object.

Remember, at this point we're still talking of the *vague* Super Objective. That is what I call it, and what my people call it. It is not the *final* Super Objective (in our use) simply because it is still formed in a reasoned, logical manner and is not yet emotionally viable beyond the innate powers of an actor to automatically feel the impassioned version of an intellectually formed tool. It is a desirable step at any rate, and I recommend that people never skip this step. It can help in *finding* the final Super Objective through the Neurosis-Provoking Moment (as it does in our use), or in some actors' use it can, by itself, even though formed through simple logic, be an emotionally viable, response-conditioning and impulse-creating tool.

Regardless of the manner of forming it, the *Vague Super Objective* at least lays out a definite direction for the character's feelings of action-taking desire for the satisfying of whatever problem is experienced by the Life Object. If found satisfactorily by the actor it maintains *the same source feelings*, and if said aloud would have *the same feeling sound* as the former tool, the Life Object, since in ideal use, even though worded as an *action* tool, it should still be felt more as an urgently desirable action which when dominated by the Life Object problem (which can't be completely gotten rid of) is *impossible to accomplish* to the desired degree. In that manner of using this first "action" tool, the two top tools (the Life Object and the Vague Super Objective) work together with an astounding emotional clarity and effect on the actor.

I should mention at this point a manner of searching out and forming the wordings of both of these first tools. I call it "*body-finding*", which will be described later, in the section discussing the *Beat Object*. When the "body-finding" process is employed to bring the body into the experience from the beginning of tool-forming it is one way of assuring that the Objects of all levels of their use can successfully dominate and agitate *all* action processes through keeping the "problem" paramount to and vitally affecting all action in all moments of roles.

However, back to the interrelated Life Object and Vague Super Objective as they can now emerge from whatever manner the actor chooses to employ in finding and forming them. Here are some examples of very obvious and very directly related wording types for a few personality types:

IF THE LIFE OBJECT IS….	THE VAGUE SUPER OBJECTIVE MIGHT BE….
The love I'll never find! (Hopelessly)….	Make somebody love me! (with the same hopeless feeling)….
How ignored I am! (with clenched-teeth determination)….	Show them I'm somebody too! (with the same clenched-teeth determination)….
How much everybody else gets! (with jealous, angry feeling)….	Make them give me my share! (with the same jealous, angry feeling)….
How inadequate I feel! (with desperation)	Show them I'm trying! (with the same desperation)….

Actors who can achieve ideal inner emotional agitation for their characters' experiences and their own feeling sources from just one such combination of two logical and intellectually formed

62

tools working together can certainly proceed to the next basic items of the system, the separate *Units* of the role, as I shall do at this point.

(The tool mentioned above, the *Neurosis-Provoking Moment,* which I teach to help actors form more deeply affecting Super Objectives, will be described in the next subsequent chapter, since I want to cover the entire *Directed Subtext* and its main tools in this chapter.)

The next basic breakdown item in the system as Stanislavski conceived it, and as it is still taught by many today, is the establishing of the separate *Units.* It is referred to as Step 7 in that "Plan of Work" outlined on those pages of *Creating A Role.*

THE UNITS OF THE ROLE

In any role there are certain major turning points—new and changed circumstances met with and needing to be coped with by the character for a period of time; discouragements which vitally affect its life for an elongated period; renewed determination sequences; etc. *Units,* in the system concept, are not intended to mean "Act I, Scene 8", etc. Units are *the larger divisions* of the role which are determined by quite different circumstances as they affect the character's experience for periods of time.

While the character always has its life problems throughout, with the Life Object and the Super Objective always centralizing its experience into particular "conditioned response" experience, there are distinctly different types of good and bad periods which exist for sometimes quite long stretches of its trip. It would be confusing and lead to vagueness if an entire role were to be prepared without dividing it up into its easy and hard times, its obstacle-fighting times, its setbacks and its few successful, easy-flowing periods.

Remember, in our own lives too there are sudden and unexpected developments which we periodically suffer or can happily exploit for a time. There are lawsuits, divorces, family problems, accidents and other such major things which change our life patterns for periods, just as there are more pleasant occurrences

63

which have the same pattern-changing effects on our temporary concerns. They need to be dealt with in acted roles just as they do in our lives, and the best manner of dealing with them—since they modify with their changing conditions the whole spectrum of our characters' behavior patterns—is to *break down the overall role into its major parts, its "Units"*, finding where the changes occur and where they end with the beginning of new major "units".

Each unit, once its content and its duration is clearly determined, needs to be assigned its focus. It needs what is called a *Unit Object*. With the basic emotional feeling of the character itself dictated by the previous tools (the Life Object and the Super Objective), the Unit Object should focus the character's attention on the subject matter of the Unit for the duration of its affecting the character's life.

I suggest to my people that all the Units of the role (sometimes perhaps three or four for most leading roles) be determined before considering their contents or their individual, separate sets of "tools".

Then, after finding where each Unit starts and ends, proceed to deciding a Unit Object for the first Unit and a *Through Line of Action* for that first Unit, to define the character's desired action for that total Unit. Stanislavski called the Through Line of Action Item 6 in the aforementioned Plan of Work, but in developments by some of us since his death the Through Line of Action has been taken out of the area where it simply duplicated the Super Objective and has been moved to the place of functioning in the over-all system where it can serve to excite the content of the separate Units, serving a more unique and more individual purpose thereby.

(You may observe in that "Plan of Work" referred to here that all of Items 7 through 13 really relate to the Through Line of Action. Remember, he was a scientist and, like you and me, a student continually growing and redefining. At the time of putting down the notes which appear in that book he was still changing and modifying his system. Since his death, without losing the basic "spine" of his system, many of those ideas have been further modified and made simpler or perhaps more effective in redefinitions by others. In its position now, applying to the separate Units, it would not require so many words to describe its function.)

In the finding of Through Lines of Action for the Units is where some actors emerge as far more interesting than others. While one actor might for a Unit choose something as simplistic as "Get away", another might, because of a Unit Object like "What he's doing to me!", choose "Make him stop suffocating me!" or perhaps "Make myself strong enough to leave!" I think the last two would be found to be more exciting and make the actor using one of them more interesting.

Here are some examples of combinations of Unit Objects with their possible resulting Through Lines of Action, for the purpose of clarifying the manner in which they can take the core personality of a character through the shifting tides of given circumstances offered by a role involving a marriage failure, dissolution and eventual reconciliation—without losing the core personality of the character:

THE UNIT OBJECTS:	THE THROUGH LINES OF ACTION:
(When the marriage is obviously failing:) "This gawd-awful mess we're in!"	"Get myself out of this snake pit!" or "Show her I can't take this crap!"
(In the divorce-details talks:) "Her goddam greediness!" or "Her shyster lawyer!"	"Hang onto everything I can!" or "Show her I can threaten too!"
(Living alone after divorce:) "How wrong this feels!" or "How ...ing dull life is!"	"Get my stupid head together!" or "Get some yelling back into my life!"
(Living alone after divorce:) "How wrong this feels!" or "How ...ing dull life is!"	"Get my stupid head together!" or "Get some yelling back into my life!"

It should be evident that in dividing the role into these major parts (its Units) the actor will be able to more easily refine the separate contents of those parts and create more separately interesting involvements for each than would be possible if the Units were not broken down. It should also be noted that a character who apparently can't feel much love at any time (as this one apparently can't) can be kept within its own personality paramaters and its spectrum of experiencing in this manner, whereas if the actor doesn't employ the Unit breakdown procedure there's the possibility that the core personality might be taken astray by the shifting conditions, resulting in simple "situation-playing" throughout.

The behavior patterns of the character prior to the divorce decision should be conditioned by the core personality, not the simple conflict; the living alone period could present the temptation to throw away the character's personality and use some standard version of loneliness or loss; the fact that the character does in the end call his ex-mate and suggest a reconciling, without the Breakdown process could suggest a whole new set of standard cliches of a love-needing type. The Units and their Through Lines of Action as suggested in the examples above have clearly maintained the character's personality, while affording the character the conditioning to adapt in its own manner to the changing circumstances without becoming lost in a sea of standardized generalities.

THE OBSTACLE

At this point, many actors like to consider the addition of an *Obstacle* in one or more of the *Units* if what the author has written implies one or requires behavior varying substantively from the character's basic patterns. This is sometimes evident in a sort of "in-and-out" or "on-and-off" form. This tool can serve especially where the character is forced by circumstances beyond its control to go against its basic grain for an entire Unit or throughout part of a Unit in order to cope with external conditions, surroundings or other influences requiring the character to hold itself back from manifesting its own feelings in order to get, keep or avoid something important to it for the duration of that Unit.

Again Webster's definition of an Obstacle is exactly right for the actor: *Something which stands in the way; an obstruction.* That's what the Obstacle for an actor and for a character is—a fact which stands in the way; an obstruction.

You'll find this exciting tool mentioned many times in Stanislavski's works, sprinkled through his writings but only occasionally given any title as an actual "tool". The later refining of it into a "tool" has afforded actors a manner of incorporating *a second reality* (over and above the Unit Object and its Through Line of Action) which may have nothing to do with the true emotional life.

The concern with the character's problem (the Object) and its manner of trying to cope (the Through Line of Action) contribute a continuing focus. The addition of an Obstacle, something probably in no way related to either of the other two tools, helps the actor achieve more interestingly varied moments as at times the character is overwhelmed by the deterring thought (the Obstacle) and at other times must exert strong determination to overcome that deterring thought to do what has to be done.

The Obstacle can be used as a thought brought back time and time again; *to overwhelm, to overcome, to subdue or even totally stop for a moment the character's desired action-taking as that thought demands temporary recognition and produces its moments of entirely different feeling experiences.* Certainly those actors of the "Action is all" school of thought, who don't choose to focus on Objects to a dominating degree, should use something similar to the Obstacle to bring some added dimension in terms of the personal experience of the character behind the sometimes one-dimensional action.

The Obstacle serves best—and obstructs more interestingly, in those moments when it intrudes upon and impedes action, if it is worded as *a simple fact* which brings *a definite feeling moment of its own kind* which is different from the feelings of the Object and the Through Line of Action. As previously mentioned, very obvious Obstacles are sometimes stated or implied by the author at different moments of a role; sometimes, however, they need to be added by the actor to justify and enhance the experiencing of any apparent nonsequiturs in the original writing.

(Often, when an actor has prepared a role with an Obstacle somewhere in order to justify what seems to be a moment or sequence of behavior not consistent with the over-all character, if questioned by the director as to why such a "tool" has been necessary, it has resulted in a needed revision by the author on the spot and bettered the script. In such a case, in spite of the author's revision, the actor may want to continue to use the Obstacle of his choice to give the moment in question added dimension and more substance.)

THE DIFFERENT KINDS OF OBSTACLES

There are *internal* Obstacles (something about the character and its own experience) and *external* Obstacles (something about other people, things, God, laws, nature, etc.). Following are some examples as they might be chosen to obstruct *totally unrelated* Through Lines of Action and distract from also totally unrelated Unit Objects:

UNIT OBJECT	THROUGH LINE OF ACTION FOR THE UNIT	OBSTACLE FOR THE UNIT
How much I have to do!	Make him leave me alone!	He looks so pitiful!
More of her damn doubts!	Show her I do need her!	Her mom still hates me!
How invaded I am!	Make him move out!	I know I'll be lonely!
This hellish month!	Keep from falling apart!	The kids are so worried!

This "secret of the character", when used in some moments to obstruct and at least particlly overcome the chosen preoccupation (or perhaps completely distract the character for whatever duration of time may be decided by the actor) will automatically be shared with the spectator to the degree that it is in feeling use by the actor.

While the Obstacle can be an important "second reality" tool for the dramatic actor, it's also a handy item for a comedy player. In a comedy role requiring that the character must attempt to maintain a false exterior with some difficulty an Obstacle can provide the comic "problem" behind the pretense, clearly revealing for the viewer the effort to keep the "secret" which must be hidden.

With the Obstacle we've completed the main items in the Directed Subtext. We've chosen the *underlying concern* of the character for its whole life (the *Life Object*); the *action* it feels compelled to try to take throughout its life to survive or eliminate the negative aspects of that concern (the *Vague Super Objective*); we've broken down the role into its separate major *Units* and supplied each Unit with a feeling-evoking *Unit Object* and the *Through Line of (desired) Action* that it provokes. Here and there we might want to sprinkle in an *Obstacle* if one is desirable for bringing its added dimension for a period of time.

But, before leaving the Directed Subtext preparation and proceeding into the chapter devoted to the *Neurosis-Provoking Moment*—and since the title itself of this latter preparation tool implies that some form of *neurosis* must be desirable in the constructing of any personality choice (whether it be manifested obviously on the surface of the character throughout the role or not), I feel the moment has come to explain my personal bias against "positive goal" characterization and the lesser depth it produces for the actor and for the character itself.

THE DRIVING FORCE OF THE NEGATIVE CHOICE
For an actor who is easily satisfied with only a modicum of experiential feeling in performance there can always be the first and most obvious choice available—the "positive goal" character. Such a choice seems at first to spring obviously into bright and temporarily attractive clarity from first reading moments. What the character seems to want is fairly apparent to the character and

to the actor as well through the writer's progression of the story. The gratifying denouement would seem to provide enough satisfaction deriving from the achieving of a very apparent goal. Some actors, so easily satisfied, are simply not aware of what they are missing. They will prepare a positive goal character and as a result will in the later performance bring as convincingly as they can what is only a half-life.The character they bring may of course be a well oiled machine functioning properly and effectively. Regrettably, the spectator will probably not be watching such a character or feeling anything for it!

How much more exciting it can be for both the actor and the spectator if the tender underbelly of a *negative-driven* character is prepared from the outset to go through the experiences created by the writer. A character experiencing its own pressures, its own ungratified needs and its own survival drives emanating from a powerful *negative* problem core is a far more engrossing character in any performed work, as well as offering a far deeper and more emotionally conditioned characterization for the actor to experience throughout all its many kinds of moments.

The "positive goal" character that wants *peace*, for example, can be somewhat frustrated in its outreaching search, but it will not lend itself to experiencing the cacophony of noisy intruders, the cage-claustrophobia of close relationships, or the empty wastelands of aloneness when they are, if ever, produced by the very peace the character seeks. On the other hand, the "negative driven" character, more focused on the intrusions, the claustrophobia and the noisy environment, will experience all of these and many more beautifully negative moments; will find the more human agonies and anguishes and frustrations throughout the role; will still serve the author's requirement that peace be something devoutly desired; and will justify that goal far more surely because it is so earnestly (and far more emotionally) sought.

The "positive goal" character who obviously wants *love* will seldom experience the pain of always imminent and always expected rejection, the despair of the thing which causes love to be denied or the hopelessness of attempting to relate more fully with other characters. Instead of seeking love, the experiencing

70

of the lack of it is so much more potent for the actor and much more illuminating and involving for the spectator.

The "positive goal" character who wants *a better world to live in* (this, like the others, was one of Stanislavski's own early ideas as to possible life goals) will sorely miss the depth experiences which the escapee from a slums neighborhood childhood will feel throughout the same role—the disgust at conditions still evident around it (whether they are real or imagined); the fanaticism of the Messianic revoltist firing its blood and its senses with the religious fervor which will create prairie fires of determination to drive its fixated lifelong struggle against conditions surrounding it, even if they have changed substantially without the change being noticed or appreciated at later life points in such a role.

An electrician would scoff at anyone who tries to attach a positive to a positive and achieve any power until the negative is attached. Similarly, the knowing actor would scoff at anyone seeking depth of experiencing out of a "positive goal" character when its experiencing is limited to only its positive attempts to achieve its goals.

Actors who have read those earlier books prepared from Stanislavski's notes—*An Actor Prepares*, *Building a Character* and *Creating A Role*—have read and perhaps accepted as final the suggestions that positive goals should be planned for characters. All those examples in the previous paragraphs are still there and still being read in college drama departments, in libraries and in some acting classes. What has not been sufficiently documented is that with his exposure to Pavlov's *conditioned response* experiments and resulting conclusions *his* appreciation of the value of negative, causal fixations behind all desired action increased dynamically. Those three books mentioned, all published so far behind time in English, do not reflect the late years of his life and his realization of the immeasurable advantages of *internal objects of a more negative nature*.

Any reasoning mind, in these later decades of increased understanding of psychological process, should certainly agree that seldom is action found to be necessary without some need, aversion or dissatisfaction being experienced to cause its being taken or attempted. Therein lies the key to the importance of selecting negative-driven characters. Someone who does not have to struggle against any negatives experienced in childhood—if there be any such person at all in real life—would probably be inclined to experience the attempts to attain positive goals less deeply, less emotionally and less interestingly, and to take attainment of them for granted. On the other hand, someone who has since childhood had to fight for everything they get with gritted teeth and clenched fists of determination will experience more fully the fanaticism and emotional stresses along the way. That someone will experience with more complete gratification the fruits of the hard efforts in the moments of picking the harvest.

In the end, the "positive goal" character's involvements will in most cases direct it outward toward other characters and simple surrounding events and situations. The character is so continually focused on others, and on simple outgoing action and the achieving of result, that its own experience is difficult for it to observe and experience in any feeling manner.

There is literally no comparison. There is so vast a polarity between the two choices—the "positive goal" character and the "negative-driven" one—that the most fervent recommendation one could make to the actor or actress who has experienced primarily "positive goal" character preparation in the past is that they experiment for a time with the others—the personalities which are almost exclusively focused on the *negative* aspects which lie waiting to be discovered in any written work if the actor seeks them.

The side benefits to be derived from such exploration are so many:

While a positive goal is like a tiny, bright light shining at the far distant end of a dark tunnel, with the actor's attention so steadfastly and exclusively focused on that tiny spot ahead that it cannot experience or even notice the many, many small moments and experiences along the way, the *negative* -focussed character is constantly assaulted by its own negatives (both real and imagined) and the necessity of coping with them every step along the way through that same dark tunnel. Its feelings are constantly agitated, bringing myriad impulses which lend added interestingness to the work of the actor playing it; it finds so many and emotional opportunities which the "positive goal" character would not suggest.

In addition, the exploring of negative-focus characters will bring to the actor's work—through the formation of habit as well as single roles' results—active involvement of those parts of his own mind and body which lie dormant and closed away from habit experience in daily life. In real life we do not willingly sink into moodiness. We never send ourselves happily into despair for the sake of reexperiencing it. We attempt to contain our angers— often to the point where we cannot later experience anger consciously. We deny most of our negative processes in real life for as long as we are able to do so. If we do not find and use the avenues for these experiences which are available to the actor they will not automatically be available on call for desirable use in moments of roles. The dramatic character requires so many of these negative moments of experience, whether for only brief periods or for the entirety of a role. If they are not practiced, ready on call without fail and emotionally grounded, the attempts to touch their responses (after allowing them to lie fallow for so long) must fail when they are most sorely needed.

It is not quickly apparent to some new, inexperienced actors and actresses—some perhaps fresh out of a university or college drama department where there has been so much emphasis on the classics and early romantic works—that the negative aspects in most characters' subtexts are all that necessary. Some such actors and actresses are too often dreaming of playing *Hamlet* or *Romeo*, *Juliet* or *Helena* and playing those roles with first-impression *goal-directed heroics*. They are too often inclined to overlooking the lacks, the needs, the frustrations, the negatives of all kinds which lurk behind the surfaces of these characters. To many of these folks, these kinds of characters are "heroes" and "heroines", to be prepared with simple positive goals. The same actors tend to seek positive goals for even the *Iagos*, the *Othellos*, the *Lady Macbeths* and *Macbeths* and have difficulty in attempts to fully flesh out these characters of more obviously *negative-*

centered, problem personalities. For these folks, conditioned to approach roles more from the "positive goal directed heroics" angle, there are rude awakenings in store.

In the 1930's and 1940's roles began changing as the scientific understanding of human psychology advanced, and since that time have continued to gravitate toward negative-driven characters. Now, and continually moreso, anti-heroes have replaced heroes. Problem characters abound in created works just as they do in real life. And, more important for the actor to note, the leading roles which are designed to gain our sympathy now have their own interesting personal torments, their own feelings of inadequacy and their own built-in self problems working against the probable achievement of their goals.

Playwrights and screenwriters have long since discovered that leading characters are far more engrossing to watch and easier for the viewer to empathize with if they have insecurities, self doubts, fears, guilts and other aspects which are built into their psychologies. In other words, most of our current-day idols have feet of clay, and the contemporary actor who wants to succeed in the professional mainstream needs to practice the experience of having his characters' feet planted in the mud and forcing his characters to "flounder in the muck of their problems" if he is to be considered for the more important roles.

Negatives are driving forces, more often than not creating very positive results from very positive goals which are brought into sharper focus and heightened emotional urgency primarily by those negative forces which have made them necessary.

What I feel the actor should seek to uncover in the early readings of roles are the aforementioned parallel behavior patterns which suggest some *negative* inner experience at work behind and deep-rooted underneath all those patterns, in fact creating them. Such patterns will certainly be there and available to be recognized in any respectably important role. It is terribly important that the actor look past all those surface actions and manifestations for their cause and what makes them necessary for the character. Actors who fail to do this can miss, throughout their preparation of the role and throughout the performance of it, the type of experiencing which could otherwise produce the most

74

desirable result for both the character and the actor. It has a nice title: *Conditioned Response!*

Truth and depth of experiencing being the very desirable things they are in all acting, it is doubly necessary that the basis for truth and depth be readied and refined into a generating, conditioning form at the earliest moment, so that early truths can generate later truth discoveries and condition the actor's responses to them as they emerge.

I firmly believe that, just as in real life, without some degree of neurosis in a prepared characterization there can be little or no conditioned response! Intellectualized decisions do not satisfy the spirit of the knowing actor or actress. Such intellectually decided truths are only half experiences based on guessing, choice-making, many questionmarks as to their appropriateness, and frustrations which result from the sense of incompleteness suffered by the actor attempting to breathe life into them.

It is an accepted fact that a neurotic personality in real life is not generally able to make intellectual calculations as to its responses. It is conditioned from an early childhood period to rely instead on one single basic response structure in moments provoking reaction or demanding action. Denied the use of logic in most moments, the neurotic personality sees its own *conditioned* truth and is ignorant of the fact that its truth is a distortion which turns most simple life events into the inevitable pressings, over and over, of its most vulnerable danger button.

This is the kind of inner life conditioning which I recommend for actors—the kind that identifies the personality for the spectator and that causes the viewer to anticipate that experience after experience of that personality will provoke a conditioned response which will probably cause it even more difficulty. I would not personally want to waste my interest or attention on a character whose coping with its experiences is easy for it. Should I observe an actor failing to find the inner torments of overwhelming struggle in a role, I know that actor either doesn't understand the value of a neurotic character base or is simply too disinterested in the preparation of an acting experience to search it out.

Give me instead the actor who turns unhappiness into pain, doubts or confusion into self-torture or self-loathing, happiness

75

into an anguished ecstasy, shame into suicidal self-abasement, anger into murderous hate and resentment into the rumbling of an earthquake. These deeper experiencings are possible only with a *conditioned response* base.

As mentioned earlier, the reason for holding off discussion of the *Neurosis-Provoking Moment* until now is that it is one of my own inventions and therefore hasn't been written about in any book prior to this one, so I want it to be fully explained.

This tool's codification was the result of my deep conviction that a state of conditioned response was desirable for the inner life of a character and that something was necessary in order to turn the quite sound but still unemotional *Super Objective into a stronger and deeper force working within the actor. There was no tool I knew of for creating that state of conditioned response.*

There is such a tool now. It is called by me the Neurosis Provoking Moment. I recommend it.

Chapter Six

The Neurosis-Provoking Moment and the Super Objective

In the previous chapter we took up all the elements in the breaking down of the Directed Subtext *except* some manner of infusing what Stanislavski called the "vague, temporary or rough Super Objective" with added experiential and depth value.

In this chapter we'll take up the tool which some of you have probably heard about somewhere—perhaps in study with one of the teachers who studied with me in the past or with one of the teacher friends of mine who have observed it and who may now teach its use. Since it may have been misunderstood in part by someone teaching it (as I know it to have been in one notable case), I want to personally describe its optimum manner of use in this chapter.

For instance, one of my closest friends for many years, the late Miriam Goldina, translator and adaptor of the books *Stanislavski Directs* by Gorchakov and *Stanislavski's Brilliant Heir: Vakhtangov* by Simonov and a student of Stanislavski herself, observed the Neurosis-Provoking Moment work in a number of my classes in the 1960's, during its early stages of development. Immediately incorporating it into her own teaching, she called it by her own title—the "Neurosis-Evoking Instant". That seemed alright to me,

77

even though it was clinically inappropriate as the label . It also pleased me to hear from her that during a subsequent visit to Moscow she had described it with enthusiasm in a talk before an assemblage of the current students at the Moscow Art Theatre Institute. But later, when preparing her own role for Broadway in Dore Shary's play *"The Highest Tree"* she called me excitedly to tell me how effective it was in her preparation. What she related to me was a *happy* moment, not a traumatic experience of any kind, and I realized that such a moment could have contrtibuted very little of what the tool was designed to contribute; also realized in dismay that her description of the tool in Moscow may have been equally error-prone.With the tool personally observed by Miriam on a number of occasions, followed by the discovery that even she didn't understand it clearly enough, it seemed a dramatic example of the many misinterpretations which could be possible about this tool and its use. After that experience with my own dear friend Miriam I have taken orientation on this tool very seriously.

The "Super Objective" was first conceived by Nemirovich-Dantchenko, Literary Head at the Moscow Art Theatre and close coworker of Stanislavski, as a script analysis step. Learning of it, Stanislavski recognized that it could serve the actor in the same manner and quickly adopted it into his then developing Method of Physical Action. As an analytical step, it was to be formed through the intellectual process alone. It is still used in this manner by some actors and by some teachers of Method persuasion. And, even though Stanislavski and Chekhov, in their writings, called it *"the most important tool"* in the preparation process (in *Creating A Role*, pgs. 77 through 81; in *To The Actor*, pgs. 155 through 170), this tool remained in an almost primitively intellectual state for many years. Since its function was fairly parallel to the Through Line of Action, and since "action" was the big word in the system of Stanislavski until "Objects" moved into their important position by the late 1930's, the Super Objective's further development was delayed and it remained an intellectually formed tool only for decades, without any means being developed for transforming it into an automatic life-producing, emotionally viable tool to guide every moment and every

78

action of the entire life of a living character. The actor still had to study and guess through tedious intellectual addition and subtraction the smallest actions and experience moments of the role in order to know what to do with them. The emotional process of the Super Objective had little effect as a conditioning tool because it still lacked that one important element—conditioned response.

In 1963, after years of concern about the ineffectuality of the Super Objective, I codified the Neurosis-Provoking Moment. In the first year of its use word about it reached Dr. Richard Renneker, the then head of the Ford Foundation Psychotherapy Group and, after many observations of its working and its creative force behind the characterizations in my play "*The Cage*" his descriptions of its internal processes when used by the actor confirmed for me that I was onto something beyond even my hopes at the time of the forming of it. During that period it was also observed in my classes and tested in others by a number of other coaches and teachers, and another therapist, Dr. William E. Shaw, was attracted to work with me after observing it and the results it created for my actors. More important than confirmations of what it did in process terms was the quickly established fact that it worked for the actor!

Regrettably, even defining it in words requires a paragraph:

It is a tool which enables the actor to create a Super Objective which involves not only the conditionings and blockages of early life but also evokes certain emotional and experiential memories of the actor as well, as an imaginary childhood and a culminating event which fixed the emotional direction of the character's psychology is constructed improvisationally by the actor while remaining emotionally conditioned by the Life Object and being pulled forward at a swift pace by the Vague Super Objective toward a final moment of trauma which produces an urgently felt Super Objective!

To some of you that definition isn't simple at all, because you still don't know how it's done.

Let's go back a bit. Although most psychologists tell us that we're "a fabric woven of many-colored threads" (quoting a friend of mine, Dr. William E. Shaw) it is self-defeating for the actor and character-confusing from the author's standpoint for the actor to try to use more than one. The actor must instead do what Charcot taught Freud to do: "*Unravel the ball of yarn*" to find the *one main conflict or blockage* which has produced all the small knots in the ball of yarn that is personality. In acting terms, the ball of yarn is essentially all the experience and actions of the character and all the inner things contributing to those actions that emanate from one strong conditioning source.

By the time you've decided the Life Object for the character, establishing its one main fixation to the best of your ability, you've "unravelled the ball of yarn" of the character and chosen the deepseated problem at its core. When you've taken the next step of deciding the Vague Super Objective you've chosen the action the character must attempt to take, at least emotionally, throughout its entire life in order to cope with the problem which is its personality core. However, the personality you've formed intellectually up to that point needs to be made emotionally viable. All that research and analysis needs to spring to life in you and in the character. At that point you are much like the doctor preparing for an operation. You need one certain tool to start operating.

In the choosing of a Life Object and Vague Super Objective in order to create some degree of deep feeling source in the character you will already have departed substantially from a dull, well-adjusted, problem-free personality for your character. You already have the basis for a good dramatic character.

It could remain only for the actor to continually agitate that basic experience so the particular need and problem and the experience they provoke in the character will be meaningful and engrossing for the spectator. But think how much more satisfying it could be for the actor if the experience provoked is equally affecting for the actor. This can occur only if the actor has succeeded thus far in conceiving of and constructing a character which—even if on the outside it appears well adjusted to its environment and the society around it—is at least to a degree *neurotic* (in the case of some characters even bordering on *psychotic!*) in his preparing of its inner life.

BUILDING THE NEUROTIC CHARACTER

In sociological terms, while a normal personality has available to it at least *three* general recourses in coping with problems— (1) escaping via running away; (2) striking out aggressively; or (3) going toward the problem and endeavoring to cope with it objectively, the *neurotic* personality is limited in the main to *only one basic response pattern* in coping with stress, and often when stress doesn't exist from the outside the neurotic personality must create it inside along one defined direction from among the foregoing or some other choice.

The neurotic personality is handicapped in any effort to take resolving action of any sort, due to the fact that at some early moment in its life its psychological filtering process was unable to correctly interpret what its culture or society threw at it. A thwarting moment, a blockage occurred which, due to either real or imagined threat, in that moment distorted the learning process needed for socialization and maturity.

The actor's problem, then, is to find a manner through which such a personality can be created and made to work inside him in the experiencing of a character's life, continually enriching what he does and how he does it through the hidden (or sometimes *not* so hidden) struggle with the character's environment, real and imagined threats and the inadequacies of self in coping with all of them.

The entire profile of the neurotic personality should be understood. It is universally accepted as fact that such a personality involves interpersonal relationships; that it is the result of a thwarting moment or several such moments in childhood; that it damages the psychological outlook and the energy system; that it has its roots in the formative years; also, that there are defenses based in a conditioned response to which the neurotic personality resorts in the defending of itself against imagined foes as well as real ones.

Knowing these things to a degree but lacking the rounding out of knowledge which has since been provided by friends and advisors more learned in the scientific aspects involved, I codified the Neurosis-Provoking Moment strictly as an acting tool.

81

It was designed in a manner that would provoke a latent neurosis through a moment of blockage or thwarting of the already conditioned problem experience; that would provide the interpersonal relationships factor; that would bring to vivid life the moment that created sufficient trauma to propel it into unchangeable and passionate life; that would root that moment appropriately in the formative years; that would provide a built-in and unchangeable defense system of a single (therefore neurotic) direction; and that, in one final emotional outburst of need-experiencing, would culminate in *the finding of a powerful Super Objective*. It does all those things in the hands of actors whose emotions are free to become involved.... and does them well.

THE NEUROSIS-PROVOKING MOMENT

First, establishing in yourself the feeling of the Life Object and the Super Objective (combined, since they have the same feeling core) and *maintaining their feeling intensely without interruption or change*, do the following:

(1) Begin a swiftly improvised, totally imaginary story about your (the character's) childhood with *"I was (any early age not older than 12)...."*, then fill in conditioning details about where you lived, your parents, brothers and sisters, relatives, neighbors, teachers, friends, perhaps toys and pets, etc., and the problems already existing with each of them in that early childhood time. For example: "I was six. We lived in the last house 'way out at the end of a dirty little street at the edge of town. I was an only child, and I never had anybody to play with because all the other kids looked down on me because my folks were poor and I never had any good clothes to wear. My mother and father always left me alone too. They were always out late at night drinking and came home late and didn't even say goodnight to me because they were too drunk to even see me. Nobody would ever play with me...."

You can see the conditioning which these rapidly improvised story-building items are already creating as they spring forth swiftly from the intensely maintained feeling which is creating them. Even though the emerging story is fictitious, these details will come pouring forth at the maintained swift pace if you will simply rely on the maintained feeling of those two top tools (the Life Object and the Vague Super Objective) because, without realizing it, you are tapping your own memory bank of similar moments. The details should come readily, one after another in quick succession and at a pace which you keep expecting to falter but which does not, because the imagination is continually generated by the feeling held at an intense level. You will never know what's coming next as you bravely bring "My Uncle Tim" or "Johnny, my nextdoor neighbor" into the story, but if the base feeling is being maintained their role, in just a few swiftly improvised words, will fit the pattern which is being more and more entrenched by even these preliminary details.

(The *swift pace* of improvising all these details, and the additional details that follow, is absolutely necessary for the purpose of tapping the experiential resources and memory bank of the right side of the brain and avoiding the self-defeating "story-writing" which would occur at a slower pace.)

(2) After enough of the foregoing "conditioning" items have been related to yourself (preferably *aloud*, by the way, so the temptation to stop and think can be bypassed with the obligation to simply keep going apace), begin *the moment that finally did it to you* (caused your neurosis, you being the character). Simply start with *"Then one day...."* and, without having any idea what you're starting to relate to yourself, let the incident start forming itself in the same continuous, rapidly improvised manner, as it assuredly will. In this final "event" improvising, knowing it is leading up to a terrible moment, just keep plunging ahead with increasingly agitated details and with the actor's sense of dramatic development, as you lead up, detail by detail of the event, to *a moment when something so terrible was done or said to you (the character) that you felt totally unable to face the next moment without taking some drastic corrective action!....* and then, when you recognize that what has just been said or done to you is potent enough that you need go no further.... instead of actually *taking* any action....

(3) *Stop everything!* The unbearable words have just been said to you, or those around you are still laughing at you, or the whip is in the air ready to come down on you, or you can see

83

that terrible thing happening! Break the film! Suspend the action! Freeze the film frame! *This* is the exact thwarting or *Neurosis-Provoking Moment!* It is the moment you must learn to recognize and handle correctly.

With the feeling of those top tools intensified to a fever pitch (as it has remained throughout the NPM if you've done it right), *suspend yourself in that awful moment; attempt to break the thought barrier and simply trust the feeling filling the right side of the brain; experience nothing but the person or persons or the thing involved in that final trauma moment.... and turn your feeling to what you have to do. Then, in that tight, stiffened moment, think "I've got to...."* and let the words of what you have to do to right that wrong, right there in that brief suspended crisis moment, come out *without any editing on your part.*

If you've successfully held to the original Life Object and Vague Super Objective feeling throughout the improvising and imagining of the rapidly formed story, still maintained it during the emotionally crescendoing event leading to the crisis moment, and still hold it intensely in that last suspended moment, what words will come out after the "I've got to...." switchover to a corrective action will be *a marvelously emotional Super Objective!*

Without mentally monitoring your processes to make the words of the emerging Super Objective (the thing you need to do to correct the wrong being committed) come out well or logically, as long as you remain concentrated on the person or persons or thing causing that awful moment you'll find yourself fumblingly, stutteringly, emotionally almost yelling that you've got to "Make them stop saying that!".... or "Make her come back here!".... or "Make them stop laughing!".... or "Show him we're *not* garbage!" .... or "Make her write *her own* goddam name a hundred times!".... etc.

In that final moment, the importance of remaining riveted on the person, people or thing causing the moment cannot be too strongly emphasized. It is just such events that cause conditioned response of neurotic personality types in real life. The real life thwarting or blockage moments caused by such events include their participants—mothers, fathers, Kindergarten teachers, neighborhood friends or enemies. Most such events would not be traumatic if they did not involve other people in some respect. Similarly, it is important that the person, people or thing involved in a fictitious Neurosis-Provoking Moment be the single focus of its final moment.

Also similar to real life fixating moments is that intense, stiffened moment of changing over to an "I've got to...." thought. In real life thwarting or blockage moments of the same kind there is that overwhelming need to take action of some kind and the fact that the actual action is *not* taken, instead is repressed, is what fixates the neurotic conditioning. It is the same with our Neurosis-Provoking Moment, in that the *need to take a specific action is so overwhelming in that moment.... and the knowledge that we can't do what we'd like to is unbearable!*

Those acquainted with the brain sciences involving the right side of the brain should recognize that, through stiffening to the point where cohesive thought and careful wording is impossible in that final moment, we are essentially drawing on the right side of the brain where true experience, more than logic, resides. We are in effect filing a computerized experience for our character which can be retrieved for its performance moments simply through use of the tools which will follow—each containing worded keys for the reevoking of the personality core of the character!

So.... now you have your actual *Super Objective!* It isn't vague or rough anymore. It's definite; it's emotional; it's neurotic in the size and urgency of its experience. It's computer-programmed for use on call!

Let's examine what you have through the Neurosis-Provoking Moment and its newly created Super Objective that you didn't have before:

(1) A believable, intensely moving, sample emotional experience *as the character itself* which has caused all its life actions and all its private experience moments before the play or film, will foundation them emotionally during the role, and would continue to work in the character were it to live on after the scripted sequences of its life are over, eventually causing the manner of its death by guiding its emotionally directed missteps toward that final moment of its life;

85

(2) Automatic interpersonal relationship conditioning toward all *hims, hers* or *thems* or *its* to be encountered throughout the character's life in the role, defining the kind of people, singly or in groups, who have thwarted you in *the moment that finally did it to you* and who will always be feared or hated or needed or rejected as determined by the actual participants in the Neurosis-Provoking Moment;

(3) More particularized (instead of general or intellectualized) need and feeling—for instance, *vengeful* hate rather than just one-dimensional hate; *helpless* love-searching rather than just love-searching; *frightened fury* rather than just fury or fear; etc.;

(4) The kinds of places and objects your character needs or can't stand (because the NPM touched on several and they are held filed with all the other facets of the traumatic NPM;

(5) An ever-present wrong waiting around every corner to happen to the character; a constant, ever-present threat to the character's survival because now the character is conditioned to always expect that wrong to be present or imminent in all interpersonal relationships;

(6) In addition, a whole network of conditioned responses which will work inside the character (and the actor) so automatically that every moment of the role is a glorious discovery of unexpected depth and conviction and feeling that flows like a torrential river, never having to pause to have its direction in next moments decided!

Of course you will note that the *words* of the newly found Super Objective will be different from those of the Vague Super Objective, simply because the final NPM incident and its culminating moment have provided a more defined reality which now includes those specific people, things, etc. The new words *sound and feel the same*, however. They are simply more emotional and far more affecting than the former vague form could be.

Something I didn't know when I codified this remarkable tool intuitively was told to me by one of my more learned friends in the field of psychotherapy is that the importance of *maintaining the feeling of the Life Object and the Vague Super Objective at an intense level throughout the NPM experience* is that, as we are "reliving" our (the character's) imagined story, we the actors are *personally* involved much more than we need realize. While figuratively "holding down the single feeling key of our organ" to keep the single sound (the single feeling in our emotional memory bank as we have experienced it and know it) coming out and directing the imagination as it improvises and touches inspirations, we are inevitably touching stone after stone of our own associative memories stored away long ago and throughout our lives in that particular "feeling file folder" in the dusty attic of the right side of the brain. Most of these details we won't recognize or associate with any actual personal experiences as we arrive at them and pass them by so rapidly. (We should be traveling too rapidly in our improvising of the details to stop and attempt to associate them with anything from our own life.) Some, however, we do recognize as being produced by specific past experiences in our own lives. That is how close the NPM can come to pulling out our emotional experience! We are not even seeking our own past experience, and should never do so intentionally in the NPM.... but it is there waiting and is sometimes touched through the associative processes of intense feeling.

It is important that if and when people or experiences out of our own life do suddenly appear in an NPM improvising because we have touched something quite personal—and they will occasionally, it's important that we *guide ourselves away immediately!* Efforts at conscious remembering out of our own lives must not be allowed to stand in the way of the much more free imagination. Conscious examination of a real life moment would in fact destroy its associative effect. It is enough that for a moment the association is there, perhaps vividly. Simply change the person or place to another reality quickly and go on. The point is, whether we recognize the sensory parallels out of our own emotional memory bin or not, they are always there adding their own acute personalizing influence to the character's experience step by step as they weave in and out, as they do tend to do. They invite our stopping to bring long forgotten moments back more completely. We *must not!* In fact, if the temptation to do so can't be resisted, abandon the NPM construction and go back to it afresh after you've done all the personal memory exploration you've stopped for.

87

Since some readers may find the power of the NPM difficult to accept and may remain a bit skeptical about its great value, there is an exercise I use in some of my class sessions dealing with the NPM. I call it "The Hot Seat".

THE NEUROSIS-PROVOKING MOMENT HOT SEAT

If experimenting with the NPM in a class, at a point where most members of the group are at least sufficiently practiced in how to construct the tool, each member could be asked to do the following:

(1) Plan an emotional character type of any kind. As you already know, I would personally recommend a good neurotic type, but any type will do;

(2) Choose the Life Object that feels right for that character and a Vague Super Objective of the same feeling. Then construct an NPM and come out with a Super Objective, using the previously described procedures, so it can work;

(3) Then decide what thing that character would appropriately have done recently (the new Super Objective, pressed to its extreme, will easily suggest the right kind of thing) that brings you onto front pages tonight; that makes you worthy of being before a group of news reporters (which other class members will become when you get into the Hot Seat) *for a press interview.*

(4) When it's your turn, get out of your seat and go into the Hot Seat chair *in the feeling of your Super Objective* (in other words, just as the character would because of its inner feelings). When you sit down, first, start by telling the "reporters" around you what you've just done that occasioned this press interview (since they won't know yet); then tell them how "It probably began when I was six...." or something like that, to lead into *reciting your NPM* details as closely as you can remember them, with the feeling that created the NPM in the first place intensely held throughout this relating of the event. At the end of relating the NPM's culminating event be sure to also tell the Super Objective which emerged from it. You might bridge into quoting it with a phrase like *"And in that moment I knew I had to...."* or something similar. Then, maintaining that intense Super Objective feeling still, ask for any questions they'd like to ask.

88

(5) When someone is in the Hot Seat the questions thrown in quick succession by the "reporters" should have *nothing to do with the event or the character's NPM*. Instead, they should be thrown loudly and clearly and rapidly—so quickly one after another that the person in the Hot Seat has no time to think of a logical or appropriate answer. This is crucial to the success of the Hot Seat testing of the NPM's effectiveness! After all, we are testing the *conditioned response* faculties of this tool.

(6) The questions asked by the "reporters" should be short and quick.... "What's your favorite color?.... Color you hate?.... Favorite food?.... Food you hate?.... Kind of car you drive?.... Favorite song?.... Favorite poem?.... Favorite movie?.... Favorite movie star?.... Favorite piece of clothing?.... Favorite room in the house?.... Favorite girl's name (or boy's name)?.... Favorite time of day?.... Favorite book?.... Favorite city? .... City you hate?.... Club you belong to?.... Kind of pet you have? Favorite page of a newspaper?....", etc., etc.

(7) There should be someone in the group who either takes shorthand or speedwriting notes or can operate a tape recorder, to take down the rapid fire questions and the reflex answers.

(8) When the questioning is stopped by the group's moderator and the answers are examined one after another it can be an absolutely mind-blowing experience for everyone present as, having heard the details of the NPM earlier, they observe what the NPM and its Super Objective have produced!

For you too, at the end of the struggle to answer every question quickly, without employing logic or anything else beside the conditioning working inside you through the NPM, the discoveries of the NPM's moment after moment powers will be startling! If you've held to the intense feeling of the Super Objective throughout the questioning and responded quickly enough to avoid intellectualized answers you'll discover that every response has been ideal for the character!

What will impress you especially is the miracle that some titles you haven't thought of for years will have come out so automatically. In some cases you'll even have responded with words that you didn't know *were* actual titles of books, poems, operas, etc. Others in the class will know them, probably. Foods, colors, car models and other items which are foreign to you in real life will have emerged as the character's favorites. Movies or songs long forgotten or never even more than idly heard of will have come out swiftly as the character's favorites or most abhorred ones!

After the class has examined each answer and related it to its being produced automatically by the NPM you and the others may well get some chills and goosebumps from what has apparently happened. You have essentially been a different person for a time, with the conditioned responses of that different person which you have created with the help of an NPM and the Super Objective it created!

A NEUROSIS-PROVOKING MOMENT EXAMPLE

Since the lengthy description required by the NPM may still leave some confused as to how to employ it, step by step, and how it is directed forward by the strong feelings of the Life Object and the Vague Super Objective, let's take as an example character for the purpose of illustration the character for whom the *facts* were listed in Chapter Three:

If the actor listing and appraising the author's facts in that role were to settle on "*slum-suffocated*" as a label for the personality of his caged, identity-craving, status-frustrated and primary circle deriding character he might, after some exploration with his mind and body of the attitude and feelings of that slum-suffocated personality, hit upon "*The stink of the gutter!*" as a sufficiently hated and feeling-evoking Life Object.

With that Object for the life of the character held strongly in mind, upon looking for an equally feeling-expanding Vague Super Objective which would satisfy by inclusion all the character's personality aspects, the actor might well hit upon something like "*Show them I don't belong there!*" or even something more simplistic and directly related like "*Get this damn stink off of me!*"

to bring its inherent values and an emotionally-enforced truth to the Super Objective which the NPM would produce in its final crisis moment. The following swiftly improvised story of such an NPM and its background of conditioning environmental influences might result.... *if* the actor steadfastly maintains the strong feeling

90

of the Life Object and Vague Super Objective at pitch throughout the improvising of the moment:

"I was eight years old. My family was gutter poor. We lived in a dirty tenement building in the rotten slum section. My father only made enough when he was alive for kerosene for an old heater and spaghetti without any meat in it for meals. My mother didn't work because there were too many kids to take care of. My brother Joey and I had to sleep on the living room sofa, and he was always dirty and smelled so bad at night I couldn't sleep, and I couldn't wash the smell off the next morning before going to school...."

(The actor might have noted in swiftly passing that while the *character's* brother in the script is named Don, the name of the NPM brother emerges as *Joey.* A Joey out of the actor's own past may well have come into momentary conscious memory after the name flashed into the improvised story. It's quite possible that the actor's remembered Joey *did* smell and therefore was locked in that particular associative memory file of the actor, whether the actor remembered that Joey smelled or not. The point is, the right side of the brain, left to its own resources, does in fact remember. Let's assume, anyhow, that there was a Joey in the actor's past. He would want to guide himself away quickly from trying to remember that Joey as he would continue his improvised story:)

"My sister Angela was a whore by the time she was thirteen. Two of my older brothers were in the reformatory for thefts all the time, and my older sisters all got married and had babies one after another and kept themselves dirt poor taking care of them. Mom's brother Rico and Dad came home drunk every night...."

(The actor might not even note at this point, but some readers of this example might, that brother Joey's smell and the drunken smell of Dad and Uncle Rico have automatically crept into the story, probably because of the Life Object's use of the word "Stink" and its amount of conditioning of the improvising imagination:)

"We never had good clothes or anything of our own, and we couldn't even afford notebooks or tin lunch pails for school like the other kids!...."

(At this point the actor might feel he has enough of the early conditioning environmental people and things stored up and at this point should send himself into a specific moment's beginning.... without knowing what will come through the swift imagining process:)

"*Then one day....* I was in the school hallway, and tried to talk to a girl in my class.... Billie Mae...."

(Billie Mae, too, may have been a real person in the actor's past. It's probable, since she has been brought into the story through his associative processes after being long forgottern, that she figured in some moment related to the one at hand in the actor's story. But he would not want to stop and dwell on the real Billie Mae. He would want to guide himself away and continue:)

"She told me to leave her alone, but I kept trying to walk with her to the other class. Finally she pushed me, and said '*Get away from me! You're nothing but scum!*....*"

(If the actor stops the NPM at this moment because he feels the moment will be sufficiently impacting, the new Super Objective, emerging out of this suspended freeze-frame moment of needing to right *this* wrong, might come out—after the actor in a trigger-tight state thinks "*I've got to....* "—"*Make HER feel like garbage!*" However, the actor might not be satisfied that the girl's comment would be sufficiently emotion-evoking for him and that he should continue the imaginary crisis for a few moments longer to create a culminating experience of added impact, continuing to intensify as he proceeds:)

"I pushed her back and told her I was just as good as she was! All I wanted to do was talk to her, for Christ's sake! But then she turned to her girlfriend in that frilly yellow rich-girl dress and said '*Do you smell what I smell? I think it's a dirty rat out of the sewer. They shouldn't let sewer rats into this place!*'.... and they both laughed and walked away!"

(If the actor is satisfied with this further aggravated moment and stops the NPM at those words and the laughter, the Super Objective which emerges from this later, different point of the same story might be, instead, something like "*Show 'em their perfume smells worse!*" or "*Show 'em I'll smell better'n they do*

92

someday!" or, because of their laughter being more impacting, *"Show 'em who's gonna laugh last!"*

Consideration of any one of the foregoing new Super Objectives should confirm that it answers by inclusion the total of the facts listed in all the appraisal categories and affords the actor an acutely emotional basis for the required attitudes and conditioned responses to a very moving degree.

The Neurosis-Provoking Moment should be recognized as being vastly different as to form and result from the "History of The Character" recommended by some teachers. The latter, as most know, is a written biography of the character's prior life which the actor prepares to fit the given circumstances and actions of the role, detailing imaginary formative years, the adolescent years and the period of time preceding the written sequences of the role.

It is my deep conviction that what is lacking in such an approach is *that all-important causative moment and its resulting conditioning* which would make any such constructed biography far more meaningful as it results moment after moment, event after event, from a truly neurotic and experienceable source rather than simply being a product of the actor's intellectual process and therefore being subject to single-dimensioned inspiration and dull, labored logic.

The formative years were felt by most psychologists some years ago to be between about five years old (when school attendance begins and new peer relationship experiences disturb and confuse the previously held concepts of life) and twelve years old (when new kinds of exposure outside the home and the previously more impressionable feelings of the "child" experience a new altering of concepts of environment as the maturing psychology finds the power to develop logic and reasoned response).

In more recent years those same formative years have been judged by the same psychologists to be of shorter duration and to be ended earlier because of the extensive exposure to broader issues, through broadcast media and freer discussion throughout press, radio, television and public forum media, of more basic issues which impact upon the developing minds of the young.

However, whatever the range the actor forms the habit of using in constructing NPM's, as long as the beginnings of familial and social confrontations can be consciously experienced to send the psychology in a reactively traumatic direction, then the residual basis and power of the childhood trauma can, as it does in life, distort the learning process into a more meaningful and more productive biography if the actor desires to use the NPM approach.

The Neurosis-Provoking Moment is not a new thing except as codified into being an acting and role-preparing tool. Ever since the science of psychotherapy and psychoanalysis emerged it has been sought in treatment of patients for the purpose of catharsis through reexamination. Writers in all literary and dramaturgy fields have recognized its dramatic value. The play "*A Far Country*" and the film "*Freud*" which it generated was based on the neurosis-provoking moment of an actual patient of Freud. A sled called "*Rosebud*" denied to William Randolph Hearst in childhood after an accident was presented in "*Citizen Kane*" as the item which caused that outraged child to grow to adulthood wanting to "Make them give me everything I want!". Those who have toured the Hearst Castle in California know how much that "everything" included later from all over the world. Arthur Laurents's play "*A Clearing In The Woods*" centers around a neurosis-provoking moment in the childhood of its central character Virginia and the later life draining of its poisons. William Inge's play "*A Loss Of Roses*" actually relates Lila's neurosis-provoking moment from childhood near the end of Act III.

A leading psychotherapist, observing the preparing and use of the Neurosis-Provoking Moment in a number of acting classes, said of it "*It mixes together the recognized psychic ingredients of personality; brings them to the boiling point in the cauldron of a traumatic experience; and turns them loose to explode!*"

SOME ADDITIONAL NEUROSIS-PROVOKING MOMENT EXAMPLES

Lastly, to better exemplify the crescendoing and emotionally enriching results obtainable through the use of NPM's, here are some possible step-by-step progressions which might occur if the actors were to use this tool in preparing three different roles:

94

(1) Desperate for Acceptance; (2) Pressured; (3) Mean and Vengeful:

PERSONALITY	LIFE OBJECT	VAGUE SUPER OBJECTIVE	SUPER OBJECTIVE
Desperate for Acceptance	"How shut out I am!"	"Make somebody love me!"	"Show her I'm *not* a trash can!"
Pressured	"Their goddam demands!"	"Make them leave me alone!"	"Show them I've stopped listening!"
Mean and Vengeful	"How to survive in this jungle!"	"Get them before they get me!"	"Make her write *her own* name a hundred times!"

The character desperate for acceptance will perhaps have been progressed through an NPM involving a final encounter with a wealthy boy or girl who called it a "trashcan".... the second, in the process of building this pressured character, may have involved a childhood full of parental scoldings and pushings up to a final moment of scolding lecture by a parent... while the third will probably have been constructed through violent street childhood experiences up to a moment when a teacher, reacting to the already formed violence-prone student, embarrassed this boy in front of his street hoodlum peers.

It should be easily observed that by creating that final conditioning moment in each of the foregoing cases there are all the ingredients of personality which would be gleaned from the written role as well as, after the NPM and emerging of the new Super Objective, *a generating "catalyst" which defines and makes more specifically experienceable all the facts given by the author and created by the actor thus far.*

That generating catalyst which mixes all the ingredients together in a usable form is the Neurosis-Provoking Moment. The secret of its immense value is that it works much like a formatted disk inserted into a computer. It conditions—almost beyond the power to believe!—all output from the character containing it as its emotional core.

It seems to me that to ignore the need for a formative moment when seeking emotional depth for a character's later development, and to assume that the character's psychology has simply evolved at some unspecified time, is to leave unexplained, beyond experiencing and beyond use, the driving forces of its very life!

The Neurosis-Provoking Moment has over the years been responsible for many highly praised performances and has in some cases helped reap awards for those performances.

I recommend it highly.

Section III

The Creative Subtext

"*An actor's talent is like a blinding beam of pure white light which, when directed through the prism of an expert technique, will send forth a glaxy of the brightest colors the world has ever known.*"

—Cletus Young
Student of Mr. Parke

Chapter Seven

The Beats and Creative Manners of Preparing Them

For those who don't know what the words *Creative Subtext* mean, it is that part of the performance of a role which involves actors with the *separate moments*, one after another, and the devising of specific approaches or "tools" for the experiencing of them *in uniquely creative and interesting manners which will deepen the actor's involvement and enable him to bring more of his own available excitements to each moment for himself and for the observer.*

This is the aspect of preparing roles which has, throughout the history of the Stanislavski and other methods, created most of those table-pounding arguments among coaches and teachers and their disciples; has created confusion for actors as to which way is "right" or "best"; and has meant the difference between bit role and top stardom careers for the people who have chosen one way or another.

Teachers and coaches who feel they have no growth still ahead of them or who feel that they in fact know it all will say their way is the *only* way. You may believe them or not. On the other hand, the teachers and coaches who know they will still grow because they keep themselves still open to new ideas, new ways, changes, developments and discoveries—those teachers will teach what they now know works, to the best of their abilities, while still searching. For them especially to feel that their current approaches are the only desirable approaches is therefore ridiculous. For actors to believe the same thing is a mistake.

There is so much confusion in this "creative approach" area. I for one can't with good conscience say that my own way, as outlined in this book, is going to remain my way in its present form forever. However, I'm willing to spell out my own present approach and outline the history of discoveries and developments which have contributed to its current form.

Again we must start with Stanislavski. Even he encountered those table-pounding arguments, right under the roof of his own theatre, with regard to the creative processes employed in the productions at the very birthplace of "the method". There is available in his diary comments about those difficulties and disagreements among himself, his literary and business partner Nemirovich-Dantchenko, their designers and the leading teachers instructing in the several Moscow Art Theatre studios at the time which can be found in Volume 9 of the quarterly *Tulane Drama Review* in an article about the preparation of "*Ghosts*" at the MAT. In that article you can detect that the creative side of even Stanislavski's own endeavors had its constant disagreements.

Also, you should remember that you're studying an *art*, not a machinery-assembly course. If you are a mere *actor*—a simple *doer of things*, as the dictionary has described us, you may be satisfied with copying and duplicating someone else's creations all your life. But if you are an *artist* as well you are more probably a fanatic Messianic revoltist aimed at replacing the current, the established, the formed, with something you alone are privileged to discover.

I find myself quoting often a little maxim of Picasso's which defines art very nicely. You might find it reassuring to remember it when considering the truly creative aspects of acting and justifying your continuing search into new and better ways:

"Art is the lie that makes us realize a truth!"

At this point in preparation of roles we're entering into that phase of the work where you must know how to *lie* effectively to both yourself and to your audiences, in order that you may bring an *exciting and impacting* truth rather than an unexciting and easily ignored one in given moments, so that your audience may realize better and with more impact on their sensibilities the *underlying* truth which you and the author wish to present. This is what creative acting is all about.

THE BEATS

If you are to gain clarity in the separate moments of roles for even yourself, the first step is to break up the Units (for which you will already have found Unit Objects and Through Lines of Action) into their many smaller, separate *Beats*.

The things that happen to the character, and the actions it takes in response, also the thoughts and feelings which dominate and cause those actions, change from moment to moment throughout roles. Each moment, whether quite short or perhaps more elongated over several pages of script, requires a new shifting of the character's focus, attention to a new object, person, experience or whatever else will be most productive in terms of involvement choice. To allow yourself and the character to let these changes remain vague, to dovetail them helter-skelter and without definition, to fuzzy them out with sameness throughout, would be defeating to each separate development step the author has created and to the separate ideas the actor wants to bring to each moment and its experiencing.

Sometimes a new Beat begins because of something another character says or does; sometimes a mere look from another character changes the scene's focus for your character; sometimes it's the opening of a door and someone's entrance. In other words, a Beat almost always changes because of an external stimulus of some sort. Something outside the character itself is usually the trigger for the new focus, but there are exceptions when the character itself moves to a new thought without any outside cause. As the character's thought-focus changes, a new thought-focus—a new Beat—replaces and ends the former object of attention.

When you begin to use beats in breaking down roles you may have a tendency to change Beats with almost every line of

101

dialogue. You've detected the slight differences in degrees of anger or pleading or frustration, etc. But as you become more familiar with Beats you'll find that, even though the *degree* of intensity may have changed slightly here and there—growing more intense here, becoming less intense there, seeming to disappear altogether for a moment—*the Beat may not have really changed.* The character still has the same thought in its mind while those variations come and go. In other words, you will learn the wisdom of considering the finding of longer Beats, at least to the extent they can apply productively. You will learn that, just as in life, the character should not be so easily diverted from its one main concentration focus or the feeling substance of a longer moment. You will observe, if you don't already realize, that a single *thought* usually exists for only one brief moment while *feeling and its cause* exist for a much longer time.

For example, who of us in real life stops arguing just because we grow quiet and walk out of a room? In our mind the argument is surely still continuing. Even if we storm out, get into our car and drive away, perhaps even go for a walk in the park, aren't we still arguing with that other person or resenting something that was said by them? Remembering that constructed characters are no different from our own behavior patterns should bring the insight that in storming out of the house the door will certainly have been slammed, the baby's tricycle on the walk will have been kicked, the car door will have been slammed, the key in the ignition will have frustrated us by sticking in our shaking hand, the tires will have screeched on the driveway asphalt as we slammed the car into violent getaway, the car will probably careen around the corner dangerously at the end of the block, etc. Even later, if we do go for that walk in the park it's probably in an attempt to cool our temper. The Beat, still going, will find cans, bottles and quick food trash to kick along the path, the children playing in the swing area may well be yelled at, the park bench may be broken from the violence with which we throw ourself onto it, etc.

By elongating Beats to the points to which they can be elongated *while still not forsaking one single excitement,* we can more closely duplicate the processes of our own lives.

Many actors suffer the worry that they may not be beginning new Beats or ending previous ones at the right spots. This is not a new problem for actors who use them in breakdowns. However, the desirability of shortening or lengthening a Beat can be tested and the changing point can always be changed when inspiration suggests a better spot with its better reason for the change. Often we discover such reasons. It is so easy to change the point at which the Beat shall be changed and just as easy to discover that a new and better content can be planned for it.

Some actors worry, too, about elongating their Beats to so great lengths that they may in performance miss some interesting little moments provided by the author which elongation of one dominating concern or focus can cause them to pass over unaware and neglect in later performance. Of course this is possible, and it is something to be aware of. However, a chosen focus in a Beat is much more elastic and flexible than some actors realize at first. An actor deeply involved in a particular thought-focus—at least if via an Object rather than an Action—can still briefly experience those little moments of slightly different kinds and use them to the degree that they warrant being used while still keeping the character's main concern foremost in the mind and feelings. There is no need to completely stop to involve with some little pyro-technic distraction of the type that some actors and actresses confuse us with so often. Those little moments will generally be recognized and used in some spontaneous manner and form, as if mere momentary impulses, by the more gifted actor.

CHOOSING THE BEAT'S CONTENT

While I recommend the use of *Beat Objects* to focus the actor's and the character's attention and feelings on the most important and most productive concerns in all individual Beats, there are other approaches recommended by teachers of acting for use in elongated moments of roles. My preference derives from my observation that while *sense memory* (an alternative) by itself is in my estimation limiting and one-dimensional and an *action* (another alternative) without something behind it is in my esti-mation hollow and unsatisfying, both can be included by inference in any good Object. Further, should the actor desire to create a

103

more total mind-and-body experience for creative result in a given Beat, the Object lends itself so wholly to the process of finding and using what is called a *Creative Psychological Objective* (another tool for use in special Beats which I highly recommend and which will be explained later).

Those teachers who advocate the use of a single Sense Memory in some or many beats of roles are of the persuasion that such a device has certain body-involving and experiential value which can involve the actor with a "substitution" experience to the extent that the Beat will be more interesting. It is simply my own conviction, though, that most Beats provide sufficiently involving thought and feeling matter organically and emerging strictly from the character in the situation, allowing moments to be experienced through the character's own response conditioning if these elements are captured in effective feeling wordings of Beat Objects. I would prefer that the initial consideration of a Beat's content be in terms of the character's own reality.

Some teachers still advocate the use of *actions* in the separate Beats of roles. Some of us no longer advocate them, feeling that chosen Actions too often produce little private experience, being in the main too often focused on other characters and on mere situations, while a Beat Object produces *both* personal and inter-personal experience and prevents the sacrificing or ignoring of either.

At this point I want to remind the reader that in his last few years, between 1936 and 1938, Stanislavski was modifying his own approach with that same conviction, as indicated in those recorded comments to the cast of the opera "Werther" in Paris to the effect that the actor's attention should be moving *from one Object to another.*

Many present day teachers agree with him and in the process of teaching the use of Objects have defined their use still further.

Some actors are also taught to use other "tools" within specific Beats, such as that item called variously *emotional memory, affective memory* or *emotional recall.* (The aversion some of us entertain for this particular approach as an acting tool for use within Beats will be thoroughly discussed in Chapter Eight, dealing with "Additional Tools Of The Creative Subtext".)

The foregoing three alternatives to Beat Objects of course share with them the objective of enlivening the body in some manner appropriate for the character and bringing discernible differences among the experiences of the different Beats.

There is a shortcut available to the involving of the body with the feeling processes. It may have existed for a longer time but it has been copiously confirmed in learned writings about the discoveries in recent times of the different functions of the two sides of the brain. I, and a few others of whom I know who also teach actors, call it "*Body Finding*".

BODY FINDING WITH THE RIGHT SIDE OF THE BRAIN

The manner of drawing on the right side of the brain for a more totally involving manner of finding Beat Objects, as pertaining to this Chapter's contents, is highly recommended by me and some others for even the initial searching for emotionally conditioned Life Objects, Vague Super Objectives, Unit Objects and Through Lines of Action as well as Beat Objects for separate moments of roles, however at this point we'll be discussing this marvelous phenomenon mostly in terms of finding the latter.

While the left side of the brain is the storehouse for information and data, logic, formulae and "executive direction" of objective behavior, and of course does contain carefully file-foldered conscious memory of all kinds, the *body* is often not attracted to participate with any willingness in simple intellectual data-consulting—particularly when any emotional or deep feeling experience is concerned. Yet in each of our own emotional or deep feeling moments in our private lives our bodies have participated to a striking degree. To leave them out of our process when searching for deep feeling Objects is a mistake.

Almost every actor is aware of body positions which most often accompany different types of feelings. Some in fact simply form their bodies in those positions and remain in those positions felt (by the left side of the brain, unfortunately) to be "right" in the hope of continuous feeling involvement. These actors' work tends toward *the playing of results* and *the representing of feelings*. This manner of involving the body in our feeling process is not what we're talking about here.

The body itself, in its own manner, can instead aid in a remarkable way in the *tools-finding* process.

To begin with, the *left* side of the brain—that side most often relied upon by an "intellectual" actor—has been determined to be the file department for information, logic, directed coordination and all the processes which are associated with their kinds of learning, observation, theory, etc. The file clerks in this side of the brain are concerned with purely mental processes of intelligence and intellect.

It is the *right* side of the brain which is too seldom used by actors, usually because they don't know how to call upon it. Yet it is this side of the brain which is the *body*-experiencing file department side.

The right side of the brain *experiences*. It experiences sensations such as soft, hard, cold, warm, visual images, sounds, smells and touch. It experiences fatigue, energy charge, pain, comfort, relaxation and acute agitation through its ability to register them in the moment of their occurring. It is the part of the brain which, in experiencing nervous tension and stress in physical terms, can register these so strongly that the organism eventually suffers ulcers and other body disorders. It *feels* impulses as they occur and causes the body to react accordingly, creating the spontaneity so desirable in actors' work. In short, the right side of the brain is the one attached to *body experiencing* and is the side of the brain which must become involved in the creating of any total experience.

Sense memory is stored in the right side of the brain almost exclusively. The haughty, highly organized and precise, intellectual clerks in the left side's file department can *talk* about sense memory, but its rich file resides across the hall in the other clerks' disorganized file drawers. Sense memory is physical, not intellectual. Without it, and without the resulting reexperiencing of it in actors' work, few experiences can be total.

There is inter-relationship, for instance, between a feeling of hopelessness or helplessness and the body fatigue which is often associated with it; even the left side's file clerks can see that association. But the experience of such hopelessness or helplessness is too often based on observation and intellectual theory about behavior and nothing more if the actual *body experience* cannot be somehow involved. It is unthinkable that any actor should be completely satisfied with such a half-experience, although some are.

A fact overlooked by actors who have not learned the ways of involving the right side of the brain and its rich sense memory and emotional memory files is that, while behaviors of certain recognizable personality types may be somewhat similar, the actor preparing those many personalities for roles has not had a lifetime of *experience* within all the spectrums of all those personalities. Thus, the temptation is often there to rely on only intelligence and observation of others. However, each individual of those generalized and categorizable personality types has behaved in *its own individual manner and pattern*, as would the actor himself were he of that particular personality type. Others' patterns and body experiencings of emotional and stressful moments or entire lifetimes can apply to us to only generalized extents. Therein lies the danger for the actor who must rely only upon observation of others of those types.

The actor himself has experienced most feelings of depth and most emotions, at least in brief moments in the past. It is too bad that any of us destined for acting careers later cannot, in such emotional moments, simply step outside ourselves and observe what our bodies are doing as they participate in their unique manners in such moments.

Although seldom aware of them, we have *our own unique body agitation patterns of very similar forms* which occur time after time under emotion-agitating conditions. It is ideal if we can learn to use *these*, rather than other people's, for such moments in roles.

For a moment, let's assume the impossible—that at several stressful moments of our past life which had similar feelings and emotions of *loss* in common we were able to stand across the room or nearby for a few moments and watch, now, what we failed to observe then.

When at age four we heard the rifle shot in the barnyard and knew our pet horse had had to be killed because of an injury, all we noticed of that moment was the agony of the loss. We weren't watching our body's parallel experiencing of pain and contortion. It did certain things and moved in certain ways as we cried for a time in our despair.

Later, perhaps at seven, when our twin brother was lifted limp and lifeless from the deep well where he had fallen and drowned, again we experienced the acute loss in mental anguish terms, but again we were not aware that the body went through very similar agitated contortions to those which it went through on the earlier occasion.

Then at nine, when they came out to us and told us that the father we loved so much had just died, once more we consciously experienced the mental anguish but failed to notice the body going through its often repeated and conditioned parallel experience pattern.

Even older still, in our early twenties, when afforded the scholarship to apprentice at a summer theatre and finally begin our acting career, and were told by our mother that she needed us at home and we must give up any hope of such things until she was gone, another mental anguish moment occurred in the privacy of our upstairs bedroom. Again there was no observation of the body as it went through those same or very similar patterns of agitated parallel moments and positions, simply because our mind was so involved with what we must lose.

Updating this "body key" file, perhaps just last week our life partner whom we love deeply has had an auto accident and lies in the Medical Center hovering between life and death. In the hospital room, being more adult now, we contain our bursting feelings of imminent loss as much as possible, but each time we return to our empty-feeling house we dissolve into our anguish more freely and, while we suffer the mental agony and pain of the apparently hopeless situation, our body, of which we're unconscious because of our preoccupation, is going through the exact same or a very similar behavior pattern as in those other long forgotten moments!

Our own unique and individual body experiencings of feelings and emotions do not age. That's what science now tells us. They do not grow mature and change. They have been with us since earliest childhood. They are *ours*, and it is probable that they are quite different from any conceptualized body patterns of other people for such feelings which might in generalizing be thought to apply to us with some substantive degree of deeply satisfying experience.

As mentioned earlier, the reason for postponing this discussion of *body-finding* for the combined mind-and-body experience in the finding of tools for the actor is that it is in *the separate Beats* of roles where the choices can and probably will contribute the more physically apparent colors in the actor's work.

The "life personality" tools (the Life Object, the Vague Super Objective, Neurosis-Provoking Moment and Super Objective especially) lie barely if at all discernible (in a particularized sense) throughout the majority of moments, of and by themselves. But the *Beats*, with their immediacy of thought-feeling choices, are the actor's most important opportunities for the bringing of the clear colors and unlimited totality into play for both their experiential value to the actor and their visible physical behavior aspects of the character for the spectator.

At this point we're discussing the *creative subtext* aspects available throughout roles and, no matter what approach for bringing creative colors the actor may use, the *body must not be left out of the process*. Body-finding of "tools" will invariably create a more total experience simply because by "asking the body" to help find our tools we will gain its enthusiastic and all-knowing participation later. There is a nice, easy and effective manner in which this can be done:

THE BODY FINDING PROCESS

The feeling thought focus, still unworded as yet by the actor as he faces the challenge of turning the desired feeling or emotion of an elongated moment (a particular Beat) into the most evocative wording possible for himself, is at least recognized as to a form and can to a degree be felt. It is at this point—in this moment of starting to find the best and most moving wording for an Object to focus and generate his own experience—that the actor should seek the body's help. The wording he must seek with the aid of his body might not apply with equal or any effectiveness for someone else, but by seeking the body's participation in the phrase-finding process at this precise point the actor can with far

more effectiveness reach into the body's experience storehouse—
that right side of the brain—and form a worded Object which will
excite the body as well as satisfy the intellectual mind.

The generalized version of the feeling desired being familiar
to the actor, it simply remains for him to feel that feeling in a
sufficiently intensified degree to start the body's impulses into
movement or improvised particiapation and continue its different
versions of positions and movements as it associates them with
the feeling area being explored. Any feeling moment having many
shadings and many variations of focuses within its available spectrum, the silent or verbalized improvising for a few moments with
the constantly changing thought and feeling areas, combined with
the body movements, will produce an ever expanding list of
worded thought experiences of Object form from which the actor
may simply choose the one which most involves both the feeling
mind and the participating body.

During the mosaic-like experience of quite brief and ever
changing positions and impulses some of them may seem cliche
and seem to be produced by past observations of generalized
patterns, or even seem to be borrowed from other people's
moments of similar type, but this is to be expected in any
prolonged exploration of such experiencing and matters not.
There will be a sufficient number of original, very personal and
unique body experiences and movements resulting from such an
improvised experience that the actor will obtain a gardenful of
highly personal choices.

It is important that such an improvised body exploration toward
a worded result be in an agitated, intensified state. The body of
an actor, if unaccustomed to processes of this type, may not move
by itself and may need to be prompted to cooperate via some
conscious triggering of the constantly changing patterns by the
actor. Once invited to join in the process and constantly urged
to explore a brief moment in its own manner, then abruptly
abandon that moment and flip to another, another and another,
the body will normally oblige happily for as long as the actor
continues to agitate the inner feeling process with some intensity.

Actors who have never before appreciated the possible results of encouraging the body into whatever acting tool finding for Beats have new excitements in store for them!

BEAT OBJECTS

Stanislavski was not unaware of the importance of cause and motivation for the "actions" he recommended so strongly in his "Method of Physical Action". As stated earlier, he referred to those causes and inner motivations often under the labels "Object of Concentration" and "Object of Attention". He simply had not found the more productive manners of incorporating the "Object" into his System as the potent acting tool, of and by itself, which it has since become. After exposure to Pavlov's conditioned response theories he was seeking those more productive manners and the searching had led him to those comments to the "Werther" opera cast with regard to moving the attention from one Object to another throughout roles. That is the approach we'll deal with here because I am so deeply convinced that it is the best way found thus far for the actor to achieve optimum results.

After seeking in the dialogue and action put down by the author to find where one Beat ends and another begins, my people are taught to find the best possible *Beat Object* for bringing the entire Beat to vibrant life; for focusing the actor's concentration upon a certain, chosen facet of the situation or the character's own experience; and for awakening the ultimate of feeling and emotion through that focus in the actor's own spirit.

What is needed as the most desirable focus for the creative subtext of the Beat is the aspect upon which the character should be concentrated because of its unique personality.

With the Life Object and Super Objective coursing through our veins and enlivened and conditioned by the Neurosis-Provoking Moment, and further knowing what the Unit Object and Through Line of Action for the entire Unit would condition us (the character) to be thinking of, it is comparatively easy to discover the particular facet of each moment (each Beat) that would attract the character's mind, hold its attention for some period and generate its feelings.

Since an Object of any kind is a worded tool, and since there

111

are actors who are not particularly creative, there can in their hands be dull, lifeless Objects. However, there are also highly sensitized actors with ultimate creativity on call, and there are highly creative Objects to be found on every occasion by the latter. The quality and eventual effectiveness of such a worded tool depends upon how effectively it has been worded by the actor planning to use it. The feeling actor who has access to his own inner processes and can summon them to a satisfactory degree through feeling thought can judge whether a certain Object will serve him well or whether another, better one should be sought.

Also, the feeling actor will probably have sought the body's valuable help in forming the Object and as a result will find those Objects which the body, having participated in the finding process, will enjoy using along with the actor!

EXTERNAL AND INTERNAL OBJECTS

In my teaching I strongly recommend more *internal* Objects (some call them Self-Experiencing Objects) for as many Beats of roles as their use can be justified. I believe that an actor examining and trying the *more externally focused* and fairly interpersonal Objects in the following examples, then trying the *internal* ones, will observe the vastly different results:

EXTERNAL BEAT OBJECTS	INTERNAL BEAT OBJECTS
For an exciting moment: How great everything's turning out!.... So much excitement!....	How wired I am!.... This all-over giddiness!.... The happiest moment of my life!....
Disgusted at somebody's behavior: More silly antics!.... How stupid he is!.... Something to throw at him!.... His poor embarrassed wife!	This captive-audience feeling.... How out of place I am here!.... Someplace to throw up!....
Somebody else has just gotten the award: That amateurish jerk!.... How smug he's looking!.... How undeserving he is!.... Those stupid-ass judges!....	More goddam injustice!.... How unappreciated I am!.... All that wasted effort!....

112

In a moment of acute embarrassment:
All those staring eyes!.... How superior they think they are!.... Their snickering smiles!....

My goddam clumsiness!.... My eternal screw-ups!.... How stupid I acted!....

In a close moment with a lover:
How wonderful she (he) is!.... The one I've always been looking for!.... The way she looks at me!....

This complete-at-last feeling!.... How scary love is!.... This warm-all-over tingle!.... The end of the searching!....

For a boring afternoon:
The fake enthusiasm on all their faces!.... This stupid, boring day!.... All those mud-puddle vegetators!....

My meaningless life!.... How empty I feel!.... Something, anything!.... The things I could be doing somewhere!....

In a divorce argument:
Her non-stop tongue!.... How unreasonable she's being!.... What we're doing to the kids with all this!....

How caged I've been all this time!.... My own goddam life at last!.... The ulcer I'm getting!....

However, as much as I recommend the more internally-focused Objects—for bringing a more involving subtext experience than the externally-focused ones, I do recognize, as any actor must, that there are moments in all roles for both, and I also recognize that some actors are more comfortable in interpersonal acting styles than in highly personalized experiencing of their own characters' concerns. Either approach—whichever brings the individual the most experiential feelings for both mind and body—is good.

It being possible that some readers may not fully understand the process of breaking down Beats and choosing Objects for their elongated moments of experiencing, there follows a sample breakdown of a short monologue taken from one of my original works entitled "*Petals*" with the Beat changes marked where they might occur and the Beat Objects which might be chosen for their experiencing indicated in the margins at the start of the Beats in which they were used by one actress preparing the role.

The short play is about a Japanese girl, Tokuho, who, following exchange student college graduation in the United States, has married a young American from the small Midwest town in which

113

the college is located, only to discover later that her new husband's mother is making their married life miserable and their
neighbors and townspeople will never accept her. Born in a small
Japanese town herself but to a well to do family, she learned
English in a private school and was able to continue her education
in America. The scene from which the monologue is excerpted
takes place in their living room.

(TOKUHO reenters the room with a cup of tea,
still upset. She sits in silence for a moment,
looking down at her tea disconsolately, then turns
to WILL.)

THOSE COLD EYES!   **TOKUHO**

Please.... talk to me. I didn't mean anything about us. You know
I didn't. It's just this place.... the way so many people think here.
Like your mother this morning. I hate the way she looks at me
sometimes. So polite, but never warm. I'm still a foreigner to her.
I know she wishes you'd never married me. You know that. And
everybody on the street, in the supermarket.... "She's one of
those. She's different. She's an outsider. She doesn't belong here!"
They all think that. You know they do.

(WILL doesn't respond. He sits with his eyes
closed in a pained expression, unable to disagree
and hurting for her. After a moment she continues:)

THIS CRAZY DIFFERENCE!

I know it's complicated. I knew it would be. In my country too,
if we were married and living there. You don't look Japanese, and
I don't look American. If we were living near my parents there
you might feel the way I do. Not because of my parents. It would
be all the others, outside. My parents would know that I love you,
and they would try to love you too. Why can't your mother accept
me? She knows you love me. I know that too. It's not that. It's
just this crazy difference!

(He still sits silent and brooding. She would like
TIMES
POISONED
AIR! to relieve the tension between them as she moves
across the sofa to be closer to him.)

114

Let's go away.... soon. I have some money, you know that. And you'd be able to work wherever you want to. There are other companies like yours in any big city. We could start over there.... away from here. Maybe in New York, or Los Angeles, or some other big city, where there are all kinds of people from everywhere in the world. Here.... Well, here it's so different. They don't know what I am or how to treat me. They smile.... but their eyes examine. They speak oh so slowly and wonder if I even understand any of what they're saying. And when I go out of a room I hear them talking, and they stop when I come back. I know they can't ever accept me here. It's not their fault, I guess.... it's just something that....

(There still being no response from him, /she adopts a more urgent tone as she continues:)
OUR ONLY HOPE!

If we can't go somewhere else.... get away from your mother and just be together, we'll never be happy. At least we should.... we have to.... move out of this house! Please.... I know you feel your mother needs you now, but I need you too. She has you more than I do. I'm not complaining, or being jealous. I just want more of your time to be with me because I love you. She calls you into her on some pretense every time she knows we're alone toghether.... and you stay and stay, and I know she wants me to be alone and worry and become discouraged. Honestly, Will, I'm not complaining. I'm not. I'm suffering.... a lot. It's different. You know what I'm going through. I've told you.... in bed late at night after those other times.... so many times. I just want us to get away from what's happening here. It could be different somewhere else. Please.... say we can go soon!

(Still he doesn't respond)

Will?.... Will you think about it?

I recommend to my people that in dividing the scenes at Beat changing points lines should be drawn from one margin across to the other edge so that later, while learning the dialogue, the Beat Object of each Beat which is written at the start of each Beat and the line so visibly delineating the exact moment for the

115

change into the new Beat, with its changed focus, can better remind to divide the line study process into precise and separate segments, so that each Beat Object, with its distinct focus and feeling content, can be experienced as the lines are committed to memory. *Studying the lines one complete Beat at a time before going on to other dialogue* enables the actor to consciously practice the body's involvement with the feelings of the Beat, and form the resulting habits for it while studying. In that manner both the inner experiences and the surface differences among the separate Beats will remain and be carried forth into performances later.

The clarities which are brought by the actor to the chosen manners of experiencing the separate moments of roles will allow the spectator to observe and vicariously experience with those same clarities what is happening inside the character as the result of the situations in which it finds itself involved throughout the role.

Now, since there are some actors who fail to appreciate the desirability of breaking down roles into Beats, I will quote an exchange from recorded notes of a critique discussion I had once with an actor approaching middle age who had just recently decided to study with me after a lengthy professional career which seemed at the moment to have stagnated into smaller, less important roles:

THE ACTOR

"But I'd like to think that I've always brought all those changes.... all those beats, you call them.... without having to break them up so carefully. They're just there. You can't help noticing them. Isn't it just up to the actor to bring them out? Do you really have to spend a lot of time breaking scenes up into such definite beats and plan them so definitely?"

MY RESPONSE

"I've seen a lot of your work over the years, as you know, and while I generally like it I've always felt that you had much more to give as an actor than you realized or knew how to use. Now, I'm going to tell you something that I hope will explain something

116

you told me earlier has always troubled you. You told me producers and directors haven't really given you any chance to 'shine out'.... those were your words.... that you've had difficulty persuading them to give you those larger roles you've had in your earlier years here. Here's something you didn't know. When I was a casting director you worked on my shows several times in somewhat smaller roles, right? You wrote me a couple of times, thanking me.... thank-you notes that I didn't deserve, because you were never recommended by me for those roles. It was always the director or producer who knew your work who felt, in their words, 'He can do the job'.... 'He looks right' or something like that. Never 'He'll be exciting' or 'He'll make the role shine out' or anything like that.

"I think that you didn't realize that those moments you feel were simply to be noticed and they'd be there and the actor could simply 'bring them out', as you said, weren't clearly enough defined in your preparation so that you could do anything with them beyond just what the author had already provided.

"I want to go a little further now, hopefully without offending you. Those times when your performances have been called 'adequate'—I'll bet you hate that word—or 'well cast', which says nothing good beyond just that—those times and those words have meant that in people's opinions you were up to what the author's dialogue and action and character required.... but no more. I think you must have known what they meant, and I'm sure those reviews bothered you.

"Beat breakdown isn't the total answer to your problem, but it could make a difference immediately in the roles you're doing. Remember that nasty note you wrote me once when you were told by our mutual friend that I'd called you a 'utility actor'? You didn't know that the star of the series had taken me to task for not trying to get someone who'd be exciting in that role. I had to explain that you were not my choice, and why the director had requested you, and it turned out that our mutual friend was in my office when that phone call came. I'm sorry he was there, and told you, but I imagine he was in his own way trying to help you see what you were missing.

"The letter I wrote replying to your nasty one expressed my

117

truest feelings about you. For somebody who had never sought any kind of coaching or formal training, yet worked as much as you did in those days, your talent itself could certainly claim some credit. You had everything but technique at the time. You had looks—which you still have; you had good, organic masculine appeal; you had a good mind; and there were many roles you could serve easily, just as you were doing. I even told you that if you wanted to learn how to bring more depth, power and excitement into the way you did what you did I thought you could be an important actor. I believed that then, and I'm more sure of it now, since you're concerned that something's missing and seeking to find out what it is.

"You're customarily hired for that fine personality you bring to roles. The next step for you, even at this later time in your career, is the clear and productive breaking down of Beats and deciding what to do with each one to make it 'shine out'. You're right.... it does take some work.... but it's worth all that work later when the result gets you praise you've never gotten before and you start climbing back into those larger roles you're not getting anymore."

The actor cited went to work immediately. New and more interesting colors began appearing in all his work, finally attracting the support of a director of a major motion picture which brought him back to starring billing and he has done a number of excellent, highly praised top starring roles and two television series since!

Some years later he has told me that it is apparently still his basic personality which has always been the thing he has been hired for in roles, whether starring or series ones, but that it took Beats and Beat Objects to bring him back to top attention and to the beautiful hilltop mansion overlooking most of Los Angeles and Hollywood in which we were sitting as we talked.

OBJECTS VS. ACTIONS!

Since the whole philosophy and methodology of the use of Objects rather than Actions in Beats is still new to so many actors who have been book-trained through the earlier techniques described in Stanislavski's notes as published in those books *An Actor Prepares, Building A Character* and *Creating A Role*, and since the more recent development of the Object's use has been less publicized and disseminated in written descriptions of acting techniques, the arguments in support of its use probably need some lengthy discussion here.

Objects' main functions are the truthful, actor feeling-involving specifics they can provide.... both as long-range (total life or larger unit) focuses for thought and feeling conditioning bases, behavior patterns, psychological appropriateness, etc., and as individual moments' focuses (as Beat Objects) for the purpose of experiencing more meaningfully the obvious changes of temporary subtext supplied by the writer.'

Objects are not simply ideas for use to structure and punctuate with changes the continuing chain of living moments of a role. In any level, as Life, Unit or Beat Objects, they are the character's continuous underlying experience throughout whatever length of the role to which they apply.

Unlike the Action or Intention—and therefore not limited to the action spectrum, they are instead a constant source of problem experiencing, emotional agitation and other subtext specifics which they enable the actor to share with the viewer through their use. They lend themselves to being easily held in the consciousness, fixed and pulsating within both the character and the actor for their duration, causing myriad *impulses* to take some action while still, for the desired length of time, creating the *inability to cope meaningfully* with whatever problem is imbedded in the concentration by their wordings.

It is not the taking of any action or pushing of any intention which distinguishes the actor's moments in a role. It is rather where the mind of the character and the actor is focused, the feelings and emotions kindled by what is focused upon, and the total experience that can be produced by an Object worded by the actor to give it importance, feeling impact and the resulting impulses and behavioral moments *behind and between* the lines of dialogue and the attempts at taking action.

Writers are paid to supply dialogue, actions and events. The actor, in the final analysis, must supply the thought focuses, the feeling and the ever changing subtext experience which gives those writer-supplied elements of a story their life.

119

An actor may be quite "adequate" yet simply be serving as a functionary/interpreter of what the writer has already been paid for. A different actor may be brilliant—with insight, nuance, inner dynamics and creatively interesting facets throughout his work—through focusing on and involving the conditioned personality responses of the character and allowing them to involve and inspire his own deepest feelings and his own creative art.

Acting, in the end, is more often *not* acting; it is essentially *being*. Actors who can freely take action at all times usually forget to *be*. Their human counterparts, floundering in the muck of their problems, are not so able.

Acting is its most brilliant and affecting for the viewer when it is sharing its experience—allowing its character to be seen to suffer; to try without success to overcome what is overwhelming it; to experience inadequacy, confusion and indecision; to exhibit all the human frailties with which its viewer can more totally identify than would be possible with a totally capable, action-taking (and therefore quite inhuman) effigy of competence and logic!

It is the unique opportunity of the actor, and one seldom accorded to real life experience, to have the luxury of sharing and baring, moment after moment, those rich inner sources of feeling and emotion which are the reasons why paying theatre-goers and filmgoers flock to watch them and enjoy the catharsis of vicarious experience through being allowed to look in their windows and see the most private of events occurring in their characters' subtexts.

Objects make *being*, in its most truthfully experienced form, possible and, further, through the actor's devising of colorful and deep choices, they can make simple being a creative and affecting experience.

The feeling use of an Object affects the body moment after moment in manners not dictated by the situation in which the character finds itself but by its feelings and what those feelings send cascading through the actor's instrument to its farthest extremities, enhancing the expressive performance of the actor.

The Object also affects the voice and speech, affecting the

ability to communicate and enriching the actor's dialogue with emotional timbre and mood color.

A special advantage of Object over Action or Intention is its versatility and its varying levels of available intensity. It can explode in a moment in any or all directions; it can abate in the next moment to a brooding, soft-edged experience when not agitated by some circumstance. It simply *is*, without any manipulation or decision as to how to use it. It sustains because it hangs in the mind and feelings easily and potently. It frees the actor, even in its most agitated and intensified state or level, of concern with *how* to do something. Its many varied impulses come from it being less like the directed arrow of the "action-playing archer" —aimed so singly in one direction and forsaking all other experience content—and more like a "porcupine", for example, with its quills ready, tensed, and available to throw in many directions at once. Not being limited to a decided action but rather being the source feeling that makes any action desirable but perhaps impossible for the moment, it includes in its use all the myriad experiences which are potential in any important moment for a character. It creates, and includes in its experiencing, those frustrations, irritations, angers, feelings of inadequacy and helplessness in appropriate moments and in precisely appropriate forms for the particular personality.

The so long established technique of employing "actions" and "intentions" within Beats of roles being still today the approach most generally known by actors (again, because of the early fixing on those two tools in American teaching and the ignoring of those last "Object"-incorporating years of Stanislavski), perhaps the following approach variations may help clarify exactly what is involved.

Here are some examples of how Objects can better illuminate characters' moments and render simple dialogue and action more specific colors and experiential values than other tools might:

A businessman, in a meeting with his boss and coworkers as his boss decides who is to receive a prize assignment, can be far more interesting for the viewer and himself if an Object such as "How inadequate I'd be!" makes his detail-discussing hesitant and slightly frightened because of his personality—even though the assignment would mean more money for him—than if he uses an Action or Intention such as "Get the assignment!" There's no comparison.

A housewife, tired of marriage, children, housework and neglect, would plan a fifth wedding anniversary party with her husband in a far more interesting manner, in spite of the detail-involving dialogue, if using an Object such as "Five miserable lifetimes!" because of her personality than if she were simply playing an Action or Intention such as "Make sure everything's planned right."

A young street gang member, reporting to his gang friends about a knifing by a rival gang's member and suggesting the need for retaliatory violence of some kind on his gang's part, would be far more interesting to the viewer, in spite of his violent-sounding dialogue urging to action, if he were using an Object such as "Another stupid bloodbath night!" rather than an Action or Intention such as "Get back at the bastards!"

A corporation board chairman, sitting in a crucial meeting where the dialogue is dull and simply detail-involved would be infinitely more interesting to the viewer, even while detail-explaining with apparently total interest, if using an Object such as "These mealy-mouth hypocrites!"—because of his awareness of the eager upcomers' one-upsmanships against him and his character's conditioned guardedness against such attempts—than simply using an Action or Intention such as "Straighten this mess out!"

In other words, if the character is acutely self-doubting *that self doubt* is the businessman's situation more than getting the coveted assignment. If the character is conditioned to feeling mistreated all her life, *those five years of mistreatment* are her situation more than planning the wedding anniversary party details. If a street gang character hates himself and what he must forever do to survive then *another idiotic night of violence* is his focus and feeling source more than getting back at the other gang. If the corporate chairman is always defensive and guarded, then the *assaults on his power tower* by the hypocrites at the conference table are his focus more than the straightening out of any details in the meeting.

Again it should be pointed out that the author of each piece has previously determined that certain actions will be taken by the characters involved. Those actions are in the scripts and they will be taken by the characters. The important thing is the *how* in which they will be taken by specifically conditioned characters. Situations simply *intrude upon* characters and their personalities. They come and go. They may be different in form and substance, but they should be dealt with, first and foremost, through the manner in which a given character will deal with them as a result of its unique conditioning and resulting personality.

The bottom line is that when an actor and his character are so involved in the taking of an Action the mind may be so focused upon that action that the underlying feeling and emotional experiences which should be present to cause the action in the first place have little opportunity to come into conscious awareness!

WORDING THE OBJECT FOR BEST RESULTS

The Object being literally *a "thing" to be focused upon* which, in its worded form, not only provides a meaningful concentration for the mind of the actor but also provides in its wording sufficient feeling content to provide the actor with more inner experience of feeling nature than will be called into use in many of the moments of the role, the manners of wording the tool for optimum results are important.

A question-worded Object focuses the actor not on an experience but on a seeking for a solution, rendering itself almost totally useless. Full sentences stating facts, no matter how brief or pithy, would feel like the repeating of broken records in use, limiting the spectrum of experiencing that the Object should provide. Wordings that don't contain the appropriate feeling vocabulary and sentiment of the character would confuse and distort the ongoing personality and behavior patterns as well as inner involvements.

Most of us who teach the Object's use have observed that, to hang in the mind most easily and continually generate feelings most effectively, Objects should feel like just what their title implies—*things*. Composite *nouns*, often (like objects are generally described in school grammar texts, but with some apt adjectives added to generate more intense attitude about those nouns). The only notable exceptions are in wordings that, if more closely examined, are more truly adjective or adverb phrases which *feel like* nouns.

Here are some examples of the forms of Objects which—whether composite nouns with their adjectives or adjective or adverb phrases—can be taken into the mind, can be easily held there and can bring unique and exciting colors to the moments in which they are used. Note that they're divided into groups whose wordings have the same beginning word, to help the actor quickly establish in his mind the forms of wordings that can be most effective:

NOUN-TYPE OBJECTS

The way they treat me!.... The last straw!.... The dreams we had once!.... The garbage smell in this place!.... The revenge I'll get someday!.... The things I won't ever have!....

This impossible situation!.... This dog-eat-dog world!.... This eternal struggling!.... This (any adjective) rat race!.... This endless waiting!....

Those snotnose bastards!.... Those phony smiles!.... Those frightening stares!.... Those same old lies!.... Those happy yesterdays!....

These painful last hours!.... These eternal obligations!.... These stupid parlor game nights!.... These (any adjective) headaches!....

More damn small talk!.... More crap to deal with!.... More delaying tactics!.... More stupid clumsiness!.... More (any adjective) insinuations!....

My last (any adjective) try!.... My only hope for survival!.... My shattered dreams!.... My damn clumsiness!.... My screwed up brain!....

His stupid ideas!.... Her never-ending carping!.... His constant worry-warting!.... Their phony faces!.... Their holier-than-thou attitudes!.... Our only hope!.... Our last night together!.... Our tough assignment!....

Another grin-and-bear-it Sunday night!.... Another useless try!....

Another silly-ass game!.... Another hit-and-run two-facer!....
Another (any good adjective) problem!....
Aspirin! Tylenol! Anything!.... Yak-yaks and smiley talk time!....
Something to kill myself with!.... Somebody to hold me!.... A hole
to crawl into!.... A way to get even!.... Murphy's Law again!.... Air
bubbles and saccharine time!.... So many (adjective) obstacles!....
Rejection slip time!.... Prison bars and handcuffs again!....

ADJECTIVE-TYPE AND VERB-TYPE OBJECTS

How wired I feel today!.... How cruel they all are!.... How crazy
this is!.... How loud those (a choice epithet here) are!.... How
ignored I am!.... How weird his mind is!.... How disgusting this
is!.... How long I've waited for this!.... How stupid he's acting!....
How far we still have to go!.... How messy it's getting!.... How
little time I have left!....

The (any adjective) notations above are included to suggest that
individuals have their own vocabularies of strong-feeling adjectives
which are associated with intense experiences and attitudes of all
kinds. Some of these are perhaps four-letter-word adjectives which
are habit with certain actors; others are simply cussword or, failing
that, perfect Webster Dictionary words that are just as feeling-
intensifying for others. The point here is that a good adjective
can bring a deeper feeling experience to whatever it's applied to,
and it belongs, almost always and carefully chosen for its power,
in a good Object. The actor who adds a good, descriptive adjective
always profits from the more intesting colors it will bring.

CREATIVE OBJECTIVES / THEIR HISTORY AND
DEVELOPMENT

After finding the Beats and finding their Objects throughout
roles we are at that point where most of the coaches who teach
specific methodologies start disagreeing with each other. Similarly,
their students clash over terminologies and creative approaches
running the gamut from ridiculous absurdities to profoundly
beautiful theories and back again to ridiculous absurdities.

No matter what your coach may teach you; no matter how it
sounds; no matter how you translate it in order to learn and use
it; no matter what it involves.... it also has to work; it has to work

well; and it has to work in preparing and playing roles. If it doesn't work for *you*, even though it appears to for others, you should keep searching until you find one that does. Some of the strictly *creative* tools work more effectively for some people and not well or at all for others, no matter how effective the tools themselves may be. The unique and individual processes of different actors' individual personalities and the parameters within which they can experience imagination stimuli vary so universally from actor to actor that what works ideally for one may not work for all.

What *is* important in considering creative tools is that one or more means which can be ideally used by each actor on an individual basis should be found and practiced to perfect its use. Each should find his own, because find it or them he must. Most actors can bring "adequate" involvement, concentration, imagination and performance to most roles; if they cannot bring those things they should not be actors at all. It is the actor who can bring *much more* who is destined for attention and respect in his profession.

And it is that actor who can bring much more who should develop in himself the learning and use of those methodologies, those "tools" and those degrees of self-extending which make it possible for him to bring those extra brilliances easily and with ultimate effectiveness.

Let's start with the word "Objective". Stanislavski's own *original* Objectives were of the following simplistic types: "To help"...."To stop him"...."To get even"...."To get home"...."To be accepted". (Note that they were very, very generalized actions and nothing more in that early form.) Probably a few coaches still teach their use in that form. However, even Stanislavski, so long ago, moved on swiftly from that beginning point, and others have since devised new forms which they consider to be far more effective.

Stanislavski's own form of Objective became much more interesting and more effective when he explored the incorporating in different manners of the "Magic If" approach which he had, again, moved on to from the original, less rich, "As If". At the point where he began involving the more colorful "Magic If" *similes* in his Objective teachings he began using the term *Creative*

Objective, recognizing that the tool was indeed more creative in surface result therewith.

In *Creating A Role*, the last of the trilogy of his notes to reach print, on pages 51 through 56 there is discussion of what these more creative objectives could do in terms of involving the feelings and moving the body. At the time of making the notes from which that last book was edited by his American translator-adaptor Elizabeth Reynolds Hapgood he was simply putting down the most exciting form of use for the Creative Objective of which he was capable at the time.

Certainly, any coach who still teaches that early form of Objective can legitimately claim that he or she teaches the Stanislavski System (at least that part), because that is the way it was when Stanislavski created the tool.

But the Ford dealerships that dot main thoroughfares in every city in America can also claim, this year, to be selling Fords, but they're certainly not selling that model that Henry Ford created in Detroit in 1892! The 1892 model barely worked at the time, and there are not too many of them on the streets anymore. The design has been bettered; speed has been increased; the separate parts have been changed and adapted for better service and dependability. Like Stanislavski's Creative Objectives, new designs have made refinements on the original.

It was in the 1930's that Stanislavski discovered the vast difference between general verbs like "get", "hurt", "find", etc., and what he came to call *action* verbs. (Sometimes in his writings you can observe that he also called them *active* verbs on occasion. A little inconsistency among the labels and titles he gave his tools appears to have been characteristic of him—or characteristic of the translating/editing of the versions available in English.)

In that period he came to recognize the special advantages of verbs which could help activate what he called the "psycho-physical" process. Such recognition is reflected, but not sufficiently stressed, in the last book mentioned above. It is too bad that so many of his own examples in print on so many library shelves still today remain complex action verbs, in fact quite generalized ones. For example, "To help" is so general that there are millions of ways of doing it and it would mean nothing at all to the actor's body. Similarly "To hurt" offers so many, many manners in which that can be done also.

Since Stanislavski's death others have refined that important "Action Verb" key to psycho-physical process to the point where the body finds such verbs more specific and moving and can in fact help find the right ones for its own associative memory/sense memory responses. The body needs to recognize the exact nature of a word in *purely physical* terms in order to respond to it actively on call.

Only the left side of the brain is sufficiently aware of what words like "help", "hurt", "get" and others of the same kind entail. However, the body knows what to do with words it helps us find like "hit", "break", "pull", "chop", "caress", "throw", "pinch", "squirm", "shake", etc. Stanislavski was headed in this direction, surely, and there are teachers who in fact respect the Action or Active Verb so mightily that they teach it as the one tool necessary to find for single Beats of roles.

For those who might be skeptical about the action verb's effectiveness, in whatever form—whether used alone or incorporated into a more complex tool, I'm reminded of an interview with one of our top stars, Paul Newman, conducted by and printed in *Look* magazine some years ago following his directing of his wife, Joanne Woodward, in the film *"Rachel, Rachel"*. In the printed version of the interview he was quoted as saying, in his own words which I remember essentially, that if one can find an active verb to describe a scene's experiencing by a character you can always give the actor the right direction. He mentioned the phrase "pinch it" as being something he kept digging away at Miss Woodward about, and went on to say that when she sucked that sensation into her body there was a certain physical quality that was achieved—including her laughter becoming pinched and a bit self-conscious, her mouth becoming pursed, her reactions becoming crimped and, in an actress as good as Miss Woodward even her toes turning in! That's just one published example of what a good Action or Active Verb can certainly do when an actor's talent can use it ideally. Keep the Action Verb in mind. It figures importantly in a tool to be discussed shortly.

Also bear in mind that another group of coaches and teachers

128

believe that an Object suffices, without any more physically creative tool ever being needed.

There is yet another group, including those who advocate the
use of the Object, who feel that for some moments (perhaps
entire Beats) of roles the Object should be used, after finding,
as a stepping stone toward the forming of another tool—the
Creative Psychological Objective. That tool, as will be discussed
in the upcoming paragraphs, comprises *a composite simile* and
a two-word *action verb* aimed at doing something to it.

The first step in the forming of a Creative Psychological Objective is to find, with the help of the body's associative memory
processes, what we can simply call the "simile".

Actually, a simile is something which is like something else.
It is a sensory parallel, in acting terms. In dictionary terms—at
least in one dictionary—it suggests that a whale is a simile for
the word "big". Many of you have heard the phrases "Mad as a
wet hen", "Dirty as a rat" and "Sly as a fox". These are a few
of those that have crept into common useage. A simile is usually
more definite in imagery and experiencing terms than the word
to which it is being likened.

Again credit must be given to Stanislavski as one of the first
who recognized the values of similes. Sprinkled throughout his
notes and the resulting published versions of them are references
to the use of such *sensory parallels* and the more "Magic Ifs" in
substitution for the Objects because they were observed to have
more physical value for the actor's body than the simple reality
thought when more creative body result was to be sought.

Another printed interview with another of our leading American
actors, Rod Steiger, which appeared in *Playboy* magazine some
years ago, quoted that gifted actor in one of his very rare moments
of talking about his approach to acting, as relating that in a scene
from the film version of "*The Big Knife*", in which he portrayed
a movie mogul as a homosexual, upon seeing a woman entering
a conference in his office he thought of her as a garbage can that
hadn't been cleaned in ages.

In Robert Lewis's excellent book *Method—Or Madness* there's
a fine example of two different actors' interpretations of a moment
from Tolstoi's "*The Human Corpse*" in which the character is

129

standing before a mirror getting ready to shoot himself. One actor, according to Mr. Lewis, used his own dramatic interpretation via trying to imagine what he himself would feel like in such a moment, while the other, Jacob Ben Ami, is said by Mr. Lewis to have used the Simile (whether he called it that or not) of preparing to step into a cold shower. One can imagine how effective that Simile of anticipating those "Ice needles" of cold water must have been.

These three examples, by adding an *action verb* to the *similes* of Messrs. Steiger and Ben Ami and by adding a *simile* to the action verb "pinch" discussed by Mr. Newman, would constitute the ingredients of what is called the *Creative Psychological Objective* as some others and I teach it today.

Incorporating the psychologically appropriate feelings of the character and similes which are recognized by and appeal to the body, along with an action verb, to which it also enjoys responding, the "CPO" (the shorter title we give it in my classes) can make the Beat Object on which it is based and from which it is formed a more vivid, *physically exciting* experience whenever the actor decides to use it.

The label "Creative Psychological Objective", in strictly terminology terms, is of my own conceiving. I understand that it is taught in essentially the same manner but called by different "tool" labels by others. (You see, the CPO has reached its current point of development *since* Stanislavski's death and therefore is one of those branches that have grown from the central trunk which fixed certain words in methodry but had not yet conceived of this particular combination of items so did not provide a label that would satisfy future discoverers. As with other "tools" formed since those early books were published, coaches and teachers have formed their own labels, and most of them, even dealing with the same things, are different.)

Stanislavski taught *Creative Objectives* and *Psychological Objectives* as separate tools. He also taught *Physical Objectives*. All began as different tools in his explorations, but even he in later years observed that while the simple Physical Objectives served in one respect they weren't always appropriately psychological at the same time. Similarly, the Creative Objectives were sometimes useful in exclusively creative terms while not sufficiently related to the psychology. And some purely Psychological Objectives were not productive in physical or psycho-physical terms as desired. Sometimes confused actors, even in later years, striving to use the right choice from among these at the right times, worried about whether one had enough of the other in it or the other had enough of the one. This is perhaps why the more creative version of Objectives remained on the sidelines, neglected, for so long as methodry moved forward into the last Mid-Century here in America and perhaps elsewhere. The three versions of Objectives were simply too much trouble; caused too much worry in actors' attempts to understand their unique and different purposes; and were therefore "sidelined" in many coaches' teachings. Many coaches, desirous to incorporate some form of Objectives into their teaching, simply used the word to describe either the Action aimed at a desired result or the Desired Result itself.

In my early years of acting study and also in those first years of teaching, as well as in my own personal explorations with different forms of Objectives, they seemed needlessly complicated to me too. Then it finally occured to me that, whichever choice among the three might be made it should be all three things— creative in that it should involve the body and psychological in that it should be appropriate to and movingly effective with the character's psychology. Hence, my title choice: *Creative Psychological Objective.* (Used in my classes, that title was found to be too big a mouthful for some and it has since been called "the CPO" by my people and me when what those letters stand for is understood.)

No matter what form it may be presented in, in an acting study situation, and no matter what it may be called in that class's terminology, this is one of the Stanislavski-inspired but later developed "tools" which can add astonishingly vivid and visually impressive colors to actors' work; turn what could be less than exciting moments of roles into highly entertaining ones for both the actor's inner experience and for the observer; and convey—

far more detectably than most other similar tools—via the sensory qualities of the simile experience—the specific emotional (or other) inner experience of the character.

This, remember, is the tool which Stanislavski didn't have the opportunity to completely put together. It has been put together since by some of the rest of us—in different forms, of course, but aiming to accomplish the same things: to involve the body more creatively in the actor's performance, through physical and psycho-physical memory processes, and to persuade the body out of ordinary, sometimes uninteresting behavior and movement habits into creative, always more interesting and more meaningful accompaniment to thoughts and feelings of characters.

It has the capacity to reach into our associative memory bin and extract for use *a composite rather than a single sense memory source*; for that reason its intensity is more variable from moment to moment (as true life subtext is); it affords an unbelievably wide and varied spectrum of experience through the double truth— the reality and the sensory, affective parallels included in its final form; and it is exciting to observe!

FORMING THE CREATIVE PSYCHOLOGICAL OBJECTIVE

After wording the Beat Object into a form which evokes definite feelings within you, the next step is to find out what that Object suggests to the body in its own sense memory and affective memory terms. To do this, first close your eyes (to shut out the visible realities around you); then think and feel the Object in an intensified degree and encourage the body to respond continually during an improvised movement experience of its own as prompted by the intensified feeling. Once this body-improvising is in progress you should "tune in" on the strange impressions of things, sounds, colors, smells, textures and body sensations which are appearing dimly. It takes a moment only for these to begin appearing, even though hazily. One could continue this process for a long time and most of the impressions would remain dim if we did not force ourself to "zoom in" on one of the impressions even before we know what it is and, by "zooming in", bring it into bright clarity for ourself. For some these impressions are clear immediately and this "zooming in" is a fairly automatic process resulting from remaining sensitive to impression. For others it may require a disciplined thrust of forcing an impression into focus.

(This process may require some practice for many contemporary actors whose senses have long ago been allowed to atrophy in our eye-oriented culture and mind-only survival patterns. However, the lost art of "listening to the body" can be cultivated through practice.)

The phenomenon which many actors can't readily accept is that the body-improvising can root out what are perhaps the most important associative memories of sensory parallels *almost instantly* upon beginning its participation with the intense experiencing of the Object. It has instant access to the exact file drawer in the right side of the brain, and can produce a mosaic of the right impressions immediately. Don't bypass the impression which seems a total nonsequitur and seems to have absolutely nothing to do with the Object's experiencing. That very early bypass may miss out on the most potent sense memory that will occur during this finding process. Force yourself to "zoom in" and bring to clear form the very first impression which invites your attention! Without your having any basis for accepting it as productive, the body has determined that it is something off one of the filecards of sense or experiential memory associations stored among your probably long forgotten experiences.

Perhaps a living thing will come first—even though, like those that follow, it will be dimly recognizable and you won't know what it is if you don't "zoom in" and bring it into clarity. If there is some impression, force yourself to "zoom in" on it. Perhaps you'll sense a sound, or a glob of color or texture. The important thing is, something will come dimly and it should be quickly brought to clarity because, without your understanding why, it is important and will assuredly be productive. It is a memory stored away by the body, by the senses, by the experiential or emotional memory long ago. If you vaguely at first see blood, or feel satin, or smell perfume, or hear wind or see ocean waves, and are tempted to pass such an impression by, don't. Trust it. It can be used by your body in its own way because it is already in that moment being associated by the body with what it experiences from your intense Object feeling.

Now, once you have the first simile, set it aside. You won't need to write it down because it can be remembered vividly, perhaps because it is so puzzling, after a moment. You must *not* have this first simile in your mind as you move on.

Now, return to intensified thinking and feeling with the original Object wording repeated to yourself and turned up to pitch level. The same process should be repeated. Again you're looking for a simile...a sensory thing or experience as described earlier. Again "zoom in" immediately as a dim impression comes.

When you have your second simile, the two should be combined. Ignore the suspicion that neither makes any sense at all. To your conscious mind they probably won't. Don't think you've failed if they sound improbable and rather silly to your brain's left side clerks. Combine them! You may then find you have either a "bloody rainbow" or "rainbow blood" (if in testing the experiencing of the strange combination you prefer one way over the other because, strange as it still seems, it is more potent for you); you might now have "perfumed albatross" or "albatross perfume"; it could be a "waving piggybank" or a "piggybank wave"; maybe a "highchair wollipog" or a "wollipog highchair" if after testing you prefer the latter.

Don't waste your time or divert your purpose with ridiculing the marvelously illogical combination of your two similes or try to modify them into making more sense to your very logical left side brain clerks. The body, and the clerks in the right side of the brain, know what those words mean, and it's part of the phenomenon involved in this "tool" that you will too as you go forward with the next steps of forming it. In the end, both you and your body will know how to use it.

You see, you need not consciously remember, for example, that once in early childhood you saw the blood around your little dog's body after it had been run over by a car and your body formed a *revulsion* reaction behavior pattern during a long moment of that experience, or that once you saw a rainbow reflected in a little stream in a gutter as you watched your little paper sailboat swallowed in the gutter's whirlpool drain, and the body formed a *loss* reaction behavior pattern in that moment.

Similarly, you don't have to remember consciously at all that, for another example, your fat aunt's perfume made you sick at your stomach as she leaned down to kiss you once, and the body formed a *stomach-wrenching* reaction behavior pattern, or that once when you got bawled out in school by a teacher it was over your poor reading aloud from *"The Albatross"* and your body formed another reaction behavior pattern which it hasn't forgotten and associates still with many similar moments.

It was some years ago when the discovery came that actors using only one single simile, through whatever process they might employ in the finding of it, tended to search into that single memory exhaustively but with only their conscious mind. Some may have proved effective, but many did not, simply because they were not recognizable to the body as being attached to any but their physical sensations.

The new addition of a second simile to be tied to the first has been discovered to involve a larger amount of the appropriate sensory parallels stored away in the brain and even more surely connected with long forgotten affective and experiential memories which caused their filing there in the first place rather than being instantly forgotten. The second simile in fact seems to bring more than the two being used, because together they appear to be bringing out an entire filefolder of similar experiences.

Perhaps Jacob Ben Ami had discovered, or at least sensed the same thing when he used the "ice needles" of that cold shower in the moment of planning to shoot himself in front of the mirror. At any rate, the body of the actor is even more enriched and even more stimulated as to its parallel experiencing in creative terms by the *two-worded* simile.

The next step, again with the eyes closed, is to feel yourself *surrounded on all sides* by the composite, two-word simile formed from those two items. *Feel the combined simile tight against all your pores!* With the simile encasing every part of you in your imagination, like an either very pleasant or very unpleasant cocoon, observe the body's reaction to being wrapped tightly in the cocoon which is the simile. Feel the body moving voluntarily

135

to try to *do something to* the simile. Whether it's a pleasant simile or an unpleasant one, the body will already be trying to do something to it. In fact the body will be trying to do something to the simile with the *total of the inner muscles*. Observe what those inner muscles are trying to do. Observe their contractions or expansions. They're trying in their own way to bring it closer (because it's desirable) or get rid of it forever (because it's undesirable). Try to observe and fix in your mind with a word *what* those inner muscles are trying to in *purely physical action* terms; also the *direction* (in, out, away, up, down, off, etc.) they're working in to accomplish it. Note—because it's important—we're not saying do *about* it or *because* of it. We're saying *doing to* it directly. There is a vast difference in the result of the use of the CPO later between those items.

Observe that the chest, the stomach, the armpits, the neck glands, in fact all the inner body muscles, are trying to perhaps *pull in* the simile, or *squeeze out* another simile, or *push off* or *caress up* or *crash away* others.

This moment is when the beautiful recognition of this tool's effectiveness begins to really impress you. You recognize as you discover the total combined activity that you've had similar experiences before! You don't need to know when or where. It would be ridiculous to think that at those earlier times in your life when you were going through similar moments you would know that, in body language, you were trying to "Squeeze out the bloody rainbow" or "Shake off the perfumed albatross" or "Caress up the waving piggybank"!

Now you would have, after those steps which appear so complicated until you've practiced them a few times, a very dynamic creative tool for any Beat in which you feel both true thought-focus involvement and the addition of *creative physicality* are desirable.

Some actors appreciate the extra exitements of highly *creative* physicalization to such a degree that they use the CPO or some similar creative tool in many more Beats of roles than would other actors. There are many actors who simply prefer to work with *reality*-thought Objects in the main and only occasionally, if ever, prepare a tool such as the CPO which may seem too labored and complex in preparation for their tastes.

Since this tool, in the form described in these paragraphs, may be totally new to many readers, the following examples of progressions in finding some CPO's may lend more graphic clarification:

BEAT OBJECT	THE SIMILE	ACTION VERB	THE "CPO"
How much she hates me!....	Screaming Whirlpool	Squeeze Off	Squeeze Off the Screaming Whirlpool!
This fantastic moment!....	Silk Breezes	Curl In	Curl In the Silk Breezes!
Some way to get even!....	Crashing Haystacks!	Whirlwind Up	Whirlwind Up the Crashing Haystacks!
How stupid I've been!....	Bloody Maggots	Scrape Off	Scrape Off the Bloody Maggots!

A few things should be pointed out to help your understanding and to encourage successful use of the CPO:

(1) Don't use only the mind, without encouraging the body to enjoy the tool which it helped you find. Perhaps the body will use it subtly much of the time (only slightly creating any discernible body movement); then at appropriate moments cause it to explode or surge up inside you to the level which causes the body to join in much broader participation. The body will glory in the freedom and size of this larger participation. In any event, regardless of the size of the moment or its physical manifestation, if your toes feel like curling let them curl; if your shoulders want to hunch up don't stop them; if your hands feel like clenching or simply hanging limply at your sides let them do as they wish; if your chest wants to weave from side to side let it. The body knows what it's doing. Let it do it!

(2) Don't let the hands do the work, as they are so accustomed to doing in contemporary society. The hands must not be a single member trying to do the total of what should be kept inside the body and experienced by all the inner muscles, just as it was in the finding process. Your hands must be free to carry things, touch things, handle things, etc., while simply adapting because of the CPO into particular muscle system-directed movement patterns they might not otherwise reflect. "Rub away....", for instance, would appear somewhat idiotic, repetitive and senseless if the hands are literally rubbing away at everything rather than the total body experieriencing the very different results of the same Action Verb. The chest, the shoulders, the stomach, the toes, the armpits, the elbows, the neck glands, the eyes and even the teeth—in other words, all parts of the body—have their individual manners of employing "Rub away....", just as they did when you were finding the CPO originally, and as they did in those moments of your prior personal experiences when you were feeling the same feelings.

(3) Explore how the total CPO experience of the body handles props, dictates the way you walk, stand, sit and adjust to all its physical tasks and the manners of their execution. Trust the CPO more than the logic of Academy-trained theatrical movement which doesn't even apply for all characters and in fact obscures the different living moments of most particularized characters. The CPO will make all movement meaningful in terms of the character itself, eradicating all cliches from your work and keeping the psycho-physical inner life ever present for the viewer to sense even when it is barely visible.

(4) After the CPO has been used during the studying of lines—during which it will have become habit automatically attached to and maintained by the Beat's dialogue and actions later.... *throw it away!* That's right. Stop using it consciously. Revert back to thinking the character's *real* thoughts and experiencing its true feelings. This tool is so effective that, once the creative habits of it have been formed during line study, the body will continue to enjoy experiencing the CPO patterns

138

after your mind has gone on to truly living the moment at hand.

I am aware of the kinds of questions which may occur in the reader's mind about the different processes discussed here. Some of them have come up before from actors and actresses who have attended seminars I have conducted. I'll use a few of their questions in discussing this tool further:

There was a fairly stiff, visibly inhibited actress of fairly advanced years in one audience. She felt that the thing she had always noticed about "method" actors and actresses was the amount of "unnecessary" movement. She felt that their thoughts too often made them "twitch, wiggle, squirm around and appear undisciplined and awkward". (Those were her words.) She questioned what she called the "over-acting" she felt their creative approaches led to and felt the adding of anything like the CPO would make that "over-acting" more exaggerated.

I was familiar with her work. I had observed that sometimes it was evident that her body wanted to move but was not allowed to; that her mind was getting in the way and deciding that a certain position was too nice and tidy to be messed up. I could almost hear her saying to herself "Now, I must sit down carefully, just like Katharine Cornell did in "*The Barretts Of Wimpole Street*", etc. She certainly couldn't ever have been accused of twitching or squirming around too much!

I offered my opinion that if she kept up the habit of self-direction and self-inhibiting during her performances for the rest of her career she certainly wouldn't ever be given any roles where twitching or squirming would be appropriate, so she need not worry about those items. I had seen her play several secretaries, an Airline reservation clerk, a cousin or something in a scene at a wedding, and things of that sort; never the excitingly frustrated boss of the secretary, or the nervously agitated passenger at the Airline reservation desk, or, in a wedding scene, an important member of the wedding.

I told her that she always appeared to me to be stiff and contained to the point that I couldn't perceive the slightest hint of what was really going on inside her character.

I mentioned Geraldine Page and the twitching and squirming sne brought to the production of Tennessee Williams's

139

"*Summer And Smoke*" which brought her instant recognition and prominence in New York, also the twitching and squirming she brought as important facets of her characters, as the wife of Louis Jourdan in Andre Gide's "*The Immoralist*" and as "Princess" in Tennessee Williams's "*Sweet Bird of Youth*". Observed to be a little stiff and contained socially herself in earlier years, she had learned that she must overcome that stiffness to afford her body more freedom of experiencing in roles.

I recommended that the questioner could use at least some of that same twitching and squirming she was worrying about to bring her characters more vividly to life and assured her that she would discover how naturally it could occur if allowed and how meaningful it would be for her characters. I assured her also that it was improbable that she would ever "over-act" with it and that her roles might become larger and more important. I also reminded her that there was seldom any "twitching or squirming" in the smaller roles and that the people she called "twitchers and squirmers" always seemed to get those larger, more important roles which she hadn't been given the chance to play yet.

Another actor, in another seminar, hit upon a very big word in criticizing essentially the same item—the amount of "agitation" (he called it) evident in so many "method" performances. I had seen his work only once. I remembered that it was a motion picture in which he got the girl in the end and everything worked out very nicely for his character. However, I had had the feeling all the time that his character wasn't doing any of the working out of things for itself; that the writer had done it all ahead of time. The actor had appeared to be just coasting through the entirety of the film on good looks, confidence and intelligent line readings. I couldn't feel anything for him, because he didn't seem to realize the problems his character was facing from one scene to another. There seemed no survival energy of any kind in his performance. Other characters and the writer seemed to be doing it all. The big thing I had sensed to be missing was any *inner need* having been planned for his character to experience moment to moment.

Classes like my own spend many hours *cultivating* the thing he had called "agitation". That is precisely the word some of us who coach use often. We admonish our actors to "agitate" their Objects so that in dominating the actions taken those Objects will create the more exciting human experience colors that offer deeper involvement and feeling access.

Stanislavski himself advocated intense agitation. Those of us who have come later also recognize its importance in the use of any acting approach. One of the attributes of the CPO, in fact, is that it *agitates the body*. Without the varying degrees of agitation in different moments of roles a planned tool such as the CPO would be meaningless for the actor. It is one of the handiest classwork items I know for prompting actors into more "agitation" of the inner experience, since the right side of the brain and the body itself are so inexorably connected, and to nurture the use of both by the actor the CPO is a wonderful key.

Most roles contain chains of moments requiring widely varying degrees or levels of agitation which can at times be most apparent and at times should be more subdued and covert. In some moments in our own lives we attempt to cover our inner feelings and thoughts completely behind a social mask appropriate for the moment in order to get or keep or avoid something. However, *our inner processes don't stop* just because a surface pretext must cover them for a time. It is the same with characters. At least a certain amount of agitation should be continuing behind the surface lie. The CPO, involving the body to the extent it does, is an excellent manner of keeping that inner life apparent, even if almost subliminally, for the spectator.

Then, there are those other moments of roles—those absolutely adored by actors from the moment when they discover a few in roles they're destined to play—when characters can let out their inner feelings totally and behave in broadest degrees of agitation without any regard for other characters around them. Of course these role moments allow far more expansive use with tools such as the CPO. They are the sternest tests of actors' abilities to bring those creative extras, as a result.

What is vitally important to the actor, in the end, is that when there are those extreme or crisis moments in a role which require the character to come on full blast and practically explode its inner life, splattering it all over everything around it, and the actor knows the CPO or some other conscious technique for making them exciting to observe, then that actor is probably going to be moved upward in the billing list of the production to at least co-starring level, simply because of the creative manner in which those few extremely demanding opportunities—even if there were only one or two—were handled.

It is obvious that I recommend the CPO highly for use in bringing continuing clarity and extra excitements to at least some separate Beats of roles. Its value as an acting tool in preparing roles is equalled only by its value as an acting class means of nurturing the imagination, conditioning the actor's body and right side of the brain to work together ideally, and fostering in the actor the desire to seek creative alternatives for moments in roles where they can utilize more of the actor's unique resources.

There are of course other tools of the Creative Subtext which some readers may have learned and may be using or may not have had described for them. Since some of these can be highly effective in many roles—either as means of seeking inspiration for moments of roles or, in some cases, as substitutions for the Beat Objects so strongly advocated by me, a considerable number of them are being discussed in the next Chapter.

Chapter Eight

Additional Tools of the Creative Subtext

The Creative Subtext being the most controversial preparation phase of any acting method as a system or any acting method, period, most individual approaches offer their own versions of creative substitutions for simple reality experiences, with those items which are taught so differently by all of the different teachers being so individual and unique that there is hardly any recognizing of them as being related to any central system source. They're called by different names, even if they're basically the same tools. Some of them work marvelously for most actors willing to learn and practice their use; some of them work in the hands of only a few more gifted talents; and some of them might as well be thrown into the trashcan for all the good they do.

First, I'll take up the ones I personally find most effective when combined on occasion with some basic system for role preparation.

They fall into two separate groups—the External Characterization Group and the Internal Characterization Group.

THE EXTERNAL CHARACTERIZATION GROUP

CHARACTER IMAGES (Sometimes called ANIMAL IMAGES)

Comedians have pretty much stopped telling those jokes about going to a "method" acting class and being asked to be a wormy apple or a cool glass of milk. Improbable as it was, it's quite possible that somebody, somewhere, did go through exactly that experience in an acting class; did it seriously; and possibly achieved some result. However, if they did it in any acting class they should have been told that it was a sensitizing exercise first and foremost, somewhat akin to what the Ford Foundation and other Sensitivity Training Centers have business excecutives go through, to break down static social images and awaken stilted imaginations, and to put people in touch with their bodies again. It probably was not a characterization tool in such an acting class but merely aimed to help the class members become the kind of people who wouldn't have to tell jokes about going to an acting class and being asked to be a wormy apple and cool glass of milk.

Stanislavski tried *inanimate* imagery of that sort in the beginning too. There is quite a section in his first explorations book, *An Actor Prepares*, devoted to using a tree as an image. But he soon reduced the amount of exploration of such inanimate imagery and instead began to teach what is presently used by many fine actors and actresses on occasion for specific characters. Although they are mostly called "Character Images" or "Animal Images", they should more aptly be called *Character Images of Animate Nature*. The shorter titles suffice, but such imagery isn't limited to only animals!

Most readers who've attended any acting classes at all have encountered this item. It's one of the most universally used—still today—of all the Stanislavski-originated tools of the External Characterization category. Even it is taught in several different manners, however.

One use of Character Images is to devote classroom exercise time to exploring and miming the actual form, as closely as the human body's limitations allow, of one of these categories of animate beings: Mammals, Birds, Insects, Reptiles, Crustaceans, Arachnids, Fish, Rodents, Amphibians, Marsupials, etc. If you're taught to explore animate images in this manner it is probable that the teacher has in mind the expansion of your processes into feelings and behavior-adapting areas of more varied experience. Perhaps you have in fact needed to be reacquainted with the animal inside yourself. Perhaps you need the survival-feeling intensification which is like the animal's strictly self-experiencing aspects. Or perhaps the exercising in this manner has been intended to help you find certain feelings which have theretofore been totally strange to you and not ever detected by the teacher in your work—feelings and emotions which you can more easily associate with the animal or other animate image but have not previously realized belong in your work too.

A large number of us prefer to view this as an *External Characterization* tool, however. In other words, we teach that, perhaps at that point just beyond finding your character's Super Objective, if you think an animate image may help inspire more interesting external colors for it you can decide upon one to use and, after itemizing all the characteristics you can think of which are common to that animate being, skillfully translate each item, or at least as many as possible, into some external that is appropriate for your human character.

A classic example—Charlie Chaplin's very apparent *penguin* comes to mind. I'll use it as an example, because it is such a good one:

The baggy pants inspired by the pear-shaped body of the penguin.... The feet pointed outward duplicating the webbed feet also pointed outward and creating the waddling walk.... The big, tattered old shoes taken from the large penguin feet and their webbing.... The beak, with some ingenious thinking, can be seen to be the cane and its peculiar manner of being carried pointed forward and down much like a beak.... The little spit curls on the forehead being the nostrils on the side of the penguin's beak.... The colors of wardrobe being penguins' colors.... The head movement from side to side resembling the penguin's own.... The "after-wiggling" upon sitting remembling the penguin's habit! A touch here, a touch there.... all adding up to that unique, unforgettable total that has made "the little fellow" so memorable!

There are a number of more recent-period actors who have

claimed that they always at least *consider* an animate image when they are preparing a role. A few have gone so far as to say that they *always* use one to bring added inspirations for far more interersting colors for their portrayals than they might otherwise be able to think of.

Movements, wardrobe, sounds, makeup, hairstyle, props, body habits, little activities and manners of doing ordinary tasks in unique manners can all be inspired by a productive character image of animate type. Even feelings themselves can be adapted, and if the image is well chosen thousands of mannerisms of the image will apply excellently with very little adaptation if combined with good taste and good judgment by the actor.

The inspiration sources, from the animate being used as the character image, can include covering (fur, feathers, scales, shell, etc.)—which may vary at the different points on the image's body, remember; extremities (wings, claws, paws, fins, tendrils, etc.); tails; head shape and its several characteristics (such as bills, jaws, teeth, facial markings, ears, hair, etc.); characteristic body positions; movement patterns involving standing, sitting, walking, lying down; pastimes; body habits; sounds of the various kinds which some images might typically make; even items with which they are usually surrounded or usually involve with; etc., etc.

While there is more tendency on the part of actors to apply character or animate imagery to the classics such as Shakespeare, Moliere, Ibsen, some of Chekov, etc., we need not limit its use to such style and period works. The contemporary actor, in contemporary characters, can often benefit equally from considering and possibly using one of these images, as long as some subtlety is applied to the adapting of the characteristics of the image into strictly human form.

Sounds adapted from the image are often mishandled by people new to the use of this tool. We must remember that we should not sound exactly like the image. Instead we should use the snarl of the image, for example, to inspire a cold in the nose; the soft growl to inspire a tired groan that recurs; the woodpecker's pecking to inspire a tongue-clicking habit or fingernail-tapping; the dog's bark to suggest a hacking cough. Then sounds are no problem. No audience member should ever be overheard saying

146

"She looks like a hen" when it's supposed to be a purely human character!

It's important that, to obtain the most productive use from a selected character image, it should be considered *after* deciding the character's personality, not before. I believe that the best point in preparation is immediately after forming the Super Objective, as mentioned earlier.

It's wise, also, to practice any physical movements and any sounds adapted from the character image, to tailor them into very believable human form that doesn't even remotely suggest their source.

Here are two examples of how many fascinating inspirations can be gleaned from the use of character images:

THE EXCITING CONTRIBUTIONS OF CHARACTER IMAGES

A truck driver is to arrive home from the road one winter evening, sit around drinking beer, relax and listen to his wife telling the children's news. The role could be a bit dull, no?

The actor seeking the most appropriate and most productive character image, knowing that the many inspirations to be found through its use can make the character much more interesting, decides to use a lazy brown bear in the zoo.

First, he lists the characteristics, one after another, that he can think of. To avoid limiting himself to a few, he remains exclusively fixed on the simple listing until he feels it is complete with all possible items.

Then, he considers each and every item to find a possible adaptation into a human inspiration. The list, prepared totally first, and the inspirations gleaned from the items upon considering them individually later, might wind up like this:

BODY COVERING: BROWN MATTED FUR.... A thick brown pile jacket and dirty brown pants. WHITE SPOT ON CHEST.... A thick white winter scarf. RUFF AROUND NECK.... Jacket buttoned closed and a big collar turned up....

EXTREMITIES: FURRY LEGS AND CLAWS.... Thick gloves, for driving, with some fingers perhaps tattered because of the bear's claws; heavy boots for the thick legs....

HEAD CONFORMATION: LONG, POINTED NOSE.... A billed winter

147

cap, also brown.... SMALL, POINTED EARS.... The winter cap must be ear-flapped, with the flaps up from the ears as people sometimes wear them.... SMALL, BEADY EYES.... Small eyeglasses for looking over the mail that's come since he left on his trip.... MESSY HAIR ON TOP.... Greasy, mussed hair pulled back by cap and scraggly-ended....

BODY POSITIONS; MOVEMENT PATTERNS: LYING BACK WITH LEGS SPREAD.... Sitting spreadlegged and slumped in that position.... HOLDS THINGS IN BOTH PAWS.... Holding the beer can in that manner at times.... LIES ON SIDE.... Position to lounge in some of the time to listen to his wife's account.... HEAVY, LUMBERING WALK.... Same for the driver.... HEAD ROLLING FROM SIDE TO SIDE.... A manner for driver to react to what he hears about the children .... SWATS WITH PAWS.... An adapted gesture carefully used some of the time in reaction....

SOUNDS: THE GROWL AND THE ROAR.... Heavy "tired" and similar source sounds.... Throat Clearing habit.... Noisy throat sounds with nose-blowing....

BODY HABITS: SCRATCHING.... Rubbing stomach; scratching an unshaven face stubble after not shaving on the road....

SURROUNDING ITEMS: ZOO BEAR'S LEASH COLLAR.... Sun or driving glasses hung around neck.... FEEDING PAN.... Snacks with beer, to be sorted and chosen as they are "pawed" for selection....

There are many more items the actor could find with additional searching, but even the foregoing offer a fascinating list of suggestions which probably wouldn't have been inspired so well and so easily in any other manner.

Of course the *tail* would have been listed, and it might suggest for this role a greasy rag hanging from a jacket pocket of the type which truck drivers carry for handling the oily and greasy parts of the truck. But this tail, and other tails, must have a bit of special discussion:

Tails of the many different kinds often prompt new users of imagery who don't know better to have belts tied in back or something of that sort. Since it's highly unusual for anyone to tie a sash or buckle a belt in the back—and especially let an end hang down obviously—such use is ill-advised. Care should always be taken to turn a tail into something which is absolutely appropriate for a human, just like all the other items. Again, the actor in the above case would not want an audience member to be overheard saying "That's a bear!"

A second character might be a perpetually busy and worried female clerk in an outer office. After some body improvising with the patterns and movements of hurried and nervous clerks the actress preparing the role decides on a Plymouth Rock, henhouse breed of laying hen. (The hen has probably come to mind in the spread-winged, hurried movement pattern moments of the hen; not the moments of sitting on a nest, although those moments are available for inspiration source material as well.) The following ideas, at least, might be found:

BODY COVERING: MOTTLED GREY FEATHERS.... Grey or mottled sweater and skirt, or tiny print, grey tone dress.... BODY CONFORMATION OF A HEN.... When sitting, doing so in a manner that makes dress bunch up like a hen....

EXTREMITIES: LIGHT YELLOW, BUMPY LEGS.... Light, maybe even yellow-toned stockings with a few wrinkles.... THE SPREAD-CLAW FEET.... All Fingers spread with worry as the woman works under self-imposed pressure.... WINGS.... Arms extended worriedly as she scurries around .... THE SCALED LEGS.... A wrist-length sleeved dress if not a sweater suggested. If a sweater, it should be rolled up on the wrists to where the feathers might begin on legs....

HEAD: BEAK.... Perhaps a small yellow pencil stub in mouth at a few moments.... RED CREST ON TOP.... One or two ribbons or a red comb near the top of the hair.... SHORTER FEATHERS ON TOP.... Simple, short hairdo close to head and maybe pompadoured back.... SMALL, ALMOST ROUND EYES.... Granny glasses for working....

BODY POSITIONS: HEAD LOW LOOKING FOR GRAIN.... Head bent out over desk much of the time.... HEAD COCKS UP IN EXCITEMENT.... Same....

NEST SITTING.... Leaned forward nervously with arms lowered to sides and a little to the rear, perhaps clasped on chair in nervousness....

MOVEMENTS: WADDLE WALK.... Waddling adapted.... RUNNING

.... Arms out at sides.... ARRANGES FEATHERS WHEN SITTING....
Nervous arranging of dress when sitting down.... PECKING FOR
FOOD.... Bobbing head with others' talking or even in silent
thinking moments.... Leaning far over the typewriter or paperwork
like a hen searching for something to peck at.... Bobbing head
as papers are scanned word by word.... Perhaps nearsightedness
from too much office work....

SOUNDS: CLUCKING..Private thinking sounds.... CACKLE....
Sounds of detail paranoia occasionally.... CACKLING WHEN DIS-
TURBED .... When buzzed to come to boss's office, making
paranoid sounds from worry and insecurity about pencil, pad,
work disturbed, etc....

HABITS: PICKING AT FEATHERS.... Constantly rearranging of a
bodice or a pin and looking down at it, or using a chest-pocket
pen or pencil and having to look for it often.... BLINKING OF
EYES LIKE HENS.... Occasional shutting of eyes to open them
wide, cleared....
CACKLING AND BODY FIDGETING WHEN LAYING AN EGG AND
JUST AFTER....
Little cackles when possible to provoke them legitimately, then
self-conscious shifting of the body into a settled position in chair
again out of embarrassment....

USUAL SURROUNDING ITEMS: STRAW NEST.... Maybe a yellow
pillow on chair for settling onto.... CHICKEN FEED PAN.... A
planter on desk, which she mutters to occasionally and putters
with absent-mindedly, peering at each small plant one after anoher
like a chicken selecting which morsel to pick at....

The imaginative actress might find even more little or big
inspirations for character externals from any good character image
such as this hen, and be very proud of the extra colorful aspects
they would bring over and above the emotional preparation for
the character's personality and moment to moment life.

THE MOTIVE CENTER

Another valuable external characterization tool used to provide
excitingly authentic externals from a body and movement standpoint is a tool some of us call the "Motive Center".

It is an outgrowth and development from Michael Chekhov's

original "Imaginary Center", which you will find described in his book *To The Actor*. As the tool has developed since, it is often chosen to bring to more authentic and more vivid life those characters whose bodies are deformed or whose personalities, physical problems, retarded states or mental illnesses have warped their bodies to a substantial degree. Of course it is not limited to those characters, however.

The tool's origin in Michael Chekhov's approach stems from his desire to help actors attain classic form for their stance and movements, which in his concepts meant something akin to a ballet dancer's perfect form. The "Imaginary Center", as he taught it apparently, was a spot in the center of the chest which would essentially lift the body of the actor to the point of elevation where the neural muscle system would flow gracefully at all times with the resulting coordination supplied by that one single point on the body.

It remained for his longtime roommate, Eugene Vakhtangov, who also taught at the Moscow Art Theatre, to decide that by moving that one single imaginary center to different parts of the body there could be other and quite different results for characters who need not and should not move so gracefully. It was his change of Checkhov's idea, and the re-labeling of it as "Motive Center", which has enhanced its potential use for so many and varied characters.

It is in the Vakhtangov manner that, as a "Motive Center", it can bring rather miraculous results and authentic movement patterns for so many different purposes.

The *Motive Center* as I'm describing it here is an imaginary spot or object on or in the body at some point, through which all feelings, thoughts and experiences such as seeing, hearing, smelling, even touching, are channeled creatively, both incoming and outgoing, for the sake of creating certain characters more organically by, in effect, relocating the center of the entire neural muscle system, through the actor's imagination and to the extent that the imagination can convincingly accomplish this.

When such a tool is used, not only are the larger movements affected—as in standing, sitting, walking, etc., but also we discover through the Motive Center the exciting little adjustments amd

151

movements which would not be possible to conceptualize intellectually or find with equal authenticity and effective result in any other manner.

Some coaches, myself included, have found that, as Jerzy Grotowski teaches in Poland during this period, the *voice resonators* are perhaps the most important parts of the actor's body in the search for an ideal Motive Center. It is the actor or actress who can experience the sensation of actually *talking through different parts of the body* at different times who can obtain the best results from a Motive Center. Ridiculous as this may appear to the less imaginative, it is indeed possible and it is in fact rather necessary for the actor to have this ability to imagine doing this in order to fully utilize this tool and reap all its possible benefits.

You might like, at this point, before even reading on, to set the book aside and try first to talk out of the side of the mouth softly; then out of the middle; then the other side. That much is easy, of course, since you will still be talking out of the mouth itself.

Next, however, try talking out of these spots, convincing yourself along the way that you are actually sending your voice out through them: The right nostril; the tip of the nose; the bottom of the upper palate; the top of the bottom palate; the middle of the right cheek; the bottom of the chin; the front of the teeth; the tip of the tongue. Can you do these? If you can, and have already observed the "instant characters" such use of the Motive Center has created, try these more difficult ones: For the previously discussed truck driver home from the road, instead of the bear Character Image, explore what talking through a large "beer belly" produces for the entire instrument; for the role of Helen Keller, as in "*The Miracle Worker*" at her early age—denied sight, hearing and speech, explore what happens throughout your entire being when trying to make (non-talking) sounds through an empty cave in the middle of the head with a small roller bearing rolling around on its floor through which all sensation must be channeled; for Cliff Robertson's Award-winning role of "*Charly*" in the television picture of that name some years ago, see what a spot under the right jaw about three inches back from the chin (to bring the retardation of that fascinating character) can bring

152

into speech and body movement inspirations; and for "Stanley Kowalski" in *"A Streetcar Named Desire"* try an imaginary iron bar stretching across the back of the character's neck from shoulder to shoulder—and discover that one of your arms will hang limply at your side in that gesture which became a Marlon Brando mimicing position in the years just subsequent to his portrayal of that character in the Broadway and film versions of Tennessee Williams's work

If you have achieved some success in channeling all your experience through these latter Motive Centers you've experienced the heaviness and deep voice of the truck driver but also discovered the new way the Motive Center brings for any sitting down and "settling" positions; the different way that the beer can would be held; the difficulty in getting up from a chair; the slumped position in sitting after the Motive Center has been consulted for the final adjustments. (Vakhtangov, with the Motive Center, discovered the value of retaining Chekhov's "final adjustments" phase, such as in sitting being conscious that when sitting there is the "I have now sat" phase which follows the sitting down moment. In those final adjustment moments can be found some interesting little surprises!)

If you achieved success with the Helen Keller try you've experienced the strange sensation of wanting to hear through that small roller bearing; of trying to make first sounds through it; of experiencing the touching of something not with the fingertips but with the roller bearing, etc., as well as the experience of channeling the fury of deprivation of Helen's problem through the same spot as it made your body twist and turn in frustration.

As "Charly", with that suggested Motive Center, you found your body slanted; the feeling of the droop and uncontrollability of the right jaw; the slurred, difficult speaking; the feeling that your wardrobe should hang to the right; also the unique manner of using your arms and hands—all of which this Motive Center probably provided during your testing.

As "Stanley Kowalski", with the imaginary iron bar across the back of your shoulders, if you successfully managed to imagine talking through it, you found your body and arm in that Brando-mimicing position; your walk like his; your sitting down and standing up the same; your handling of a beer can similar; and if you were to try that famous "Stella!" outcry you'd find that it sounded somewhat like his!

When testing the Motive Center, find out what it does to your body to listen through it, smell some aroma through it, experience the character's feelings of various kinds through it, walk through it, stand with it, sit with it—and don't forget those final adjustments in each case when finishing sitting or standing up. Then pick up some props and feel how the Motive Center determines they are to be handled. Try the Motive Center's unique manner of dialing a telephone, listening to an imaginary speaker at the other end of the line, and then putting the phone on its cradle again.

Whether you use the Motive Center consciously only in the *finding* of all its product—using it to discover all the forms of movement and the total experience, then discarding the conscious use later (since the body will remember to use it in the practiced manner)—or choose to still use it very consciously in performance for a more extreme character, it works marvelously either way.

The experience aspects are not the only benefits to be obtained from an appropriate and well developed Motive Center. It, like the Character Image, can be a source of some wonderful external ideas for characters.

While the relocating of the neural muscle system center—which you're essentially doing when you use a Motive Center—creates a so complete experience for the actor *inside* those externals, it is the result in *external appearance, movements, speech and other inspirations* which come in profusion from Motive Center use for which this tool is created to primarily serve.

From the Motive Center experience the actor can find, in addition to the movement patterns discussed earlier, so many inspirations for wardrobe, hairstyle, makeup and props use.

That human being who seems to be warped a little in an interesting way because of its personality usually has the hair parted to fall a certain way or straight backward or forward—and the actor can simply *feel through the Motive Center* the way that will be right! The wardrobe of the character will want to be a little askew in a certain way, and will *feel through the Motive*

Center to be wrong in any other way. The head drooping as it will in some direction, the hat or cap will want to be adjusted a little as well. With the shoulder affected by some Motive Center the wardrobe will automatically suggest a special manner of going along with that condition. Props will want to be held in one way and no other because the hands and arms are formed in a certain way by the Motive Center. A successfully created Motive Center character very clearly makes all these decisions for you!

Visualize (or try), for instance, a *"chrysanthemum-at-the-shoulder"* clubwoman who in effect "chrysanthemums" everything she does—simpering through it, gossiping covertly through it, walking with its self-conscious one-sided erectness, sitting with its left-side uplift apparent as she presents her importance before her peers, listening through it to the guest speaker at the Thursday tea, sniffing sideways through it to find out what perfume her neighbor is wearing, and speaking with the slight breathiness which the relocated Motive Center causes. The actress using this Motive Center would observe that her lips would be pursed a little, her chin would want to rise to the left a little, her hands clasped politely in her lap would want to be a little to the right or left. Such things are automatic results and are easily observed in first experiencings with this tool.

A selfconsciously macho muscleman, for another example, with a Motive Center of, say, a *big neon "Superman" V lying across the top of his pectorals and extending out to the outside of his biceps* would find his speech more guttural and forced, his armpits tightly pressed, his hands curled apelike, his body swaggering when he walks, his sitting position stretched wider, his hair feeling like it must be flattened to his head, his legs spread appropriately for the selfconscious macho effect when he stands, his mouth feeling itself widened at the corners, etc.

We need not go down the entire list of fairly obvious real life Motive Center people around us, but we're sure to know at least one front-of-the-bottom-teeth bully, a few upper or lower palate gullible folks, some corner-of-the-mouth cynics, one or two top-of-the-shoulder movie starlets, some kidney-pain older people, one or two top-of-the-tight-behind social pleasers, etc.

155

Many actors and actresses down through the years have used this marvelous tool, and continue to do so often, after learning what it can produce for external characterization.

IMAGINARY SURROUNDINGS CHARACTERS

This one is of my own devising. Again it's a manner of gaining inspirations for external characterization. I've been teaching it for many years and it has helped some performances in theatre, film and television achieve some top honors. Like the previously discussed external characterization tools of longer standing, it too can be used with a fair amount of freedom and invention in theatre (where actors are left more to their own devising of makeup, hairstyle, wardrobe and other external items until subject to approval by the director), while for film and television the majority of makeup, hairstyle and wardrobe items are subject to the suggestion and design of highly paid people in those studio departments. For the latter two fields the actor must wait until in a top position where his or her suggestions are more graciously accepted and often enthusiastically approved.

Once one is a star the right is accorded to come up with ideas, but ideas and suggestions of the types found through Character Images, Motive Centers and Imaginary Surroundings Characters—where smaller film and television roles are concerned—are seldom that much appreciated by the department people who may be a bit jealous of their domains.

This item involves the finding of a small number of imaginary surroundings characters and drawing from them individual external characteristics and ideas which, when added to the basic character the actor is preparing, supply an unlimited list of inspirations.

In theatre especially, where the actor is expected to come up with his own inspirations more often as to makeup, hairstyle and in some cases even wardrobe, many of us have been through those agonizing times of sitting before mirrors and trying to imagine the ideal makeup, wardrobe and hairstyles for characters already planned as to their emotional lives but which remain to be adorned with external highlights—many of which we're expected to suggest.

156

If you're one who has been through this experience you'll recall that after coming up with some rather nice ideas you've partially tailored those ideas right back out of existence because, looking at yourself in those mirrors, you felt they wouldn't look right with your particular face, nose, head shape, neck, body, or some other aspect of your own unique appearance and the professional image you wished to maintain.

Instead, you might find it productive and exciting to try the following:

Imagine three or four *somewhat similar* characters, one after another, in fairly equal social strata to the character you're to play, but in different places—different imaginary surroundings and perhaps of different personality types even. Imagine them in a stationary moment, so you won't become involved with a developing story and distract yourself from inagining their characteristics strictly from an external viewing of them.

Perhaps if you're to play a bum who sleeps in roadside caves and parks at night you might imagine (1) a wino on Skid Row beside a trashcan, (2) an itinerant field worker standing in line for a job of artichoke-picking, (3) a Skid Row missionary minister supervising a bread-and-soup kitchen and (4) maybe a ragged hermit in his junkyard hovel on the edge of town.

As you imagine each individual character singly, keep asking yourself "What's wrong with his...."—his nose, his hands, his shirt, his shoes, his hair, his eyebrows, his mouth, his hat or cap, his pants, his socks, his belt and as many other details as you like until you have a big list containing many small ideas that have brought that character vividly to life.

Another question that proves productive is "What's unusual about...."—applied to the same items. You might want to also ask yourself "What's in that pocket?", "What's he carrying?" and any other question of similar nature which will further your examination of your subject and bring more inspirations.

When one character is completely constructed and its ideas and inspirations are listed for consideration later, go on to the next and construct it in the same manner.

Of course all of the ideas brought out will not be used, but you'll have a rich gardenful of new ideas from which to choose.

157

Incidentally, for higher social level characters self questionings more on the order of "What's *unusual* about...." or "What's *special* about...." would probably be more productive, rather than "What's *wrong* with....".

Sometimes you'll find yourself so excited with the multitude of exciting inspirations you can glean from just one imaginary surroundings character that you'll be tempted to go no further. Do, however. Even a member of the other gender can often be productive. Many of the characteristics found in an imagined female character for a man's role, or in an imagined man for a woman's role, can be adapted to the other sex in some appropriate manner. (Don't scoff at this idea till you've tried it!)

Before leaving the discussion of External Characterization tools, two items conceived of by Michael Chekhov should be mentioned briefly. They have apparently been used by actors and actresses whose manners of studying and whose teachers' presentation of them have persuaded them of their desirability for use: THE HUMAN IMAGE, as proposed by Chekhov, involves the obtaining of ideas through observing a human being known to or observed by the actor, listening to them talk, observing their mannerisms, etc., while THE PSYCHOLOGICAL GESTURE, which he considered to be a shortcut to characterization and which is described in his book *To The Actor*, is a manner of forming the external embodiment of the character via an emotionally conditioned body improvising.

In discussing some tools so briefly, such as these of Michael Chekhov, I simply feel that, like a lawyer in court, I must present a definite case for some tools and let others present the cases for others, knowing the reader will act as his own judge and jury, consider the evidence and make his own final judgments.

But now, as we get into discussion of other *Inner Characterization* tools, I'm aware that we're getting into the most touchy disagreement-provoking section of this or any other book on the subject. The only justification for discussing them at all, in view of the controversies which arise wherever they come up, is that not to discuss them would be even worse.

Now we must take a deep breath, get our shields in front of us securely, and hold our spears ready, for this stepping off into

158

the discussion of those additional tools we have all heard of, perhaps tried and either continue to swear by, or use only peripherally or totally discarded long ago for others we consider more effective.

SOME OTHER APPROACH ITEMS

EMOTIONAL MEMORY / AFFECTIVE MEMORY

This argument is not between you, the reader, and me. It has been raging for many, many years. I will refer you to research references along the way which amply document the ongoing battles about this approach as it applies in the hands of some and in the disdain of others.

Ribot, who gave it its title "Affective Memory", taught it to Charcot, who taught it to Freud. Stanislavski came upon it through hearing of it and, for a time, investigated its use as an approach for actors' use. He began using it with his actors but by 1934 had totally discarded it. Before discarding it he had set off a chain of events he later wished he could reverse, but it was too late.

First, *what* it is is nicely defined in *Stanislavski And The Method*, by Charles Marowitz, who opined that the most popular of the Method exercises at the time of the writing of his book was without doubt the Emotional Memory or Emotional Recall. He described the exercise aptly as *an attempt by the actor to reconstruct a moment out of past life remembered as being highly emotional, in order to recreate in the actor the feelings associated with that experience.* After his description he referred to it later as simply an exercise, a great boon for the ego, a classroom toy and a ginger-peachy parlor game. Eight pages of his book were devoted to arguing against its use. Some of us would want to use far more than eight pages, if necessary, toward persuading actors of the many fallacies of using it and depending on it as a respectable acting "tool".

It is true that Stanislavski originally taught its use to his actors. But it is equally true that by the mid-1930's he had summarily stopped using it, partly because he detected an alarming and undesirable inner hysteria in the performances of some of the members of his theatre; felt that that hysteria emanated from the

159

so acutely felt need to make the memory work each time—and that that hysteria was most pronounced in moments when the actor was trying to overcome the undependable nature of such a memory; knew that such an unhealthy tendency violated art and any truly creative bringing of a character's life; and, worse still, observed that too frequent and extreme use of emotional memory had even brought some actors of the First Studio of the Moscow Art Theatre to serious mental illness!

It was Stella Adler, one of our leading American teachers, who upon her return from her 1934 visit with Stanislavski in Paris brought word that the very founder of the acting approach which was sweeping American acting circles by then had stopped teaching the Emotional Memory approach.

An issue of *The Tulane Drama Review* of some years ago was devoted to a group of noted teachers' judgments about this process. In it Miss Adler opined that to go back to a feeling or emotion of one's own past was believed by her to be unhealthy; that in her estimation it tended to separate the actor from the play, from the action and circumstances of the play, and from the author's intention. It seemed to Miss Adler that the approach was lacking in artistic control and she stated that she could not support such a methodology. She was agreeing with Stanislavski, also with the many others who have always shared these beliefs.

Vera Soloviova, another noted coach, rendered an almost verbatim opinion to one of Stanislavski's own later quotes about this item, stating that if the actress was lacking in imagination she might resort to affective memory, but she too objected to affective memory and preferred to encourage her students' creative imaginations to go further in unknown spheres of more creative imagining.

Robert Lewis, also, in *Method—Or Madness*, argued that an actor worth his salt has stored up within himself memories of all sorts of experiences and feelings and is able to evoke the memory of similar emotions in his life without his thinking about them consciously at all. He attributed a great deal of the nonsense that had been spoken about the Group Theatre in the 1930's to this particular, highly controversial item. He was of the opinion that it is dangerous territory to tread, in any case.

I'm sure that the reader must have heard that the late Lee Strasberg, one of America's most broadly publicized acting teachers, taught the "emotional recall" or "emotional memory" or "affective memory", as he called it in various periods of his teaching career.

He learned of the item in the early period of the American Lab Theatre, and even when Miss Adler brought from Paris the word that Stanislavski himself had abandoned it Mr. Strasberg is reported to have said that he would not. It is common understanding that he in fact continued to advocate its use and write about it up to the time of his death in 1982. His continuous work with it is public record.

Yet, in the book *Strasberg At The Actors Studio* he voiced, in his own words as recorded and reported in the book, some rather significant observations and reservations about it.

As quoted in that book, his recorded comments point out some discouraging problems. He commented that out of a hundred Affective Memory experiments perhaps six might work; that even if the actor were to perform the Affective Memory correctly it might not work the first time because of a counter-conditioning which may have taken place causing the original experience to have lost some of its emotional force; that, moreover, the emotional value of the experience might even have changed substantially. He stated that an actor might be planning to evoke a happy experience and wind up weeping because the happiness might at that later in life time be gone, or the same actor might be seeking to recall something sad which would suddenly, at that later time, strike him as a joke.

Mr. Strasberg steadfastly maintained, however, that by attempting a *lot* of affective memories the actor might gradually obtain a stock of memories which would be permanent and which would become easier to invoke as he continued to use them.

The foregoing describe as nearly as possible Mr. Strasberg's own comments about the exercise he so determinedly maintained in his teaching! There are those readers who should observe rather easily the hit-or-miss aspect of this item as a dependable acting tool, even as described by its foremost proponent.

By another proponent who learned this procedure from Mr.

Strasberg and who publicly maintains that she relies upon it often there has been the comment that she never knows whether it will start on time or at all upon call, how long it will remain effective, or whether it will end when she wants it to!

And there is one more questionmark which must be noted about this item: In the same *Strasberg At The Actors Studio* book the editor states that in the cases of those people who needed certain psychiatric treatment Mr. Strasberg refused to allow them to use it at all. What an overwhelming obligation this would place squarely upon the shoulders of any coach teaching its use—the determining with any accuracy *which* members had need of psychiatric treatment and, after exposing them to the "How to do it" procedure, also assuming the responsibility of making sure that they wouldn't do it privately at home!

Since many readers have heard about this item, and have perhaps explored it under a coach's direction in an acting class somewhere, I feel it is important to note the foregoing comments and opinions about this highly publicized item which most of us prefer to not use in our teaching and not recommend. I also feel it is important for the reader to differentiate between the Stanislavski-based approaches and others such as this one which, even though tried for a time by him, were discarded for some of the foregoing reasons. Many of us recommend against its use at all for the aforementioned reasons and because we prefer to teach the many far more dependable and, we feel, far more productive tools.

In addition, I for one believe that it is disastrous for actors to feel they need those preparation moments to summon forth deep feelings. Imagine the actor trying to find time for them under film conditions, for instance, where pushbutton involvement with deep feelings is invariably required in those few last seconds before or after a director yells "Action!"

Even in reading for roles, if the actor or actress needs to take a few moments of *preparing* to feel something the director will probably sense it, thank him or her and signal to the casting person to send in the next candidate. The director knows that if the actor does not have easy and quick access to deep feeling there will be delays and less than optimum result in the sometimes

162

quite brief (and often quickly reshot from different angles) takes required in filming. Even in those interviews for film roles such preparation is questionable, since in all probability, immediately after the actor must give a few career details about himself, there's the invitation to begin reading the role in the next second.

One of my main objections, also, is that an actor depending on such an approach will usually be so locked into one feeling level for the duration of the use of this item—if it's working that time at all!—that the scripted changes of intensity are missed. The actor simply isn't there in the right place or even in the person of the character to note them and respond more truthfully to them.

This item, in the final analysis, is in my estimation the main reason for some actors forever failing to find out that they are indeed fine actors and need not feel forever that they are inept students of acting. Dependence on such an undependable item and too often being unable to make it work for them can keep them from achieving ultimate confidence with all the rest of their available talents!

I have chosen to not explain the procedures of exploring this item in these pages because I have no inclination to even discuss them. There are teachers and coaches who find this exercise a handy time-killer and confidence-destroyer in acting classes who would be happy to explore the Affective Memory with any reader over a long period if asked and paid to do so.

SENSE MEMORY

Here is another item which is unfortunately controversial, but only in the manners of teaching its use in roles.

If Sense Memory needs any defense, which it assuredly does not, I want to point out that in the Affective Memory exercise, if you know the latter's procedures or if you're exposed to them at some point, you must observe that it is really the Sense Memory approach cycle involved in constructing the Affective Memory which is the key to the progression toward its reevoking.

That should speak more eloquently for Sense Memory than any other praise. It by itself is that important!

Sense Memory of one type or another is involved in *almost all the major tools* of the System, if not to a degree in all of them. It is merely taught differently by different coaches when broken down to be worked on by itself.

In my own teaching it is used, as you have previously noted, in the finding of most tools through the body's associative memory processes, and it is perhaps the main key toward reaching into the right side of the brain's rich storehouse. It is at least peripherally involved in any effective Object, whether it is a Beat Object, Life Object or Unit Object. It is one of the most productive facets of an actor's talent.

People in my classes use it most consciously in the finding and use of Creative Psychological Objectives which include those two simile keys and what they trigger in body responses, but any actor with sufficient imagination will be involving with Sense Memory throughout every moment which involves his imagination.

A Sense Memory is what the body has stored away and retains forever after we have experienced something physically through one or more of the senses or perhaps through most of them combined in a single experience. Additionally, sense memory often involves the body with some experience of its own which it associates with a definite thought or feeling or both. This is why I recommend the *body-finding* process for discovering worded tools, so that the complete instrument of the actor can be brought into play, rather than simply a feeling or thought basis for an experience which may or may not later attract the body's important participation.

Used in acting classes as an exercise to stimulate actors' imagination, it often involves examining, for instance, the imaginary contents of an old trunk in an attic. Each item discovered in the trunk by the imagination is encouraged to be explored as a sensory experiencing of its characteristics. Is it cold, hot, warm, soft, rough, hard? What does it smell like? What is the sound made when it is handled, if it has no sound-making faculty of its own? How light or heavy does it feel?

What does it remind you of? How does it make you feel? Where did it come from?.... etc., etc.

Other acting class exercisings with Sense Memory might involve, for example, lying in the sand on a sunny beach on a hot day.

164

The actor would be encouraged to note the heat of the sun on already hot skin; the rubbing of suntan oil and its soothing softness; the little tinkly sounds across the sand; the caress of the sun-filtered breezes; the smell of the surf; etc.—storing or reviving sense memories which might serve the actor in some peacefully relaxed moment of a role at a future time.

This kind of exercising with Sense Memory is more a general developmental exercise to increase the actor's appreciation of the body-involving aspects of any good sense memories.

Another sense memory in such a class might be that of trying to get to sleep on a very hot night. The oppressive heat would be noted and explored; the perspiration-wet and sticky sheets would be noted; the bumps in the bed never noticed before that immensely uncomfortable moment; the attempt to find a cool spot somewhere; the closeness of the air; the magnified night-sounds outside the open window; the tossing and turning in restive agony; the parched feeling of the mouth and throat—all being reexplored for their possible value later in moments of roles where a weighty problem makes the character nervous, tense and restless, or where the character is feeling very guilty, dissatisfied or annoyed.

One of the benefits of these class exercisings with Sense Memory is that the actor can't fail to note the involvement of the body which any Sense Memory exploration promotes.

Some teachers who recommend the use of single Sense Memories in separate moments of roles also recommend the following manner of finding an appropriate one for use in that manner: Instead of trying to find the right Sense Memory via simple result words like "hate" or "love" or "confusion" the actor should, rather, think about what such a single word feels like most often to him or her personally. Nothing sensory yet; at least nothing planned to feel or sound sensory yet in its wording.

One actor's mind might see "hate" as "wanting to bust something!", while another might in his mind redefine the same single word as "not able to think clearly". Such differences do exist among different personalities' experiences of identical words, being caused by the different psychologies' defense and coping structures. It is important that you find *your own unique* redefinition, in strictly mental terms, for the feelings for which a Sense Memory is to be sought. Then and only then, try to remember a moment not when you felt "hate" but when you simply "wanted to bust something" or when you were "not able to think clearly".

The remarkable thing which happens when this *redefining* approach is employed is that, by summoning the body's help in the redefining, a sense memory will come which is more appropriate for you personally than one could be through the one-step approach. It's even possible that you might find that the available Sense Memory inspired in this manner of finding one offers you personally as much as, or in your own case more than, the more channeled and more psychologically-keyed CPO approach which I so strongly recommend. It's my privilege to disagree, but we're all different. You certainly might explore Sense Memory use in the foregoing manner if it appeals to you.

I should mention, however, that if you're one to whom a simple Sense Memory appeals more than the CPO approach, in preparing a role there is the danger of violating or overlooking the overall personality—that recognizable emotional identity of your character. When the experiencing of a Sense Memory is foremost, without the psychological conditioning which a CPO (or perhaps some other similar tool) can provide, it's possible that the spectator may become confused as to what the base feelings of the character itself are in such a moment.

I still strongly recommend the CPO process for involving a more Sense Memory-stimulated body participation in the Beat of a role, or relying in fact on the associative memory triggerers an effectively worded Object itself can produce if found through the "body-finding" process recommended earlier.

THE SOCIAL MASK

Few roles exist where the character can show all its feelings openly all the time and still be able to *get, keep or avoid* something important to it. Those are the key words in determining situations which suggest or require the use of a *Social Mask* as a "cover-up" tool.

No matter what the true inner feelings of a character may be, there are moments and longer sequences in most roles when the

166

character must cover those feelings (actually, *attempt* to cover them) in order to *get* something (perhaps a raise, a sale, a contract, some respect), to *keep* something (perhaps a marriage, a job, some peace, an inheritance, an upper hand) or *avoid* something (being fired, being discovered, causing a fight, committing a social *faux pas* or spoiling a group's fun).

In real life we probably have friends or associates who may not really like us at all, but who treat us in perhaps one of these manners: friendly, loving, interested, helpful, cooperative or indulgent. Underneath those facades we may not even detect that there is jealousy, loathing, prejudice, sexual calculation, resentment or something else. Perhaps, on the other hand, we may know that they like us very much but, to protect themselves from becoming too involved, they pretend disinterest, casual acceptance, critical, distant, always too busy or something else.

Social Mask is a *lie*. In acting terms, as in everyday life, it is a *pretense*. It is a "represented" feeling, a "role-playing" designed to cover whatever true feelings lie behind it.

When actors attempt to "play simple results" such as adjectives they tend to theatricalize their efforts because they aren't really experiencing those feelings in any inner manner. It is the same with a Social Mask, and in using this nice tool in a role the actor should do precisely the opposite of what he must do for true experiencing.... he must "represent", "play simple result" and "role-play" for as long as the Social Mark is necessary in order to get, keep or avoid something.

This use of a "Social Mask" for the character in sometimes long moments of roles is like visiting an old friend in real life.... the process is so very familiar for all of us. For the actor who decides to use one it is one of the most natural and easiest processes of all. The Social Mask itself feels like the back porch "play-acting" from childhood days. It's important that it not be ideally real.... but it's pleasant to "perform".

Since the true character behind the Social Mask is still there, and should be apparent in its true inner experience for the viewer—while attempting to get away with a surface lie to other characters around it, the actor should employ the most obviously called for approach in forming a Social Mask for those moments when the character needs one. Therefore, there is nothing more sure to work than those self-same *adjectives* and *role labels* which create "bad acting".

In that manner, just as in life, the viewer will be able to detect the inner truths of the character hiding behind the surface "representation" and "result-playing" effort of the character as it attempts to mislead other characters. The audience member, seeing through the sham, can hurt because he knows that while attempting to be "brave" or "courageous" on the surface the character is sufferingly deeply inside. On the other hand, good comedy can result and the viewer will laugh as he shares the dynamic secret of a character's inner thought while the pretense on the surface is allowed to be ridiculously transparent.

The *Social Mask*, in its most appropriate use, is for the man about to get a divorce who can't stand his wife, and the wife who can't stand her husband one more day, who, together—as they entertain the husband's superior at a sit-down dinner, pretend "The world's most loving couple". The boss himself, sitting across from them and smiling—although he can't stand his employee and loathes the man's wife, may be pretending "Jovial benefactor" or something else on the surface.

It is also for the frightened virgin, out with a man who is known to have a wild reputation, who pretends to be perhaps "A foxy doxie", while the roue across from her, anxious to finish the evening with the desired event, pretends to be a "Harmless puppydog". It's for the friend who can't wait to leave your party because she's unbelievably bored, who pretends "Having a ball" because her husband works for you.

Note that simple adjectives are one form of Social Mask, and they work excellently for this purpose, but many actors enjoy more those catchy *labels* or *role titles* such as are spoken of in the preceding paragraph. Either way works. The choice is up to the actor who wants to use this tool.

I recommend to my people that when a Social Mask is in use it is—even more than at other times—desirable to use a CPO developed with the inner experience truths, so that the body will still be sending its sensory messages (those unique qualities of the CPO) to the viewer's sensory antennae, to insure the most

168

vivid awareness for the viewer of what is really going on inside the character behind that surface pretense.

* * *

If you're wondering at this point about certain tools which haven't been mentioned yet and which your own past study has associated with the preparation of the Analytic, Directed or Creative Subtext phases, perhaps it is because in the previous chapters and this one I've tried to cover those tools which I personally teach and recommend or feel should be mentioned in passing. The tools mentioned thus far are of course designed for the *homework* preparations to help bring as much creativity as possible to those processes.

Some items you've missed thus far may be felt by me to be more applicable to upcoming chapters dealing with *Rehearsals For Theatre And Film Roles* and *Continuing Work On The Actor's Instrument and Resources*, and will be found under those headings. For instance, I feel that the small Physical Objectives, Inner Dialogue, Inner Monologue and Private Moment, not discussed yet, belong in the latter phases. While they are often exercised with in classes as pertaining to performance moments I don't feel they should be finitely planned in the preliminary preparation.

It has been my intention up to this point to describe what I feel to be *a productive sequence of application of system tools* so each can be of optimum benefit, while attempting to convey the purpose of certain class exercises mentioned thus far which relate most directly to the preparation phase *if employed at productive points in the preparation sequence.*

Section IV

Rehearsals for Theatre and Film Roles

Chapter Nine

The Early Rehearsal Period

The word "period" in the title of this Chapter should make it apparent that most of the discussion in the chapter applies primarily to *theatre* rehearsals. Those who have done many *film* roles know in advance that any rehearsals they will have for the filming of scenes will be on the set and quite brief usually. The work in the following areas which can be brought to the one, two or three brief run-throughs before filming a scene must be automatic, firmly formed as habit and on call without too much conscious thinking about it.

In the period during which this book is written there are four or five weeks of rehearsals allowed for major stage productions employing union members of Actors Equity Association, while in film there are usually less than those four quick run-throughs for each separate shot of any kind, and they're conducted in the last few minutes before the shot is filmed.

In theatre—with the director's indulgence and approval, of course—the actor can use some of the early rehearsals to add or explore in specific areas. As long as the director trusts that you know what you're doing, there's usually time allowed for you to do it. For film, on the other hand, you can certainly do all the

173

foregoing *homework* prior to arrival on the set, but not too many of the following, due to lack of time in tight filming schedules, shots which are planned ahead of time by the director to be filmed in ways the actor can't anticipate, set limitations, shooting out of sequence because of locations and cost-saving, and in the end the terrible pressures imposed on directors by production front offices.

For theatre primarily, then, here are some things the actor might consider as he rehearses a role or just prior to the start of rehearsals to either bring deeper familiarity with the role or begin bringing the many excitements which are easier to develop once rehearsals are under way than they are in the solitary homework processes:

IMPROVISATIONS TO FIND EXTRA COLORS

From the moment you begin planning the Directed Subtext of your character—the Life Object, the Super Objective, the Unit Objects and their Through Lines of Action, the Beat Objects as you study lines, even the CPO's if desired—you'll probably, like other actors and actresses, find it difficult to resist exploring the character's attitudes and behavior at home, on the street, in group gatherings and many other places.

Rod Steiger, one of our leading American actors mentioned earlier, once said in an interview that he has gone into department stores in character and wandered around to discover his character's relationships with all kinds of objects as conditioned by its personality.

It is a natural excitement for the actor, this exploration and living of the character's subtext. Do it anywhere when the impulse strikes you, as long as it won't cause your arrest or make you lose a friend or spouse. Improvisations in the closed enironment of an acting class, too, can help deepen your experiential acquaintance with the character's own impulses, tastes, choices, etc., and can sometimes help to find mannerisms, thought patterns, tempos and other overlooked items if your earlier preparation hasn't been sufficiently thorough.

Also, if you have a friend in an acting class where that "Hot Seat" exercise with the Neurosis-Provoking Moment has been

174

conducted you might ask your friend to put you through such an exercise privately with the conditioning prepared for the character you're scheduled to play. If you do, you'll probably note the similarity between those results and what Mr. Steiger related doing in department stores. But the questions thrown at you by your friend will of course be wider ranging than the items available to Mr. Steiger on department store shelves.

STUDYING LINES WITH CONSCIOUS TOOLS

The importance of using *the conscious characterization tools* you've prepared for the character throughout all line study can't be stressed too strongly. The lines should not be learned simply by rote, without the prepared thought and feeling patterns providing at least those early experiencing of the emotional, feeling and mood realities for which they've been created. Having broken down your script into Units and Beats, get yourself into the feelings created by the Beat Objects especially for the studying of each Beat, one after another.

Working beat by beat, one at a time, is so important. Work on one until its lines are secure, all the time maintaining the Beat Object's feelings thoughout the memorizing process. Finish that Beat's memorizing before going on to the following one. If you maintain the Beat Object's feelings throughout the creative habits you've planned for the Beat the particular feeling depth you desire will be firmly associated with that Beat's duration as the role is rehearsed and later performed.

It should also be mentioned here that for *film and television* role line study this practice of studying one beat at a time while remaining in the feeling of the Beat Object for that beat throughout is doubly important! Those who've worked in these two fields know that if that Beat's action is to move from one room to another, or from an exterior scene approach to a front door directly to the entrance to the interior of a building those different locations of that Beat's duration will be shot hours, days or even weeks or months apart. The running up to the front door may be shot in Malibu or Afghanistan a week or ten weeks before the same run, with its same feelings of the character, enters the interior of the building! The actor who doesn't have a definite plan, such as a Beat Object, firmly in mind at both times, may well have his footage cut from the picture because when the interior shots were made on a sound stage at a Hollywood studio so long a time later he may have forgotten the level of intensity or even the exact focus of his thoughts and feelings which were so evident in the exterior footage shot so long before!

THIS MOMENT

The actor can develop more confident work and bring out more of his own natural resources when he is not under pressure; when he doesn't feel pulled or pushed forward at an unrelenting pace by dialogue or by a director who doesn't understand the actor's processes. The actor should try to bear in mind that "*this moment*"—this thing that's going on in the mind and feelings *right now*—must be searched into and explored for all its potential values and little colors.

Remember, you already have your characterization tools ready to produce myriad impulses, things to do, feelings to explore, etc., and you already have your Beat Object for this moment to particularize everything involved in the situation at hand. Keep yourself strictly in *this moment—not thinking ahead!* If the problem at hand hasn't gone away, don't neglect it and lose its potency by thinking of the next moment when the writer has determined that it will have disappeared. The writer has also determined ahead of time that at *this* particular moment that problem should be the one concentration focus. Seek out the adventure, the pain, the heartache, the frustrations and irritations, the feelings of inadequacy and self-doubt that are available if you simply "flounder in the muck of your problem" for as long as the planned Beat allows. There are always so many more big and little (even if very brief) experiences in a given moment than an actor can anticipate, and some of them will lend added brilliance to your work after they're sought out.

NURSING YOUR OWN IMPULSES

Sir Laurence Olivier, in an article-interview in a magazine, once said that the main job of an actor was to "keep the audience awake." Whether he said it facetiously or not, it states one of the

176

actor's responsibilities if the performed work is to mean something and maintain attention and involvement on the part of the viewer.

So many actors bypass their impulses out of fear that they may get in the way of a carefully prepared character or the continuing scene in which it's involved. But the impulsive and spontaneous actor is always more interesting than the cautious, self-inhibiting one, and his personal excitements are more free to blend with the character because of encouraging and using his own impulses more determinedly. The risk of impulses being wrong when the actor is conditioned by characterization beforehand is minimal, while the value of their occurring and being used is so great.

However, to avoid any misapprehension, please note that we're talking here about nursing impulses *during rehearsals*, not during performances of a work which has been carefully rehearsed and polished under the director's eye.

Stanislavski recognized the value of impulses and wrote about them expansively in his notes. An excellent device grew out of his work with them—the smaller *Physical Objectives*.

PHYSICAL OBJECTIVES

There is an excellent discussion of these little Physical Objectives on pages 56 through 77 of *Creating A Role*, detailing some of the work by Stanislavski on the role of "Chatski" in Griboyedov's "*Woe From Wit*". It gives a very clear idea of what the tiny Physical Objectives are. Remember, they're often the product of impulses experienced during rehearsals or found even earlier in improvising in character. They should of course be passed through the conscious consideration of whether they have value for use later if they can bring added reality or interesting moments to a situation.

Physical Objectives, as discussed here at least, are *tiny actions* of only momentary life which bring the emotional character into direct contact with the physical realities around it. They provide the little justifications for simple action, and because they are individually ultra-clear of and by themselves they often bring exciting little human recognition moments for viewers.

For instance, when the author says merely "He sits" or "She paces" the actor should find little Physical Objectives which will give the sitting or the pacing some purpose. Perhaps the character should "sit" in order to "rest my tired bones", "show them I mean business", "control my temper", or perhaps "show them I've stopped listening". Perhaps the other character "paces" to "get my head straightened out", "stop his yelling" or to "show them I'm ready to start".

Since Physical Objectives are for the purpose of involving both the mind and the body—not simply thought alone, they provide interesting moments of illumination throughout their brief lifespans. By the way, any one Beat may have a bunch of little Physical Objectives which flow naturally out of the Object. The manner in which they establish strong contact between the character and its physical surroundings, or by choice might not, is up to the actor.

As an example, there is a play entitled "*The Andersonville Trial*". In the play, "Chipman", as prosecutor, is to bring into the last day of the court the witness who he feels is his one hope of finally winning a conviction against "Wirz", the former Commandant responsible for the inhuman treatment of enemy prisoners at the Andersonville prison camp. Before the witness "Davidson" is brought into the courtroom and leading up to the start of his questioning of the young soldier, Chipman must go through certain last-minute preparations.

Here are some possible Physical Objectives which might be used in the Beat before the questioning is commenced:

Get that key sentence in mind! (He picks up the previous testimony transcript, searches for the sentence and finds it.)

Find out what he was about to say! (He squints toward the horizon, remembering the nervous faltering of that prior moment.)

Memorize the details! (His eyes shut and his head bobs as he plans the words that may key the rest of the damning details.)

(At this point Davidson is led in and Chipman
turns to inspect his condition.)

See if he's up to it! (He appraises the condition of the emaciated, frightened soldier.)

178

Give him my strength! (He goes to meet Davidson and leads him gently to the witness chair, pats him softly and sympathetically to reassure the lad prior to another grilling testifying.)

Make sure the judges notice his condition! (He looks intently at the judges one after another as he stands to one side to give all a good view of the boy.)

Show Wirz he's done for! (A flick of a half-threatening, half-triumphant look at the defendant.)

Keep him from freaking out again! (He leans semi-casually on the witness chair arm and briefly smiles encouragingly down at Davidson.)

Get this over with now! (He fills his lungs quickly and adopts a strong starting position.)

While Physical Objectives add the tiny, moment to moment details for dramatic acting, they are also a marvelous boon to comedians and comedy playing. Imagine, for instance, a drunk who arrives at his own door and, not wanting to awaken his wife, begins this sequence of Physical Objectives:

Make it stop moving around! (He tries to locate the doorknob.) .... then *Thank it for stopping!* (Pats the doorknob gratefully for letting him find it!)

Make sure it doesn't squeak this time! (Turns the doorknob ever so carefully; opens the door with the same precaution in mind; shuts it after going through it, still with the same thought.)

Get these bad boys off! (Notices his shoes and the bit of noise they're making; leans down and takes them off and spanks each one gently; decides to carry them.)

Aim myself in the right direction! (Squints to find the bedroom; laboriously plants his feet in that direction; starts to take a step.)

Keep that damn thing from squeaking! (Carefully avoids a floorboard which tends to squeak.)

Make sure she's asleep! (He stops and cocks an ear toward the bedroom door.)

(A car might honk loudly outside the house at
this point and continue for a moment.)

Kill the bastard! (After a second of wincing, fearful that the sound will have awakened his wife, he grimaces toward the window and shakes his fist at the car horn!)

For comedy especially, Physical Objectives are a nice way in which to bring inanimate objects to very funny life—treating them as if they were human, whether friends or enemies.

For effective use of them, Physical Objectives depend upon the imagination and inventiveness of their creator. With most who find they can enjoy them, a bit of practice brings their finding and use to vivid life in figuratively "embroidering" the moments of individual Beats in which they're used.

SILENT THOUGHTS

While Physical Objectives are certainly silent thoughts also, they are involved with tiny actions. There are all the other kinds of silent thoughts as well.

What I'm calling "Silent Thoughts" was originally called the *Inner Monologue* and *Inner Dialogue* by Stanislavski. Just as they were planned by Stanislavski to do, they accompany spoken dialogue periodically and often continue when there is no dialogue. Some of us since, desiring to loosen and free this item from the formal "writing" aspect which might stifle some impulsive discoveries if formed too early, call it simply *Silent Thoughts.*

As the character's thoughts arrive more and more clearly in the rehearsing of its moments, there are automatically more and more silent thoughts. They spring from the increasing onslaught of realities to which the character is introduced. They come because a next line must be led up to via a sequence of such thoughts, or a next thing the author has the character do needs to be considered, justified, decided upon, or perhaps because of private shifts and turns in the character's attention of some kinds, moment after moment.

Silent Thoughts would mean nothing if not used by an actor whose instrument, the body, is tuned to experiencing them along with the mind. The actor should try to involve the body with each thought somehow, even if ever so slightly. It's a more enjoyable experience, and a more meaningful one, for both the actor and the audience.

In real life most of our bodies respond to our thoughts with some degree of accompanying movement—far more actively than we might observe. For the actor, the art of *tuning the body to the thoughts* is imperative.

Of special value for the actor are the several tiny thoughts which can lead from the end of one speech or even one word to another. The "between-the-lines" thoughts lend added reality and truth, as well as increased experiencing for the character and the actor, to all moments or roles.

This searching out of the experiences of the "between-the-lines" spaces in involved and interesting manners should of course be cultivated as habit in acting class sessions, since many actors seem to neglect those moments and their great potential when involved with dialogue. However, here we're discussing their incorporation in roles being prepared.

Any moment without some silent thought is not a living moment at all, except for those occasional "*feeling blob*" moments when our thoughts simply can't focus. Those brief moments are extremely valuable for the actor to use on occasion too, since they are so frequently part of our human process in real life and should not be missing in the tiny moments of roles. A few words will be said about these silent *non*-thoughts following these more defined Silent Thoughts' discussion.

One reason that some of us who teach don't ask actors to write out "Inner Monologues" throughout their roles is that I, for instance, have discovered that while one actor responds ideally to what I call "Silent Thoughts" use another responds with more personal excitement to the previously discussed "Physical Objectives" use. Some might use the two together, mixing them, one following another, for best result, in fact.

The two are different. One is a consciously executed series of tiny actions; the other is some manner of talking to one's self or talking to someone else without uttering words. Silent Thoughts, in their own terms, are more along the following line as they might be discovered and later used by someone whose character is to get on a bus at a busy streetcorner:

"Where the hell is that quarter? Aha! Got the bastard! Dammit, I keep forgetting, is it Number 32 or Number 23? Oh yeah, there

181

it is.... Good ol' Number 32. Damn, crowded as usual! Oh, boy, always happens.... I stand here, the damn thing stops over there!"

(Gets on the bus:)

"Hey, you!.... Quit shoving, dammit! Okay, go ahead, fatso! Boy, some people! Oh-oh, it's that snotty driver again. Oh well, win a few, lose a few."

(Looking for a seat to sit down:)

"Garbage, garbage everywhere! Smells terrible! Over there! Nope not next to that bum. There, next to her? Beat me to it, dammit! Smells like somebody threw up in here. Watch your feet, Henry. Oh well, guess I can stand for twelve blocks again. Boy, the manners some people have, sittin' there while she stands!"

FEELING BLOBS

Now, that other kind of "between-the-lines" experiencing. I suppose there is a more academic-sounding title by which to call what it is, but I know of one therapist who uses the phrase to describe a type of occurrence in his patients which is common in all of us and occurs far more often than we realize throughout our daily activities, broodings, worryings and even in our happy and relaxed moments. Also, in exactly those two words it seems to me to best describe its form and content.

Such "blob" moments occur when a thought isn't yet formed; when a response is triggered by something and words simply aren't necessary or possible; when we are struggling to concentrate but aren't able to; and in many, many other moments. They are more automatic than consciously used in life. Therefore, many actors need to be made aware that they even happen!

Haven't you observed others when, in response to your question or statement their faces and bodies both change visibly for a rather long moment.... very clear expressions coming onto their faces and their bodies adjusting very expansively even before any actual response is indicated as imminent? Sometimes there are even two or three of these changes in these rather brief moments before any response comes. These are "feeling blobs". Even if there follows a final moment of the face and body changing to a formed and "zeroing in" appearance which lets you know that they're about to respond verbally, can't you read fairly clearly the kind of thing they're going to say? This last moment, too, is still a feeling blob or whatever you want to call it that means the same thing.

There are actors—and many of them have been taught by me, I might add—who value these little, brief "feeling blobs" as being very important in their work to duplicate this actual human occurrence. The actors I've taught understand why they occur; what kinds of things cause them; and how to use them to best advantage.

Capable actors, who have easily formed thoughts (perhaps "Inner Monologue" or "Inner Dialogue" so readily on tap every moment of a role) can still appear to be missing two elements that are so important in performed characters—vulnerability and spontaneity. Like the patients of a psychotherapist, an actor consciously using "feeling blob" moments to duplicate the quite human aspect of not having a response ready will be far more interesting—and far more vulnerable and spontaneous in the eyes of the viewer.

This moment of not having a thought focused every time a feeling is triggered should be examined and really thought about! What's happening in such a moment?

An automatic response occurs because the right side of the brain and the body, through their associative memory process, qualify what has been observed by them more quickly than the left side of the brain processes can run it through the data file. The panic button is touched in the left side of the brain to take appropriate action quickly; the call goes to the right side of the brain for help; the right side clerks and the body begin the struggle to somehow bridge the language gap between the two sides of the brain and help the data-theory-logic clerks on the left side do their job. That they don't speak the same language makes communication difficult. The right side clerks finally, with the body's help, get their message through to the befuddled left side folks and some word of response or some kind of appropriate action is produced under the now reoriented direction of the left side folks. If all this sounds complicated you should remind yourself that all this probably takes place in less than two or three seconds in normal conversation and less turmoiled moments.

It's those more emotionally agitated moments in which the actor should consider the conscious interjecting of these "feeling blobs". In those moments when others' words or actions impact more dynamically on our characters and cause more intensified responses those responses and reactions should not be so quickly formed that they bypass the disorientation and floundering moments which must be part of vulnerable characters' performances. Those moments are more truly the *experience* of the character than are the responses and reactions which evolve after a cohesive thought is formed.

The science of what is happening in the departments of the brain during such moments need not be learned. The reason for mentioning those inner processes earlier was that the actor should be aware of *how many small fragments* are basically part of that short moment when some disorientation does occur. That it occurs in real life far more often than we notice is fact. That it should occur equally often in role performance is desirable.

Those fragmented moments when thoughts aren't clear for a brief span of time and often go through two, three or four short and varied "feeling blobs" with no words necessary or possible for the character give the character so many tiny opportunities to believe its own process and give the actor so many opportunities to be more engrossingly interesting!

They aren't written by authors. They must be interjected by the thinking actor because they're part of what the actor should contribute. A writer would find his script, whether film or theatre work, taking up hundreds of pages if at every moment of the role he had to do the actor's job as well, with these kinds of paren-thetical directions:

"(John gasps briefly at the ridiculousness of Helen's assertion, then smiles for a second at how funny it really was, then looks heavenward for two seconds at her stupidity, then drops his shoulders in dismay that she hasn't understood anything he has tried to communicate to her, then, realizing he has to respond

184

in some manner, takes a deep breath occasioned by the added effort it's going to take to get his point across to her, then leans forward with a thought starting to form, then shakes his head because he knows she will fail to understand no matter how he tries, but in spite of his knowledge that his effort and his words will be wasted again, he finally speaks.)"

Moments of this type, however brief or protracted over a few moments they may be, in the hands of talented actors who know how valuable they are, are, after all, in every tiniest part, the character's *experience*. What's more, they are so uniquely experienceable *by the actor as well* that they offer opportunities for so many facets of his talent and personal resources to be employed. These moments, more than all the dialogue in the entire role, are golden opportunities for the actor!

Awareness of the importance of these "feeling blob" moments is another reason for my own bias against the too formed "Inner Monologue" or "Inner Dialogue". They are substitutes for those logically progressed, "every stone in place", too clean-cut passages between dialogue moments, and I think highly desirable substitutes for duplicating more ideally the human pattern in the moments where they should be used.

I have observed that actors who become aware of the desirability of using "feeling blobs" in many, many moments of roles are much more interesting to watch, more ideally spontaneous seeming and more riveting of attention than other actors who either don't realize they belong or simply haven't the courage to use them.

Take another moment and reexamine that paragraph of parenthesized directions which no writer should have to put into a script. Try either that paragraph for yourself, or a sequence of such small "feeling blob" moments of your own improvising. I believe you will always want to have such moments in your work thereafter.

THE LIVING SOUNDS

Watching some actors' work, one often gets the feeling that something else is missing. Often, rather than some of the foregoing items, it's the absence of *the living sounds*—the kinds of sounds that punctuate everything we do and say in real life. Thoughts produce sounds. Feelings produce sounds. Body conditions produce sounds. Reactions of all nature produce sounds. In fact, most experiences in real life produce sounds. Some actors use sounds in their work automatically, while others must be tutored into finding them. In any event, the majority of truthful experiences demand them for completeness.

How important are sounds in real life? They are so important in the field of psychotherapy that they are studied just as closely, or even moreso in some cases, as the spoken words of the therapists' patients. They are the "animal within".

The spoken answers of patients are one thing, while the little or sometimes very large sounds that precede, punctuate or follow words and partial sentences are another, often negating the very essence of what the patient is trying to say. The spoken words are often evasive or even outright lies, or at best may be half-truths. The sounds, on the other hand, indicate clearly, if studied, that something entirely different is going on inside the patient.

Like the previous item, sounds are most often a form of "feeling blobs". A graphic example was demonstrated for me by a therapist friend once. First he handed me a slip of paper with just six words on it taken from the transcript of a session with one of his patients. On the paper was the question "How did your week go?" and the single word response "Fine." But then my friend played that portion of the taping of the session!

After the question came a soft, deep sigh of malaise, followed in confused succession by an exhalation of despair, a lost moan of trying to gather an answer that would mean something, then a half grunt of irritation at being required to encapsule an entire week in an answer and not wanting to bother to do it, then another sound of "What the hell!" nature, finally the single word "Fine," which was followed immediately by a couple more sounds of far more deeply felt despair.

You certainly must detect in this exchange how closely the sounds experience parallels, in fact is produced by and emanates from the "feeling blob" experience!

While sounds in real life are sometimes unconscious *results* of the inner experience, for the actor they should be used more consciously to not only enhance expressiveness and bring a more complete experiencing of something but to also create a more truthful experiencing of the *next* moment.

In an acting class exercise sounds can illustrate their effectiveness ideally. If the actor is asked to improvise some ordinary moment out of daily life with only sounds and does so he will be surprised at how many inspirations come that might be overlooked without their being triggered by exploring in terms of sounds. The sounds will bring ideas, will cause a heightened sensory experiencing of everything, will automatically move the body through that heightening of the sensory perception, and turn otherwise dull moments into individual adventures along the way.

The use of sounds should be nurtured in acting classes so that the actor forms the habit of using them. Then, apropos of the "rehearsal period" being dealt with in these paragraphs, they will automatically be brought into the actor's work as moments of roles are being rehearsed. They belong in characters' lives as surely as they occur less consciously in our own!

SURROUNDING REALITIES

A very important checkpoint, and one sometimes overlooked by actors until directors remind them, is to double-check in early rehearsals—or in last moments before the filming of scenes for motion pictures—the "surrounding realities" involved in scenes which may have been noted earlier but which may have been forgotten while concentrating on the enriching of the emotional experience of the character in these early phases.

It is always good to go back and check the facts presented by the writer as to surrounding realities which should not be overlooked and which should be actively incorporated in the character's moments.

Now is the time to remind yourself of the cotton lint and chaff that should fill the air in Tennessee Williams's "*27 Wagon Loads Of Cotton*"; the dust that should rise from the dirt road running past the shack and fill the air when a car passes; the mosquitos and flies that are constantly biting; the oppressive heat of the midday sun; etc.

Quite often the director is too preoccupied with other production details to notice that one or more of these surrounding realities are not yet being incorporated by cast members as the action of a work is being blocked. Not only will the adding of these extras at an early point in rehearsal bring you some lovely little moments and add increased authenticity; it will also create many organic blocking items that, later, may be difficult or impossible to incorporate after the performance's blocking has been set and polished without their being included.

I once directed the film star, Billie Burke, at a point quite late in her life, in a play going the rounds among most of the eastern summer theatres which booked star packages. There were so many beautiful little physical details involved with the surrounding realities which were brought by her from the very first moments of rehearsal and as rehearsals progressed more were added daily by her. Observing her to be somewhat forgetful in offstage life, I was surprised that, once found, every single little item of relating to her physical surroundings was repeated at precisely the spot where it was first added, which was not even true with the younger cast members who seemed to have no memory problems offstage! Her offstage memory problem being no secret, I asked her over dinner one night as the production opening approached how she managed to so ideally remember all those tiny details while some others often forgot them. Her reply might suggest a fine way for others to do the same thing:

"Darling, all those years of film taught me that if I was going to do some little things in my scenes they had to be memorized along with my lines. I learned that on a film set you're just so busy with so many new details from the director that you can't come up with them at those last minutes. So I've always jotted them down exactly where I want to do them and memorized them as if they're part of my dialogue. It works that way for theatre too, doesn't it!"

It certainly does.

THE SPECIAL REALITY OF OTHER CHARACTERS

Other characters in dramatic situations are often the main realities to which some actors relate. Some actors appear to be "vacuuming in" everything the other characters do or say to such an extent that they wind up with little reality in their own character's experience.

Of course there are also those actors who spend so much of their preparation and rehearsal time on self-involved characterization that they seem to fail to see or hear the others in their scenes. Neither of these two extremes is wise.

Somewhere between these two lies the true path to scenic involvement with other characters and use of their contributed realities while still maintaining the character's own experience as the central point and conditioning core.

Remember, the emotional line of your own character, formed ahead of time in the very beginning of your work on the role, will carry it through early rehearsals into being deeply focused on its inner involvements and some amount of interaction with other characters as well. It will usually have been the match which ignited the first fiery exchanges in those early rehearsals, and it is one of the major advantages of having used a systematic approach in role preparation that, with characters planned and brought so immediately, the exchanges start easily and quickly because each character brings with him or her so much for other characters to play against and with.

(In this respect, I'm again reminded of film, where of course most if not all of characterization work must be prepared ahead of time. I know one director who always tells his cast members to "Bring something from home!" and another, saying the same thing with a Russian accent, who admonishes his people to "Make from yourself something before you come!")

I have found it profitable, once I know the actor has "brought something from home" and "made from himself something before he comes", to allow actors time to search out some of the items mentioned in a number of the early rehearsals before zeroing in too tightly on other characters if they need to later at all. In those instances where I have allowed the reverse it was extremely difficult to add extra colors to the individual performances later.

Of course, once a rehearsal is under way it is important to reserve a part of your awareness for observing and using what the other character is doing unless your character should be so self concerned that such attention isn't appropriate. Failure to recognize that in many scenes other characters are responsible for what is happening to your character can lead to important oversights and produce admonitions from directors. The audience member will be listening for nuances, observing little slips, catching many subtle shadings of the other characters' feelings and attitudes, and your character certainly should also. The "illusion of the first time" depends on your character never knowing what's coming next.

So, at least to the degree desirable within the context of each character, one should always be looking behind others' words for their meanings; behind the actions of others for their deeper implications; and behind other characters' social masks for their "animal within". In real life we do it because survival and security depend on it. In acting we should do it because good acting most often depends on it.

OUR CHARACTER'S OWN PERSONAL EXPERIENCE

Having just stressed the importance of interaction with other characters, it's important at this point to mention the even greater important guideline: In spite of the desired amount of relating with other characters, the maintaining of your own character's *personal* experience must come first. Any character whose experience depends totally upon what happens to it in the process of relating with other characters or the simple events around it is one which has no valid purpose in a dramatic work!

A leading American actor was once asked in a magazine interview *"You have the reputation of not looking at other actors very much.... Why is that?"* The answer, which nicely sums up what this discussion is taking up: *"Why should I look at other actors? I'm looking at my character's problems.... they're more important."*

While this may sound too cut and dried for some readers and may cause an actor of the "always-eye-to-eye" persuasion to sneer, I feel it's an excellent pinpointing of the difference between what makes for an attention-holding and interest-riveting performance and allows the actor inside that performance to be brilliant, and the approach that makes a pedestrian performance occur in the hands of the less interesting actor who always works eye to eye with other characters.

190

There are in fact those actors who simply cannot grasp conceptually any character that can be *with* but *not focused on* other characters around them. They experience a need for direct interrelating with other characters at all times. This is too bad, because such an actor will often persist in looking directly into other actors' eyes even when they're describing memories, experiences, dreams, unhappinesses and all varieties of personal life experience sharing. This, in my opinion, is as ridiculous as it is patently false.

If I were to describe the Nebraska wheatfields and my little dog "Shep" out of my own childhood, I'd want to be *reexperiencing* those things as I talk about them if they're worth relating at all. If I were to have the eye-to-eye habit so firmly imbedded in me that I had to look into the other person's eyes during my ralating of such details I couldn't see, couldn't reexperience and certainly couldn't be fully sharing much of those details at the same time. If I look away from the distraction of the other person's eyes, on the other hand, so many details of memories and experiences come streaming forth into the images I'm visualizing as I talk about them that they bring countless little body results as I talk which in their own way convey more than mere words can. The listener who is with me will be given so much more than if I were simply talking to them directly.

It's really quite simple: Eye to eye work is always merely communication with much action content involved, while involving with imagery and memory visualizing in such moments is "privacy in public" which the listener is privileged to observe and more fully share.

At least in moments of involvement with our character's own life, both memories of the past and dreams of the future must lie beyond the horizon. That is where past events and people disappeared to in those other times and other places, and that is where, out in those distant vastnesses, lie those things our character is envisioning among future hopes and dreams as well.

This manner of private experiencing in public, whether in the presence of another character in a scene or simply in the presence of an audience of spectators, produces the ideal condition for fullest involving of the imagination as well as an acute sense of being *there*—in that time and place being talked about—rather than being here and simply communicating with the words which can convey far less. Even the working out of urgent problems of the character, dealing with life-affecting facts, conceiving of plans and programs of activity of any kind and, especially, the tiny moments of simply searching for the right words or phrases as we struggle to speak meaningfully, are best served by holding *them* before us as our concentration points rather than holding onto another character's eyes.

In interviewing actors for my classes I often encounter actors who, in the test reading, overuse eye-to-eye contact. Some cases seem to be the result of past coaching; some suggest some forms of personality problems which I know I will have to attend to later. If such actors can easily understand the reasons that too much eye-to-eye work is counterproductive, respond, and in the interview come to enjoy the values to be found in the more personal and more interesting values of more "privacy in public" in the presence of another person, rather than every moment needing to "talk to" that person, then I feel encouraged to work with them. This item is really that important in my estimation!

It is amusing, even though a little tragic at the same time, to watch an eye-to-eye trained actor endeavor to play in the foreground position before a camera, in which position it is impossible to look into the eyes of another character standing almost directly behind the actor, in the background of the shot. Actors trained to focus on more important aspects of the character's own life at all times do not encounter this problem at all. They know that through making their own character's problems more important than the other actor's character can possibly be they will command far more tight closeup exposure in any roles they play. Even in theatre an actor is often blocked by a director to face front when talking to other characters who are blocked to remain standing behind them, unavailable for any kind of eye-to-eye work. Pity the poor actor who, so trained and so dependent on working directly into another's face, must go through the agony of having to adjust in such moments. Some actually can't do it with any conviction!

There are many versions of what is commonly called the "Private Moment" in terms of class exercises devoted to encou-

192

raging the exploring of typical moments when the actor in real life is alone and doing something which occupies his concentration. It is interesting to observe the difference between the eye-to-eye oriented actor's experiencing of such a private moment and the personal experience-oriented actor's version of the same type of moment. The former is often quite visibly ill at ease and experiences feelings of obligation to perform for the observers, because his orientation requires communication and response so sorely at all times. The latter, on the other hand, has little concern for what any observers are thinking because his own experience is so full and satisfying.

Carried to its inevitable extreme as it often is, this eye-to-eye working must remind some older readers of the actors we all knew in New York many years ago who were studying with a teacher who was an alumnus of the Group Theatre. We called them "duck-walkers". Their coach was so dedicated to frontal confrontation and its eye-to-eye style of acting (such as was so evident in, for instance, one of the earliest and most highly critically acclaimed productions of the Group Theatre, "*Waiting For Lefty*") that most of his students, in their studied manner of working under his coaching, actually suggested ducks! So many violent, yelling and screaming confrontation improvisations in his classes had accustomed them to always be leaning far forward with their hands flying out ahead of them and the rest of their bodies trailing behind them much like ducks.

That such body positions and approaches over-all worked for the production of "*Waiting For Lefty*", with its firebrand strike inciting content, is not the question. That they are *not* ideal body use for most other dramatic work is the problem. Yet, to this day, too often the result of too prolonged actor training emphasizing "getting something from" and "doing something to" approaches, when the exercising with these basic action and goal-directed tools are encouraged to their peaks in large confrontations, is an actor whose technique is ill fitted to the professional demands of most roles he will try for.

The main value of any prolonged period of peak level confrontation improvising in acting classes, as I see it, is to accustom actors to achieving those single level experiences with the use of their inner resources and feelings. For some beginning actors this kind of coaching might, temporarily, be deemed by a coach or teacher to be helpful. However, there must come the point at which the actor should be cautioned that in most roles he will be called upon to play there may be just one or perhaps two moments where such levels of violent confrontation are desirable. At that point the actor should be encouraged to seek the other levels and the other experiences which will more appropriately and beneficially develop his talents toward the more subdued subtext experiences which are more typical of the majority of moments in roles. In my own classes I prefer to bypass this heavy "do something to the other character!" phase, even with new actors. I feel it serves only a very temporary purpose if any at all and I have found no more than perhaps one or two young actors, in my many years of coaching and teaching, for whom it might have been a temporary stimulant for developing the use of the actor's strong feelings had I felt it wise for even that purpose.

A problem so often apparent in this same eye-to-eye group of actors who have learned little but those intense levels of "direct confrontation" work is the constant need to talk with their hands. Their hands flail about, constantly reaching forward toward other characters, continually trying so huffingly and puffingly to "get something from" or "do something to" them, helping to create that clumsy, awkward appearing "duck walking" form mentioned earlier. It's a manner of behaving seldom seen in real life characters anywhere outside these particular acting classes. It is a shock to the young actor who comes to believe in this style of acting when he later is told by intelligent directors to abandon it summarily. The knowing director is aware that the actor will bring little or none of his own character's experience when the hands are so davastatingly involved with "talking to" or trying to "get something from" other characters rather than being free to take part in the experiencing of the character's own problems.

We're still talking about *The Character's Own Personal Experience*, remember, but simply discussing here some of the manners of acting which make it fairly impossible for the actor to wholly involve with it.

Eye-to-eye working defeats much of the character's inner experiencing; hands-talking adds to that problem. If the actor hasn't cured himself of these habits prior to the early rehearsals in theatre, or before even walking on the set for a film role, the director surely will.

There are other items which could be taken up as checkpoints for the Early Rehearsal period. Some, certainly not overlooked, will be taken up in the following section devoted to the Later Rehearsal Period since I feel they can best be attended to in that period. (I should repeat, however, that *all* of the details discussed for either rehearsal period for theatre must for film be checked and readied before walking on the set!)

Chapter Ten

The Later Rehearsal Period

After the creative habits brought to the role through conscious techniques and tools have set in and seem secure enough that they can work without further conscious employment by the actor, it is a natural process to give less and less attention to them and more and more attention to the interaction among the characters and to those private concerns of the character in their real (rather than still concentratedly creative) terms. Good actors do this automatically at a point, however there are often newer actors and those who rely too heavily upon a continuous and perhaps worried employing of technique items. The latter folks need persuasion to "throw away all conscious tools" at the right moment along the way and thereafter bring their characters' living thoughts, moment after moment, instead.

THROWING AWAY THE CONSCIOUS CREATIVE TOOLS

In most cases it will not even have been evident to other actors or the director that any creative tools were being used and focused upon from the beginning.... only the actor will have been aware of such creative focus.... so the shifting of focus from them to the realities of the character will not attract any attention. But it's something the actor should do, in all but a chosen few moments where the creative tool can beneficially be consciously used for special effect during performances.

The creative result of the early concentration on the tools aimed at creating that result will remain beyond this "throwing away of the tools" as the actor begins to more truly *live and believe and experience* as the character.

It was Stanislavski's unwavering belief throughout the latter years of his teaching and directing career that *creative thinking* should come first; *creative work* second; and last of all should come *realities of the character in their true form.* When his actors tried to work in reverse of that principle—seeking simple realities first, then later attempting to add creative elements, seldom were any of their too late creative efforts able to eventually catch fire and remain in their performances. A vast number of us who teach and direct feel precisely as he did with regard to the most productive sequence. And when the actor works in that sequence the lovely thing is that even after this "throwing away of the conscious tools" the planned and practiced creative colors will remain!

It should be stated that many actors differ in their positions with respect to this "throwing away of conscious tools". Some believe in throwing them away *totally* and thereafter thinking only the reality thoughts of their characters. Some others believe in only *partially* dismissing their consciously creative tools and are able to easily maintain their sense of reality and truthful experiencing while alternating their involvements between the scenic realities around them and the creative versions prepared for each experience ahead of time. Then there is the remaining group who are confident enough and expert enough to *remain continually involved* with creative tools during actual performance.

The decision as to the ideal manner for the individual actor (of either throwing away the tools or maintaining their use, or perhaps using them in that off and on manner mentioned) must be made by the actor and based on his observation of what works best in his particular case.

THE ILLUSION OF THE FIRST TIME

Of course you'll have had endless and tiring hours of going over and over the same scenes in rehearsals, if it is for a stage performance. If for film even, at least you've had those hours of studying lines and forming approach ideas, then those quick one or two run-throughs prior to the filming moment. In spite of all those hours of preparing, what happens on stage in performance or in front of the camera during actual filming must create *the illusion of the first time.*

The illusion must be created that the dialogue isn't written down anywhere; that a sentence, or even the finding of the words to continue and finish a sentence, hasn't been practiced or in any way previously formed. Even where dialogue words aren't separated by authors with many dots to suggest insecurity, indecision, vagueness, corrections, attempts to be explicit or use the most expressive word here or there....and even where sentences are written fully and without any such distortions between their capital letter starts and their period endings, the actor still should always have to search for certain words and phrases from time to time, just as the author probably did when writing. (Of course it goes without saying that the words the actor "searches out and finds" must in the end be the author's.)

An answer should not be ready when our character is asked something. Just as in real life, our characters must think first, even if only very briefly and then form the response.

Similarly with the incoming experience.... the hearing of things said or the seeing of things which happen, it is often a temptation or habit of the actor to hear or see something with one single "final result" experience in that moment, forgetting that in real life the same moment of surprise, for instance, would probably contain about four or five tiny, fleeting parts of the taking in and reorienting processes before the final thought or feeling or reply are formed. (It should be borne in mind that this could be overdone to the point of being obvious, therefore some taste and judgment should be used.)

This "illusion of the first time" is an ultimate goal in any acting performance. It must be constantly practiced by the actor, since the actor's art most often involves working many hours over the

script—researching, analyzing, studying, preparing its subtext—
and then rehearsing it many times.

Nothing which falls short of accomplishing this most important
illusion has the appearance of truth.

THE ART OF NOT PERFORMING

History records entertainment events in terms of numbers of
performances. Signs outside theatres announce "This Performance"
as being sold out or something else. Critics write about the
performance of the actor. But the actor must view each
performance as something quite different.

Human beings can "perform" many things. Like actors, they
usually perform things they have learned how to do, things they
can repeat, things that become easier and easier to perform each
time they're repeated. For the actor, however, that feeling of
simply "performing" should not be enough.

In the first place, the word isn't synonymous in any respect with
living or *being* or *surviving*. Instead of survival, for instance, it
implies doing something with ease. If there's too much ease
visible in the character, chances are there isn't much surviving
going on, or discovery, or deep concern about how and when
things may or may not happen. Also, there's certainly *no* illusion
of the first time!

The actor who strikes brilliance knows that the moment at hand
is all the character should be concerned with. It was in this
context that Stanislavski once remarked that for the actor a chain
of living moments should be much like laying separate pieces
of railroad track in sequence, setting your train on the first length
of track and starting the engine. The train will go forward by itself,
passing over each carefully laid length of track one after another
to the end of its run.

The actor should look forward to each so-called performance
with a sense of adventure and a beautiful, soul-satisfying
helplessness and surrender to the fact that certain events are going
to transpire *in spite of the best efforts of his character*; not
because of any sense of performing. He should look forward to
the meeting of the obstacles and jeopardies which he of course
knows ahead of time will come, and look forward to having to
overcome them afresh each time they confront his character.

200

The director who observes an actor setting his moments too early can skillfully discourage such fixed, inflexible and ossified repetition in subsequent rehearsals, so the actor can continue to explore his moments. The discoveries and additional excitements brought by this protracted freedom will naturally be sifted for their values by the director. In a theatre production there is normally plenty of time for the final decisions as to what shall be retained and what shall be set aside.

True living moments occur when living and breathing human beings are surviving in their own manners in events which are happening for the first time, the outcomes of which are important to those human beings but are not known in advance of their occurring. The more gifted actor can experience this over and over with that "first time" feeling. The less gifted must recognize that, after lengthy rehearsals and all the preparation leading up to the "performance" of a role, the greatest joy for an actor lies in then forgetting all that went before and *living* the prepared experience rather than performing it.

Section V

Continuing Work on the Instrument and Resources

Chapter Eleven

Development Aimed Explorations and Exercises Recommended for Class And Homework

This particular chapter would not be such a challenge if it were simply an orientation talk to be given before a group of actors with whom the teacher would later have the opportunity to work in many class sessions. It is difficult to cover as much territory as this chapter's subject matter deserves, with its many variations so dependent upon the personalities of individual actors and their particular needs. A lot may unintentionally be left out, and a lot will be written about only partially when it would require volumes to ideally express everything involved.

Also, with acting study being the continuous research activity it is, there is so much that we who teach are still developing further!

Aside from teaching established techniques which are known to work for most actors, teachers also have the ever present responsibility of finding specialized solutions and treatments for individual problems of their individual students. No two actors are completely alike. Life patterns, psychologies, intellects and intelligences—with their resulting conditionings of this or that sociological aspect and absolute galaxies of desired images—have fostered the growth of some aspects of individual actors' natural resources and talent accessibilities while stifling others. There are so many, many "adjustments" which have to be found to bring into ideally creative balances the personalities, the behavior patterns, the conditioned and sociologically self-conscious bodies and the abilities to observe and interpret wide spectrums of characters.

This particular section of the book, rather than being part of the system as I teach it for preparing individual roles, is more a syllabus of manners in which the actor may develop his own resources and his ability to use them at will.

The instrument-expanding exercises employed by individual teachers are so many and so varied that here I'll simply be itemizing certain problem areas which need to be coped with now or eventually by all actors and actresses and suggesting manners of working on them one by one. I'm sure there will be many which I've forgotten to include here, and probably many, many different exercises that coaches employ for achieving the development goals involved in each problem's eradication.

RELAXATION

This is a hot item! It's one of the prime prerequisites for good acting and the greatest problem actors must struggle with in the early periods of their careers. If there were a primer written for beginning actors it would, or should, be the first lesson!

In their earliest experiences as actors most feel an overwhelming obligation to do everything so well that their talents can be immediately appraised and respected, and the fear imposed by that obligation alone is enough to tighten the instrument beyond the point where it can function fully and effectively. For some actors that feeling of obligation and the attendant tensions never go away. Most recognize the importance of finding an answer which will work for them and then using it or anything else that works for them whenever they need to.

It's so easy to pontificate that any actor can be relaxed if he knows securely that he and his character are doing something appropriate, doing it well, and believing it sufficiently. Of course that's the desired state. Unfortunately, for those who can't achieve that state of mind often enough there's no one device or means

206

of relaxing the instrument which is exactly right for all different personality types and the tensions which have been formed by all the different mind-body combinations which have been formed over the years due to "image-maintaining" mechanisms. What a rocky road some actors have to travel, over and over again, to arrive at the magic kingdom of relaxation—for exactly those reasons. In each role preparation, in each attempt to live those prepared moments in performance, and even in those auditions where the actor must read for roles lie so many of these image-encountering and image-conflicting moments which revive at least one or two tensions or perhaps a whole bundle of them at once.

If you have a system for approaching roles that works for you you can certainly forget more easily at least those self-doubt feelings you would otherwise experience in all your work without the results that system preparation can achieve. As your ability to involve yourself with the character's problems increases your thoughts of self, and the nervous tensions that come from those latter thoughts, are less evident.

When there is a psycho-physical basis for an actor's tension—and of course there usually is, then I have found a simple *"relaxation of the mask"* to be one of the best manners of working away those tensions either briefly if possible or continually over a longer period if necessary. If there are long established social or emotional tensions that keep reoccurring in the actor the result is probably quite visible on the face—at least to the discerning eye, even though it may be difficult to observe in many cases and is probably passed off by family and friends as simply the actor's "look" and "usual expression".

Actually, the face is a complex *mask* formed over the years by problem-experiencing, conditioned social self-presentation and the constructing of defense networks. The exercise I recommend is one which, step by step, can relax each area of the face that is usually tensed by the "social armor" of the human being.

Involved are *the eyes*—which are important for our survival against dangers and the most used of all parts of the body in our eye-dominated culture; *the crease running from the outside of the nostrils down to the corners of the mouth*—formed by our most often presented expressions because they are part of our desired social image; then *the corners of the mouth*—which we are conditioned to control simply because we sense, quite correctly, that they most often involuntarily divulge our true feelings whether we like it or not. (You can surely recall moments in your own past when, after wearing a fixed social smile for too long in the presence of others your cheek creases and mouth corners actually ached!)

Commence by closing your eyes (unless you're somewhere where it's impractical). Focus on the muscles involved in relaxing the bridge of the nose at the top point where it lies directly between the inner corners of the eyes. Imagine starting to relax the bridge at its very center and continue down the sides to the inner corners of both survival-tensed eyes. This first phase will bring the feeling of moving from the top of a triangle to the two outer ends at its base.

Then continue the line of relaxation down the cheek-edges of the nose, then along the crease as it leads downward to the two corners of the mouth. This step is a terribly important one, in that to do it implies that this "self presenting" part of our mask isn't even necessary in this particular moment. You should feel a goodly amount of your tension draining away by this point.

Next, consciously relax the two corners of the mouth itself. The sensation by now, probably mental as well as physical, is that you can dare to be open in this moment, receptive to whatever may come and sensitive to external stimuli without any need of the defense-network armorplate which should be gone from your face by now. Fear is the main source of tension, and tension is what keeps actors from feeling relaxed.

The nice thing about this exercise, aside from its effectiveness with most actors, is that it can be repeated as often as you like until relaxation is complete, and it can in fact be used during an actual performance, or in a meeting with a producer or director, without anyone observing it! We tense these three main areas in life quite regularly without much if any of the tensing showing to the unpracticed eye, so we can just as secretly *un* - tense them with equal secrecy. Do the sequence again and again, whenever you feel the need. (The eyes need not be closed. It simply helps the exercise if they can be.)

Now, to prove to yourself that you can do this exercise and that you can even use it during a performance if need be without any loss of expressiveness or feeling, bring yourself to a feeling of intense hate or anger with whatever technique you like or by simply "pressing the button" to get there, as one of our leading actors recommends. Then continue to experience those feelings as you go through this exercise in its proper sequence. The only physical change in your countenance which you will feel as it occurs progressively is the relaxing of the externalized version of your feelings into a different external expression but one which applies just as aptly and even brings an unexpected and perhaps more unusually interesting surface for the feeling still held strongly within.

Then try the exercise while experiencing other feelings of your choice. You will not only discover that it works in the same manner with all kinds of feelings and that an inner result is experienced from the relaxing; you'll possibly discover that along with the sad moment may come the beginning of soft tears; with anger or fear may come even a more intense (although different and more relaxed) experience of those kinds of feeling!

You see, as the face relaxes, the feelings are taken more into the inner spirit. They remain, which is what's important, while the tensions disappear.

In the book *Strasberg At The Actors Studio*, mentioned earlier, Mr. Strasberg recommends some other relaxing exercises on pages 88 through 93 of the paperback edition. You certainly might try them.

SELF ACCEPTANCE AND SELF REVELATION

So many books have been written by learned men and women on this subject that your study of this item, which is so important for actors, will be one of the main continuing pastimes throughout your life.

I personally recommend at least a certain amount of social therapy and sensitizing for all actors. There are what are called "Sociological Games" and also "Sensitivity Training Experiences" such as are nicely described by Dr. Everett L. Shostrom in his book *Man The Manipulator*, in which he describes how small sensitivity

209

training groups can provide opportunities to experience ourselves more fully in relating with others at deeper, more intensive levels in the experiences such groups can provide; to observe more definitely the manners in which people relate to each other and how we ourselves may relate to all others in more objective manners.

A quotation from that book, published in a University of California at Los Angeles Sensitivity Training brochure, states that as we come to see ourselves more realistically with respect to our values, our goals, our habits, our behavior patterns, our personal strengths and weaknesses, our potentials and limits, we can obtain a more accurate image of ourselves as it applies in interpersonal relations.

The aforementioned brochure maintains, and Dr. Shostrom agrees, that we may free ourselves to function more effectively through such group experiences and be less excessively burdened by many unrealistic assumptions about our personal adequacy, our worth and our social acceptability.

Following my own experiences on several occasions at one of our most noted Sensitivity Training Centers on the West Coast some years ago, from time to time I've conducted some scheduled informal evenings of various forms of these experiences for my people. Acting being the very public art that it is, it is so important that the actor accept his totality—his perhaps imperfect body; his perhaps limited intellect; his perhaps inhibited behavior; and all other aspects of the instrument that he must allow to be observed and judged by audiences and must, even before standing figuratively naked before audiences, do so before the industry hiring people who may or may not afford him the job opportunity. For these reasons, I felt my actors should have the opportunity to explore the Sensitivity Training experiences. Observing the benefits gained by those who participated, both at the time and later in their subsequent careers, I'll describe some of the particular experiences I selected, even though rather more briefly than they individually warrant:

TWO SOCIOLOGICAL GAMES
One of these is the "*I'm the worst person in the room*

because...." game. Someone says these words and then completes a brief sentence expressing a guilt-gathering problem but not going into detail. That person then remains quiet and turns to his clockwise neighbor. The neighbor looks directly into his eyes as he attempts to interpret only what he thinks the "worst person" into whose eyes he's looking means by those few words. There is no judgmental criticism or advice-giving on his part; no chiding and no attempt at reassurance. There is just the attempt to interpret and understand what the "worst person" means.

The subject is gaining insight into the many different impressions about his actions and behavior patterns that are held by others as the guesses are voiced one after another around the room, while the interpreters are, by focusing so steadfastly on the subject person, bringing into focus more dramatically their perception of the workings of personalities other than their own.

After all present have interpreted his comment the "worst person" talks for a bit about what he did actually mean by his words. The around the room participation, without judgment, advice, criticism or indulgent reassurances leaves the subject with the warm realization that it is alright to harbor such guilts and their sources and that people can accept those sources of those feelings.

In many instances during the interpretation process tears will come to the eyes of the "worst person", created by an interpreter's keen insight into exactly what lies in the "worst person's" mind. When one or more interpretations are so close there is frequently a draining of some of the poisons on the spot and, if this doesn't happen then, later in his divulging what he did mean, the "worst person" is encouraged to really bare his innermost thoughts because of what has gone before.

Each person around the room has his or her turn as the "worst person" as the same procedure is followed for all.

Remember, these are not strangers gathered in such a group, as would be involved in a typical group therapy session with a psychologist or analyst. These are people who have known each other for some time, usually. At the end of this particular "game"— if one dare call it that—there is much more warmth in the room and occasionally someone is prompted to get up and go hug another person with whom there has evolved a far more meaningful contact and a greatly increased understanding.

In the same session, preferably following rather than preceding the "Worst Person" game, it could be productive to use the identical procedures with "*I'm the most perfect person in the room because....* " This version of the game, too, has its obvious social sensitizing result.

One of the "fun" (deceptively so) games is "*The Substitute Cast*". While it truly is sociological in its potential impact on the participants, it feels more like a harmless little parlor game for bringing the members of an ensemble company closer together and for promoting group understanding in any company which will be working together over a period of time.

Two people stand or sit near each other in the center of the group. They never speak as the scene is "played". The others around the circle, instead, in clockwise order, will supply the short speeches and responses for the center two. Their speeches and responses are what the circle members supplying their dialogue feel the individuals *would* say if they were doing the talking.

The dynamics of interpersonal substitutions are shockingly impressive on the people in the center for whom the dialogue and the obvious thought patterns, orientations and personality manifestations contained therein are being supplied by people who know them. The center two are hearing themselves through those other people's words, for the first time in some cases.

Even when laughter comes from time to time as the result of a bit of dialogue which is instantly recognized by the group as being precisely characteristic of one of the two there is no resentment or bad feeling result possible. The experience is a lighthearted one, sometimes affording comic result, but it is also a nice, incisive way of discovering others' impressions of our predictable patterns.

There is another, not much touchier experience in the "*Revenges*" game. Again, and in spite of any borderline touchiness it might contain on occasion, the result can be illuminating for both the revenge-detailer and others around the room, one after another. For the revenge-detailer there is an increased perception of how patterned his or her social retributions have become and how similar are the actions and reactions that suggest to him the need for some form of avenging.

The first "Avenger" starts by saying "*If somebody treats me wrong, I....* " and continues with just a few words to end the sentence. Others around the room, preferably in *counter* -clock-wise order, make brief guesses as to the exact forms the speaker might employ. (Of course all the guesses are based upon past observations of the speaker's patterns in such moments, so they have telling effect on the speaker as they are presented verbally.)

At the end of the circle of comments the speaker explains in greater detail what is most often done and the feelings and reasons usually accompanying such actions.

Each person around the room is given his turn as the "Avenger", but after the avenger the next subsequent person is always basing the suggested revenge on the kind of treatment which constituted the basic revenge of the person who has just gone before them. The sociological value of this sequence, in its somewhat different form from the earlier "Worst Person" and "Most Perfect Person" games, is that each person, after voicing his own basic form of revenge most often resorted to hears a packageful of the kinds of resulting treatment he may expect in response to his own actions.... many of which he will recognize that he has encoun-tered in the past.

There is another area of Sensitivity Training which might not even have dared to be mentioned some years ago but which, while not for everyone, can be so beneficial for actors that it bears at least some discussion here:

NUDE SENSITIVITY TRAINING

The actor's body is, after all, his acting instrument along with his mind. That was always true, and the only change in recent times is that more and more of the actor's body is on public view in more and more roles. Many years ago it was unthinkable that more than a hint of a bare spot on the body was acceptable to theatre and film audience members. Even then most actors were a bit self-conscious about their total bodies, even when they were comfortably covered from neck to feet as they usually were in those former times. The self-consciousness in those earlier years was caused by a roll of fat here that wardrobe couldn't cover; a too small breast that too often was detectable through even those beautiful Edith Head gowns; a thick neck that a tall starring actress always wanted hidden; perhaps a mole on a cheek or a too small chin or thin, unmuscled arms on the actor seeking a boxoffice star career. Even in those days, acute body self-consciousness existed in some form in most actors. Even then, some amount of nude sensitivity training experiences could have lessened those concerns, but such a solution would have been laughed at or would have sent someone into shock.

Those times are long gone. With them have gone much of the wardrobe that actors could hide behind earlier! In even many of the top boxoffice productions on Broadway and in films, let alone the sensationalist offerings in both, there are sequences involving actors and actresses with little on but makeup.

Today's actors can't hide their bodies and those real or imagined imperfections which embarrass them when noticed. Even when fully clothed, the long skirts that hid fat calves on women are seldom what the Wardrobe Designer comes up with; the short sleeve shirts of leading men no longer cover the absence of any bulging muscles; the bare-chest scenes and the bikini swimsuits offer no hiding places for anything the actor or actress is concerned about. These days, in whatever entertainment field the actor may choose to work, that roll of fat, that underdeveloped or overdeveloped bosom, those birthmarks, those fat calves or thighs, that round stomach and nearly everything else is going to be right there before the audience and the world for all to see.

Actually, all these things are nicely in style now, aren't they! Sometimes they are equally considered along with talent and rightness in other respects for casting in roles. But it's difficult to tell our brain that and make it stick.

Acting being the inexorably public art form that it is, our body flaws, whether real or imagined, can be covered or reshaped cosmetically, for the most part, and still concern us mightily to the point that they also stifle our creative imaginations and the self acceptance we must have to free our total beings.

It was for the addressing of these kinds of problems that Nude Sensitivity was conceived of in the first place. Therapists of all persuasions recognize the values—for many self-conscious, inferior-body-feeling people. which includes so many of us!—of experiencing the easy release of many tension points and catharsizing of many fixed fears connected with their bodies through participation in a few such sensitivity training sessions, of course under skilled guidance by conductors or leaders schooled in the expert handling of all the phases of such experiences.

While these very respectable Sensitivity Training Centers utilize many kinds of body-acceptance experiences for their therapy values—including mutual body-slapping to open each other's body pores; manners of touching others and being touched by others without inhibition or discomfort; body-shaking of one person at a time by whole groups to encourage the delirious feelings of vulnerability without danger; peer support experiences such as being lifted and held high by a group or being passed in a circle and always kept from falling by other people's linked arms to discover the support which will generally be there; etc., the nude experience which I feel is perhaps the most dynamically cathartic is the exploration by a group of each individual's entire body, one after another, to bring the one whose body is in that moment being explored the ecstasy of knowing that moles, thin or fat parts of the body or what he or she considers to be deformities of any kinds can be easily accepted by peers as they are felt to be explored and passed on from.

Of course Nude Sensitivity Training is something to which not everyone can commit himself or herself, but our society has evolved to the point where for some years such training has been available in many centers headed by recognized therapists, and they know how to help all kinds of people, including actors, rid themselves of many of these body worries.

In one such session some years ago I happened to bump into an actor friend who has in recent years played top starring roles in film and television. At that time in the past he was a huff-and-puff, self-consciously macho-tense young newcomer. Tenderness and softness of any nature were foreign to him and always caused him to experience easily discernible malaise. He confided that he

215

had put off attending such a weekend experience in spite of urgings of his "shrink" to do so, but had finally come to "see what all the shouting's about", I think he said.

During the customary rest period after about two hours of the nude session, while most were lounging around and talking, he simply crouched on his knees at the edge of the circle and, with big tears streaming down his cheeks and no effort to conceal them or wipe them away, he murmured "I haven't felt like this since I was a little kid!" It was soon after that that his first big opportunities came. His single-dimensioned huff-and-pull macho manner had been softened and all the other desirable colors had been allowed into his work as an actor. I think he still today benefits from that first occasion of lessening his tensions.

I've noted, as have all his fans, that his body now is not at all the selfconsciously muscular body it was when he achieved first stardom, and if he were to ever be concerned with his body image it would be now. He obviously isn't. He has said since that his two weekend trips to Esalen, in Northern California (Yes, he went back another time!) were the turning point in his career, and I know he believes that deeply, as do I.

BODY HABITS CORRECTION

There is a far less confronting manner which I have found for dealing with body concerns and helping actors become aware of how they have often in the past obstructed some of their process freedom, created unnecessary limitations in their characterization and performance experiences and formed habits and mannerisms that don't work to advantage with otherwise excellently prepared characterizations.

The phrase *Body Habits Correction* might suggest that only the body is concerned. But the fact that body habits are vitally connected with *self image* concerns is the big problem in any attempt to help actors overcome those habits which were formed so long ago in the interest of presenting an acceptable self.

The actor who exhibits certain body habits which recur often and constantly get in the way of and obstruct some of his processes generally has some psychological problems of identity, self image or desired social image type creating those habits. Any

216

such problems—even if conscious, which they seldom are—are probably very well hidden, but the body habits they have helped create are not.

Rather than attempt to discuss any of those psychological problems that can and do create body habits and mannerisms, I'll save the reader's time by getting to a form of body habits therapy I have found which helps to focus the actor's attention on the body and movement mannerisms, illustrates the manner in which they affect his work, and, after bringing them out into conscious awareness, offers a manner of working through the problems they've created.

First, let's assume that we're already conditioned to think certain things about ourselves in our manner of relating to our environment by the time we reach those formative years when we begin to believe what parents, friends, teachers, relatives and neighborhood friends are quick to tell us—over and over, in much the same words—that we are. That would be bad enough. But it doesn't end there.

Also in those childhood years we've already encountered other people's viewpoints on certain *physical* aspects of our being. We've probably spent hours of worry in front of mirrors hoping to convince ourselves that those things others are saying about our body are groundless. Unfortunately, standing there before our mirror, instead of telling us those other people are wrong, our mirror confirms what we've been told. There really is that problem—that telltale clue, that distortion that is bound to hold us back as we approach adulthood and strive for life goals. Of course it can't occur to us at the time that those physical differences between us and others around us wouldn't seem so bad if they weren't by this time closely connected in our minds with things that are bothering us about ourselves in purely psychological identity terms as well.

For example, if too many people have told us that we're "lazy and good for nothing" then, looking in the mirror, we will also note that our body which has been called "weak" or "sickly" is indeed "lazy and good for nothing" also. Or if we've been constantly scolded for being "so selfish", looking in the mirror, our body which has been called things like "pimply" or "scarface"

217

is also "selfish". The associations are formed, and we immediately go to work to develop body positions and movement patterns that are intended to cover up those physical shortcomings and lessen the chances of being rejected because of what they tell people about us.

For people who later go into other professions this curious association of supposedly projected image with apparently unacceptable or at least unfortunate aspects of our body would matter less. For actors, however, the result matters! It really does!

The actor is called upon to play many different kinds of roles during a productive career. Those many roles demand an instrument which is as free as possible from any limiting conditions and unshakeable mannerisms, be they real or imagined.

Most actors have a whole catalogue of unconscious mannerisms which result from those long ago found solutions which seemed at the time ideal cover-ups for whatever bothers us about ourselves, whether psychological or physical. Those mannerisms will remain with us throughout our lives if they aren't consciously dealt with. For actors, they come back to plague in moments when directors make perfectly innocent demands or suggestions that feel uncomfortable for us. In the end we of course have to do what the director says, but we're either vaguely or even agitatedly upset as we force ourselves to do what has been requested, without understanding why it's upsetting to us. Later, in performance, we approach those moments with a conscious dread because of the discomfort and embarrassment they bring with them. We are self-conscious as we go through those moments.

There are more of these "body habit problems" in each of us than we realize until someone—perhaps an observant acting coach—helps us to bring them to conscious awareness and work to overcome the acting instrument restrictions they produce.

Here's the exercise which I formed with the help of a therapist friend and have used in my acting classes with many remarkable results:

Each actor can be asked to prepare a list of, say, three or four parts of his physical body that he doesn't like. After some moments each individual sits before the class and mentions the first of his three or four items. He's asked to show the class clearly what it is. The slight flabbiness around his middle might be called by him a "fat blob middle"; the hump in his nose might be called his "ski jump nose"; the receding hairline might be called his "clown makeup forehead"; his two larger than normal ears might be "rabbit ears" or "donkey ears" to him. He will probably grin sheepishly as he points out the characteristic he's talking about.

After he's stated and demonstrated his first item, he's asked by me (1) "What's *wrong* with having a.... ?", to which he'll probably reply with an unpleasant adjective or character label that it suggests.

He's then asked (2) "What does it make *you feel you are* because you have a.... ?". Again he'll probably respond with an adjective; a different one usually. Then, (3) "What do you think *other people* automatically think someone is who has a.... ?" Again an adjective or unpleasant label. (These key words are being jotted down by me as they are said.)

Finally he's asked (4) "What do you *do* to keep people from noticing your.... ?"

It's exciting to an entire class made up of people who've watched each other's work and become aware of certain repeated body positions and mannerisms—this moment of finding out why the actor walks the way he walks, sits the few ways he customarily sits, uses his hands in certain ways time and time again, etc.

The person being interviewed feels little or no embarrassment as he goes through this questioning and comes out with all those unflattering labels and adjectives with deepest honesty. Even when showing the onlookers precisely what he's talking about he still feels no threat. And when he's showing them the special walk he uses to keep people from noticing whatever he's talking about there is usually warm recognition laughter from those who've seen that special, sometimes slightly strange walk so many times before. Because of the manner in which the questioning is conducted and the unthreatening atmosphere made possible by the fact that the discussion is—or so it seems to him—purely *physical*, whenever there's laughter at something (which is quite common among the observers as details are shared) he can easily share in it.

After thoroughly discussing that first item that he doesn't like about himself the actor is asked to move on to the second, and so on, with exactly the same procedures and sequences being repeated for the second, third and fourth items.

Of course there may be those two or three people who "don't dislike anything" about their bodies. Pressed a little, there are usually a few things that "*used* to bother" them but "don't anymore". They usually feel they're being completely truthful, and probably are. While the others, more conscious in varying degrees as to what physical items still bother them, have been able to come up quickly with those adjective and label associations, the person who "isn't bothered anymore" will have to reach back into distant memory not only to come up with what used to bother them but also to remember why those items bothered them in those earlier times.

These latter people's mannerisms and frequently repeated body positions are usually just as fixed and often as easily observable as those of the folks who are more currently conscious of them. And, once reminded of the items and their *raison d'etre*, they can glean just as much benefit from the interview's reexamination of them and what is involved in working on them.

It would be difficult for anyone to come up with highly individual "working through" solutions for each person singly. Each would require special approaches of his own. But, in addition to the fact that this area is possible to dig into in a spirit of sharing and unthreatened self-exposure in this manner, there is also a manner of achieving some very interesting and effective results through the "interview" exercise and what can be scheduled afterward.

During the itemizing and discussion of those items the actor will have amassed a list of some twelve to perhaps sixteen unflattering labels and adjectives in responding to the questions which have been planned to produce exactly those different responses. The response words will be read back to the actors, one after another for each person, and each person will then be asked to pick the word or label that they *dislike the most*. It's fairly easy for both the coach and the others present to know ahead of time approximately which word or label is going to be selected. Normally, it will apply to the mannerism and source which is the most pronounced in the actor's work. So, if the actor seems suddenly evasive and picks a word which very apparently seems less confronting to him the coach should help guide him to the more obviously affecting area.

If there's still time in the same class session there is some exercising which I would recommend. Otherwise in a next upcoming session (which is much better because of allowing a fuller preparation), each actor is asked to prepare *three characters* whose personalities are to be constructed in the following manner: (1) a character who *hates, but has to live with being* that labeled personality; (2) a character who is *proud* of being that labeled personality; and (3) a character who is *the complete opposite* of that label. The actors should be asked to jot down those exact descriptions, to make sure they prepare correctly.

The actors should be sent home with this assignment if possible, so that their preparations can be more thorough and so that they can return for the subsequent class with wardrobe items, props, hairstyle plans and whatever else they will require for the bringing of those personality types. They should be told ahead of time that their characters' improvisations will be placed in some appropriate location where *total strangers* meet for the first time. Conferences, little seacoast summer resort hotel lobbies, airport lounges, railroad or bus waiting rooms and similar locations serve ideally.

They should be told to prepare every possible manner of "showing and telling" and "broadcasting" that they are the kinds of personality they are in each label's case. To make this kind of "caricaturing" perfectly clear ahead of time the coach might equate each improvisation with the "performance" of a Lodge member or regional sales manager who, introducing himself to another attendee at some national gathering, immediately sails into his life story, his family information, where he's from, his car model, his tastes and his dislikes in a rehearsed manner in order to speed the process of achieving the other party's interest and attention. "How are you? I'm John Quincy, District Sales Manager in the Toledo office. Had to come down here to get away from my wife and six kids upstairs in one of the Royal Court rooms. They're off to Europe Thursday so the rest of the week'll be all mine.... A little golf, some fishing, some pickin' up girls...."

that's why I brought the Audi. I'm ordering an Ouzo.... you like Greek beer? My wife and I spent two weeks in Athens last Fall and got to like it. Doc says I drink too much, but what the hell! Oh yeah, what's your name?"

Of course this kind of garrulous bore is ridiculous, but any of us who has attended those national conventions and conferences has met several of this ilk and has known their entire history and the name of their children and their pets, in similar first meetings, while still having our hand shaken.

The actors should be asked to prepare their "acts", their "routines" (since they're being asked to *caricature*, so they'll prepare fully). They should plan what to talk about to "broadcast" who and what they are—business, home, foods, names to drop, places their characters would obviously have been, books they'd have read and would recommend, movies that would appeal to them, types of activity they'd be anxious to get to now that they've arrived at the location.

In any good, serious acting class it will offer a nice change of pace and the people will probably look forward to the next session anticipating the comedy that will obviously result.

For the coach it's a more serious result that can be achieved. In the process of observing the resulting work from three different angles, the coach can judge the best steps in order to help eradicate the actor's body habit problem or to help the actor utilize it or its source in some constructive manner, now that it's been brought to conscious awareness.

In one of the three characters resulting from the foregoing approach the habit or habits will be very pronounced, while in another it will be modified or not evident at all. These results, so evident to both the coach and the others in class who observe the work, will point directions for further work.

Two other, perhaps more important benefits of this exercise, are that (1) the actor will have found that those kinds of characters and moments of roles which have caused body-use embarrassment in the past are easily within comfortable experiencing and (2) there will probably have occurred a significant break-through on the part of the actor into some new and possibly important characterization areas.

EXPANDING THE AVAILABLE SPECTRUM OF IDENTITIES

The challenge continually faced by actors is the observing and interpreting of psychological patterns other than their own. This is the core of a continuing study in any good actor, and one of the places where it can best and most comfortably be undertaken is in acting classes, with certain preparation tools making it possible to experience the thoughts, feelings and patterns that are found in those other character types. Stanislavski often stated that "Every role is a character role."

One of the handiest devices of which I know for opening the actor's door to wider characterization horizons—while accomplishing significantly more than that at the same time—is a class exploration which I call the....

DESIRED IMAGE AND NECESSARY OPPOSITE

No matter how we spent our very earliest years—and sometimes precisely because of how we spent them, at some point we began "role playing" in our daily lives. As our goals and concerns changed, their achievement demanded new masks, new costumes and new behavior patterns to complete the newly embarked upon "performances". We applied ourselves assiduously to equipping ourselves for the trip to each new goal.

The actor might pause for a moment at this point and think of the image he currently wants to project socially. As you read this, observe the way you're sitting. Are you sitting that way because that's how an actor sits, or how an honest person sits, or how a people-pleaser sits, or how a king of the mountain sits? Now, if you've just changed position, look at that new position you've unconsciously settled into. Isn't it just one more of the limited few that spells (again) actor, honest person, people-pleaser or king of the mountain? I'd wager that it is.

Examine what you wore in public today. Wasn't it calculated in some manner to present the same image? And your hair style? And the way you walk? The car you drive? The colors and fabrics and styles you wear? It's all there, as if you've made a very careful list, studied it, memorized it, and are the "very picture" of what you want people to see you as, rather than what you know you really are inside.

223

What actors, more than people in some other professions, must recognize is that all those surface calculations, all those bits of "window-dressing", have probably blended together into a hardened, shell-like outer layer of limitations, obstructing many natural impulses and richnesses which can't break the surface shell to come out.

The *Desired Image* is a lifeless cocoon that holds too many actors in its hardened casing. A perceptive coach, upon noting that an actor is so imprisoned, should immediately find some manner of helping to break the cocoon and encourage the actor to either discard it and walk away from it or at least climb back into it only when necessary for some social purpose.

If an actor is continually observed to be bringing little more than conceptual work to characterization, with each attempt producing little more than carefully executed ideas with little or no true inner experiencing behind those "character pictures", it should be a clear sign to the coach that there are parts of the actor's inner truths and emotional experience which are being denied and laid aside from any degree of use either in the planning of characters or the performance of them. It should also be recognized by the coach that there can never be true feeling experience brought by these image-playing actors until they dare to explore and subsequently fall more in love with their own inner truths than with the cardboard characters they otherwise bring.

There is a class experience which I personally use on occasion, and recommend. Like the title of this section, I call it the *Desired Image and Necessary Opposite*.

All members of the class are instructed to spend some length of time considering specifically what their own "desired images" are. Each is instructed to combine in "one label" of about two or three words the probably several personality characteristics which they want people to view as their totality.

For example, a gregarious and attention-seeking class member might ponder for a time over words like *likeable, interesting, friendly, Good Joe*, perhaps even *stimulating*, then eventually become conscious that he must add some more and different words such as *attention-needing, sophisticated, athletic* and maybe more words which seem unrelated but all part of what he wants to be recognized as. It will take him some time, but eventually he might decide they can all be combined (only because the coach has said to) in a fairly all-embracing label such as "Hotshot team prodder", and be pleased with the image this label implies for him.

The next step in such a class is to have all members come forward individually and state their individual labels, then explain what the adjectives and nouns mean to them individually. There is much insight to be gained as to the individuals' psychological orientations through this step alone, but in addition it brings clearer self-observation to the individuals through their having to put into words their desired image makeup and its component parts.

When all class members have stated and discussed their image labels they should then be directed to form into words what would be *The Exact Opposite* of those labels. Some members will come up with labels which are precisely that—exact opposites of their desired images. However, some will inadvertently come up with labels which they personally feel to be opposites but which to other ears, hearing their words, seem unrelated. Those apparently unrelated opposites should not be changed, because in some such cases they will be what the individuals believe themselves to more truly be, behind the desired image masks.

It is common for, say, the "Hotshot team prodder" to come up with a "Stupid" or "Clumsy" "Deadbeat"; for a "Hypersensitive Extremist" to come up with a "People-Hating Injustice Collector"; etc. It is unusual for the "Mysterious, Elegant Lady", on the other hand, to come up with a "Self-Centered Rat Trap" or an "Identity Hitchhiker" or something else so seemingly unrelated. Either of those latter labels might, however, be exactly what the actress thinks she is inside, and should be accepted without question.

This exploration, like the "Body Habits Correction" one, should be afforded two separate sessions in a row for optimum effectiveness. The same procedure is followed in the preparation of at least two characters for two separate improvisations to be located, again, in a place where participants are meeting strangers for the first time.

They should be asked to prepare (1) a character totally based on the Desired Image label and (2) a character totally based on the Opposite label, with, in addition to the emotional tools chosen to bring such personalities, the previously listed items as well—wardrobe, props, hairstyle, catch phrases, topics of conversation, appropriate sitting, standing and walking manners, etc., again planned so as to "show and tell" and "broadcast" for others the exact personality they are and make sure the others get their message in every way possible.

If there's time in such a class and this is known ahead of time because of the smaller group involved, for the *Opposite* character *two* versions should be planned. For one improvisation it should be *proud* of what it is, while in the other it should be *unhappy* about being what it is.

What is so remarkable to see is that, for fairly obvious reasons, the *Opposite* and normally disliked image characterization will be so rich and full of beautiful highlights, shadings and feeling experience! Often this happens because the actor is working on what he is personally ashamed of being inside; sometimes it's because he has studied the undesired image categories so thoroughly in the process of avoiding any association with them that he has a full catalogue of those social adversaries' patterns.

I have found that the *Desired Image and Necessary Opposite* exploration is a quick device for introducing actors caught up in image-presenting to a whole new gardenful of personality experiences, and often it is a means of quickly bringing into their work those more deeply felt inner experiences and impulses which have been laid aside and hidden long ago. With the encouragement of the coach and the after-class praise of the actors' peers of what occurred in those "*negative*" characters, the dynamic changes hoped for in the actors' use of themselves frequently begin immediately.

THE NURSING OF IMPULSES
This is discussed in the "Rehearsals" chapter, however I would strongly encourage that separate class sessions be devoted specifically to a manner of exploring moments in improvisations which

226

might be called "Embroidering The Moments", "Between The Lines Experiencing", "Barnstorming Around", "This Moment's Moments" or whatever the coach wants to call them as long as they're announced as, and held to, the continuous courting and exploring of the many, many impulses which could occur within characters in given moments of the improvisations.

Such directed improvisation emphasis helps to cultivate spontaneity and appealing freedom in actors' work.

The nursing of impulses is really such a simple and easy thing once it's suggested by a coach, no matter what kind of exercising or practicing device or approach is scheduled in an acting class for the encouraging of them.

Actors need to know that their impulses—those unplanned needs or desires to do something not provided in the written dialogue and action of a role—are desirable for their characters just as they are observable moment after moment in real life.

The actor should be taught to be confident enough to encourage impulses to come and be sufficiently aware of them when they do that they can be used and enjoyed as valuable additions in so many moments of roles.

OBSERVATION AND RESPONSE

These two, also, are items which may be taught and exercised in so many manners in acting classes. There is need for both in every developmental step of the actor's training and in the preparation of and experiencing of every role the actor will ever play. The subject of these two important items is fairly covered in the earlier chapter dealing with rehearsals but, again, I want to warn the reader, as I do my class members, to not form the habit of *overusing* these two items at the expense of the more important personal experience of characters.

FORM AND MOVEMENT

A certain amount of feeling for form and movement cannot be taught. It lies like the fluid of truth itself at the bottom of the well when all the water of technique has been drained from it. It flavors, refines, distills, and is what makes an actor a true artist

227

just as it would another practitioner in any visual medium—whether it be painting, architecture, dance, landscaping or graphic design.

The aesthetically aware actor saves an immeasurable amount of time for directors during the preparation of a production, whether it be theatre of film. Of course if they have to, directors will take valuable time to show the actor just how to stand or sit, but they really can't afford that time and seldom are willing to do it twice. Even the highly involved actor or actress, if not aesthetically and scenically aware, runs the risk of being extremely limited in many directors' estimation.

Any true art requires some *composition*, and any meaningful art requires *focus*. How often we see one inept actor or actress unconsciously change some carefully formed composition and as a result find ourselves watching an entire scene suffer because of an inadvertent shifting of focus or the destroying of a certain beauty of form. The ability to *help* create beauty or *help* present some composite truth theatrically—and to be able to enjoy such helping without letting it take away from the inner concentration of characters—must ideally exist in the actor who would qualify as an artist.

Stanislavski taught form. Vakhtangov taught it. Chekhov taught it. Yet today few of the teachers of the System or Method teach it at all. The most famed leaders down through the history of theatre arts have taught it. Brecht's entire Epic Theatre was based substantively on its use. (The latter's "A Formation" made it possible for him to focus entire audiences on propaganda and over-all ideas he wanted to communicate in his works.) The German director Reinhardt's success was based in part on his feeling for huge spectacle and on his constant and brilliant employing of focus, form and movement. The busy stages of Shakespeare, Marlowe and others would be impossibly cluttered and unclear, and the beauties of their works would be lost completely, without consummate attention to form and composition.

Some excellent manners of developing the actor's feeling for these aesthetics of human body form and composition have been contributed by Michael Chekhov in his book *To The Actor*. Actors find his "moulding the air", "radiating" and "floating" exercises very helpful. They're lengthily described in that book, so I won't duplicate his descriptions here.

However, classwork on Brecht's "A Formation" hasn't been all that effectively outlined elsewhere, so I'll describe the kinds of classwork which might ideally employ these concepts:

EXERCISING WITH BRECHT'S "A" FORMATION

Brecht and others down through history have valued the visual accentuation of body form as an important addition to simply placing actors in triangulated positions on a stage. Over and above the over-all triangle of players' positions—so arranged to rivet attention on one person who is meant to be the focal point at a given moment, the forming of the actors' individual bodies, as well, can assist mightily in the achieving of the desired result.

For actors and actresses whose senses of aesthetics are not sufficiently developed theretofore, there is one exercise which I highly recommend for providing them with a much enhanced understanding of the ways in which they can assist in focusing the viewer's attention on a single player when desired.

One actor is designated to "Take focus!" It is understood by the others in the group that during the period of his remaining the focal point they are to "Assist focus!"

The actor seeking the strongest, most visually dominant place at which to situate himself finds himself at the same time attempting to enhance and strengthen his domination of the scene through body positions which may not have occurred to him before. As he adopts one position and remains in that position until others around him have adopted "focus-assisting" positions, he gains valuable recognition of what is and what is not a strong, dominating position in relating to the others around him. It is an exhilarating experience for the one "maintaining focus" as he observes his own body wanting to lean or slant in some manner to more strongly focus on and dominate those surrounding him.

Meanwhile, the focus-assisting players are developing (under the coach's guidance if necessary) positions and forms which help focus attention on the one chosen to dominate at the time. Their focus-assisting role illustrates to them (again under the coach's guidance if required) how their bodies can be formed to assist in composition of an over-all spectacle involving large numbers of participants. They learn to consider the extensions of their own extremities as they aim toward or extend backward from the focal center of the scene. They learn how their own bodies can relate to other bodies beside, before or behind them in creating of individual attention-focused groupings involving two or more focus-assisting observers. As they practice the Brechtian "A" Formation concepts they learn that the players closest to the focal player can adopt positions which are higher off the floor in some way than those positions into which the farther away players must form for best effect. Those at the farthest points from the focal player find that they need to extend their bodies more and lie or half-lie in almost prone positions as they strain forward. That is the manner in which Brecht, Reinhardt and others have managed their individual versions of what to Brecht was his "A" Formation.

Directors must always be concerned with focusing the spectator's attention on the most important action or most important player at all times. It is a happy discovery for any director to find the actors prepared with understanding of what is being constructed visually and with the ability to quickly and easily form in a manner which aids that arrangement.

There is a three player formation, also, which can further the actor's awareness of the dynamics of the *aiming* aspect involved in assisting with the creating and maintaining of focus:

One player is supposedly being attacked verbally or perhaps threatened by another. The latter player is being *aimed* and *urged on* by a third player, much in the manner of a typical moment in which someone might be sicking a dog at someone or something. The same effect is involved. However, this exercise, for its optimum result as a form experience, should be done with hands and knees on the floor.

While the player who is under attack stretches his entire body away from his attackers, still rooted to one spot and unable to get away, the attacker experiments for the position on hands and knees (or at least one knee) which affords him the strongest feeling of attacking or threatening. With a finger stretched forward like a gun toward the one under attack, and the other hand supporting his body and supplying the most possible force itself, his legs, extending back of him, should also seek the most effective positions for adding their own support and force thrust to his attack.

When the attacker has settled into his most forceful position choice, the third player, the "aimer" or the "instigator from behind", experiments to find his own most forceful-feeling position for aiming and urging on the attacker, trying at the same time to instill his own spirit and force in the attacker's through finding a position which feels most like it is fusing the two attackers' bodies and strengths.

An actor inexperienced with classic staging and its required focus-assisting may take additional time to discover either the attacking position or the aiming position. The longer it takes that actor to consciously find the best ways to consciously arrange the parts of his body, the more effective the learning process going on, simply because this kind of work is new to him and requires conscious adapting of his body parts into a form which for some may be the first time.

Both the attacker and the aimer will generally, even if inexperienced, recognize the best positions when they are finally found and, at least in the case of actors who are not also dance trained and whose muscles may not be tuned, it is wise to end this exercise as soon as that final position is formed ideally, since the dynamics of so much force of attack thrust could otherwise cause muscle cramps if the position were held longer.

THE FOCAL LEADER

There's another exercise, of my own devising in the main, which I call *"Focal Leader"*. It's ideal for training actors for the kinds of *elongated classic movement* required in Greek tragedies and other heroic dramas. It will not seem new to any dancers or dance trained people in the group, since it comprises the same extensions, contractions and expansions in much the same manner as does ballet, modern and jazz dancing.

I use this exercise to assure actors that, even without dance training, their bodies can assume ideally graceful positions at will and maintain graceful movement over periods of time as positions are required to be changed. Of course this is an *exercise* if desired to be used as one. It is also a *tool* whenever it can serve in a role. I formed and commenced using this exercise some years ago when a production required the ultimate in classic form and my company of actors included not one movement-trained player.

The methodology involved here is that the muscle systems of our bodies are capable of flowing one into another behind an extended part of the body. If that "Focal Leader" role is for one moment of a role determined to be a pointed finger, and that pointed finger is stretched forth to its emotional extreme as well as its physical limit, the combination of the emotional urgency and the efforts of the body to assist with that urgent pointing will result in the rest of the body's forming itself into a completely graceful extension of all parts falling into their muscle-system-created graceful positions all the way back to the pointed toe at the farthest point from that pointed finger as it seems to be pulling in the opposite direction. It is the same as what occurs with a dancer's body in a moment of "extension".

When *different Focal Leaders* are used in sequence, one after another, the body adjusts to each via the same muscle system flow and becomes in each new focal leader use a perfectly formed, most graceful organism. The same can apply if the actor is constructing a stationary pose for some purpose. By employing the Focal Leader which best creates the pose desired, the natural flow of extension, contraction and expansion takes place in the muscle system and the actor, even though untrained in movement, can in this manner easily create beauty of form.

After beginning any movement from one spot to another with a first Focal Leader the actor will find that a new one must be chosen and used to take the body in some direction. At the extreme limit of stretching one Focal Leader in the direction desired, simply delegate some other part of the body to continue the body's progress forward or in any desired direction.

Throughout the experiencing with Focal Leader by one group the observing group will be constantly amazed at what happens with even those bodies which are untrained. If a videotape camera is handy, or even an instant-print camera, it can document for the players' viewing later the constant beauty, composition and form which a focused body can create through its own magical coordination!

INCORPORATION OF LIVING SUBTEXT SOUNDS

Present day actors have been reared in a world where the *conscious* use of sounds has gradually diminished before the onslaught of civilizations and languages, with the latter having become sometimes inadequate substitutes for the experiential and communication sounds which were the natural heritage of man since the primates. Nowadays we make sounds involuntarily for the most part and more in private—usually as a result of the "policing" imposed by socialization on everything but *The Animal Within*, the only part of us which has managed to avoid this socialization by remaining hidden most of the time.

As mentioned earlier in the *Rehearsals* sections, sounds illuminate our inner processes far more fully than any words can. They are generally involuntary in human beings, but for the actor they need to be used consciously and recognized for the added degree of experiencing which their use creates; for the inspirations they can bring moment after moment; and for the spontaneity and the freedom which they provide in acting roles.

Try for yourself a few ordinary moments out of daily life—first without sounds, then with sounds. Try the various phases of taking a shower; being stuck in a traffic jam on a busy freeway when you're obviously going to be late for work; nursing a terrible sunburn; watching a dreadful, ridiculous rerun of an old movie failure on late night television. You'll find in the second version—through adding sounds, moment after moment—the many inspirations for such moments that wouldn't have been found without them!

SOME LIVING SOUNDS CLASSWORK

Some actors experience inhibitions created by our culture when asked to simply add sounds to their work. They recognize the value of doing it, but are uneasy about the kinds of sounds they personally may make. It is profitable to devote some class session time to helping even the more inhibited overcome their hesitations in this area, and those more comfortable with the use of

233

sounds in many kinds of moments won't be bored. They'll enjoy the exploring of the different types of moments and possibly will set some good examples of what can be inspired, thereby encouraging more determined tries by their more hesitant peers. The following is a good "warmup" exercise for such a session:

I call it "Immediate Sound Changes". I explain that each person will be called upon, not in any special sequence, and told what experience is to be explored for its many sounds and their moments; also that they will be suddenly and unexpectedly sent into several more experiences, one after another, after the first one. Here are some examples of the sound explorations I might call out to them:

An unbearably hot night....	A splitting headache....
Trying to get to sleep on a hot night....	Waking up with an awful hangover....
Checking a script for the role you're cast to play....	Bored at a dull lecture....
	Cuddling with a loved one....
Nursing a terrible sunburn....	Cramming for an exam....

While each is being put through his series of sound experiences, the others present, even more than the person who is doing the exploring, will notice how actively the body is triggered into busy participation with each sound experience. This helps increase their respect for what sounds can produce and helps to fire their enthusiasm for using them.

While others are going through their experiences there will probably be recognition laughter. Sounds being the basically private experience that they are, the sharing is so complete through the sensory content of most sounds that the exercise will be a good ice-breaker for the class session and encourage the hesitant to go into it with good humor and less self-doubting.

Next, I recommend *solo improvisations* by all class members, experiencing some ordinary moment of daily life—anything, no matter how inconsequential—with only sounds. Men might shave, spruce themselves up for a promising date, worry through their first day as a bachelor after their marital separation, try to assemble one of those "Do It Yourself" items from the instructions. Women might put on makeup, try a new recipe, clean up an apartment, plan the invitation list for a dinner or something else.

Each will appreciate the many, many unexpected inspirations which come from being required to use sounds as much as possible and finding that the sounds produce ideas in the very moment of their being used.

For an enjoyable session of very informal exploring, the remainder of a class could be used for group improvisations for which the actors do no advance planning. No characters need be prepared; no situations are known in advance. The coach might simply announce that when the starting moment comes they will be told where they are and what's happening; that they should *immediately* begin with some sound and go from there, continuing to make sounds throughout that situation; that their situations will be suddenly changed by the coach calling out new details; and that again they should immediately begin with some sound and continue making sounds throughout.

In the same or another class there could be a more formal schedule including improvisations with dialogue but also many sounds interjected. If they're expected to plan their own situations the coach might caution them to avoid the violent confrontation areas and subject matter, suggesting that for more freedom to explore they might deal with situations such as a boring Sunday at home, a New Year's morning wakeup after a big party, irritable roommates, nurses' or teachers' lounges and other non-event subject matter. The work should be announced as purely exercising with mixing sounds with dialogue so that few if any will become carried away with a developing situation and forget to practice the sounds use.

THE ILLUSION OF THE FIRST TIME—IN DIALOGUE
Discussed in fairly general terms in the *Rehearsals* section, this valuable end result can best be developed effectively in coaching sessions under the keen eye and ear of a teacher or coach who is himself aware of what dialogue should mean and not mean to the actor.

There are many human characteristic traits in communication

235

processes which are completely overlooked by some actors. These characteristics need to be thought about, consciously incorporated in the actor's handling of dialogue, and practiced until they become automatic. They offer the actor so much: The absence of the obligation to give perfect (therefore not really human) line readings; the resulting elimination of nervousness that usually accompanies and results from that obligation; more opportunities for the character's feeling experiences behind the lines; more illusion of the first time for the actor himself in the process of delivering someone else's words; closer duplication of the manner in which someone in real life would find their way through the same sentences; and the joy for the actor in the multitudes of little experiences which result from observing and using as many as possible of those human characteristics.

Not only in final performances or roles, but also in those important interviews and readings to obtain those roles in the first place, the actor needs to form the habit of *experiencing the life behind the words* more than the words themselves. And there are some items which help accomplish this.

Since all actors *read* for more roles than they are hired to portray, we'll discuss these points primarily in terms of those all important interviews, although they apply equally to final performance experiences as well.

An actor may go for years on end reading for roles in offices, perhaps being hired for some tiny roles now and then but always cursing his luck for never rising above those tiny supporting roles and walk-ons. He wonders why. So does his agent. Neither is aware that while he may be a "good actor" and give "excellent readings" he actually brings little beyond those very well delivered lines of the characters' dialogue.

Perfect dialogue readings can actually mark the actor with the "bit player", "day player" or "walk-on" label in producers' and directors' experienced judgment during those very first moments of reading for roles.

Actors should watch the *leading* role players in film, television and theatre more closely. He should notice—even if for the first time taking the trouble to—that the top stars' dialogue sounds original; that they seem to search for next words or phrases

236

(which they of course know, but their characters don't); that they seldom speak full sentences in capital-letter-to-period outpourings; that they don't treat punctuation like a religious obligation; that they hesitate and struggle for brief moments, affording their characters moments of seeming inadequacy at finishing sentences; that there isn't nearly as much eye-to-eye communication as you might be habitually using; that they seem to be concentrating on their characters' problems more than on perfect dialogue; that their moments are varied and interesting because of all the other items and that your attention is riveted on them rather than on what they're saying.

Starring actors and actresses have usually cultivated the art of duplicating these human processes faithfully, and at some point in their careers have become courageous enough in reading for roles to bring those processes into their readings. At that precise point, perhaps, or soon thereafter, when called in to read for a small role they may have been sent back to the outer office with the complete script and told to look over one of the top roles. It may well be how they got their first starring opportunity, in fact. In willingly making their reading less than ideal for a tiny role they impressed the producer and director with their leading role potential by bringing *the total human being* rather than an actorish version of the dialogue.

Actors destined to rise into top roles quickly are interesting to watch as they focus more on the character's inner struggle than on the words it speaks. They avoid the melodramatics that result from trying to find the emotional experience in the words themselves. They seem to not know what they should say next. They pass periods and commas and only hesitate, after starting next phrases with confidence, to become hung up then, rather than at the grammarical punctuation points—just as most human beings do. Their bodies become involved interestingly and meaningfully in their between-the-lines moments. Their own personalities are afforded moments to involve their own highlights of character experiencing. Even their moments of listening to other characters are more interesting because they're brave enough to enjoy those tiny, important reactions as they listen, unlike the worried actor who, because he's focused on how to "act" the next line, is nervously preparing its perfect delivery while he should be still experiencing the current moment. The leading player knows that the next line will be there when it's due; not before. He doesn't rush, therefore never feels rushed and nervous.

A curious and beautiful thing happens *inside the actor* when he's employing some of these human characteristic items in his readings, also in his performances, quite apart from the role-getting advantages they offer: The carefully incorporated searching for words and phrases, especially, brings the actor the feeling that he is actually saying lines which haven't been written by someone else. He, too, is having an "illusion of the first time" experience which affords him a far greater experiencing of his character's truths in all moments.

Work on this approach to dialogue should start early and continue until all these characteristics become firmly imbedded habits and fairly automatic, thereby making both reading and performing of writers' dialogue a gratifying adventure instead of worrisome obligation and ulcer-promoting nervousness.

Opportunities for the bringing of the character's subtext and the actor's own personality and talent exist in many, many big and small moments of all roles. The actor who misses them, or fails to create them for himself if they're not apparent in the author's style of writing, misses the prime ingredients which constitute the illusion of the first time and distinguish good and true acting from bad and false acting!

CONSCIOUS IMAGE-TAILORING

This particular aspect of the actor's work on his instrument and on his professional image is chiefly important toward the *job-getting result* hoped for. There are so many very fine actors and actresses who don't work, simply because there is nothing special about them until they're at work in a role. In most cases that's too late. The actor who doesn't occur to the mind of a producer, director or casting director in relation to a certain kind of role or at least a certain category of role types isn't likely to find advancement too easy or employment too continuous. It's a regrettable fact for extremely versatile actors and actresses to face, but it's true.

Stanislavski himself is quoted in the book *Building A Character* as having stated that it is important in the actor's art for each actor to understand his or her type. Although it might seem the very antithesis of his general teaching emphasis, it is not. He understood then—and in the period of this book it's even more imperative—that every actor should understand the kinds of roles he will be most often thought of to play, or the quality which is uniquely his own which occasions his being brought in for interviews for certain types of roles more often than for others.

Over a period of years of professional work it becomes more and more apparent that producers, directors, casting directors and agents all think of us in relatively similar areas. Since they also talk to each other about how excellently we did in a certain role or how miscast we appeared to be in another, it's understandable that a professional image emerges in the minds of people around us. It is important that we read the signs through observing what we're usually called to be interviewed for.

It can save many years of waiting if this awareness can come in the early years of a career. Beginnings can be quicker and progress can be more rapid. There is always time—for those of us who treasure our versatility and ability to play all roles—to "branch out" and "diversify" later into a wider spectrum of roles. Most successful artists have had to go through these "limited category" beginnings even though they deeply desired to be known immediately as versatile and capable in many different areas. Some, after wondering for years why their starts have been so slow and labored, have been confronted with the necessity of finding out their particular niches at later times; have dealt with the necessity; and have finally reached the point, after establishing their talents, where they could diversify more broadly and more often.

The actor can and should seek other people's opinions even before entering the mainstream of professional exposure. Other people's opinions are usually more objective than the actor's own view of what he is right for and what his limitations and advantages make probable or improbable. Continue, of course, to prepare for the broader range of roles into which you can expand later, but at each moment of your career try to recognize with complete objectivity what you can do best at that particular moment. In all probability that's what you'll be hired to do.

THE OFF-CENTER PERSONAL VS. THE SOCIAL SYMMETRICAL

Are you one of those actors who has been so socially cultivated that when you sit or stand you adopt quite symmetrical positions—those usually associated with social propriety? If you are, have you ever noticed that you seldom experience any particular feelings or emotions with any depth in those very centered positions?

Examine your sitting and standing habits. If they're more or less symmetrical—if you're generally quite erect and if your hands and arms generally move in the same manner at the same time as if on the same string from your center, you should consider breaking this "social body" position and movement pattern early. It limits you. Although it may be appropriate for certain characters you may be called upon to play from time to time (perhaps a Social Registerite schooled in etiquette or a self-consciously proper person), it is detrimental to the experiencing of many other characters, and inhibits intensified feeling experiences of many, many kinds.

Try this: Sit erect, first, with your hands and arms in similar positions—in your lap, folded across your chest or stomach, down at your sides; anywhere—then get a good feeling Object in mind. Experience the feelings of that Object to the fullest degree possible in that position.

Then simply lean sideways, perhaps with one hand supporting your head, and extend one leg and bend the other. In other words, remove any symmetrical positioning of the body. Now, feel the heightened ability to experience that same feeling Object that you had in mind before. I'm sure there's a remarkable difference!

Accustom your body to adopting off-center positions whenever possibe—even for characters who might be thought of as more socially oriented, in order to experience feeling depths more fully at all times.

PRACTICE WITH PSYCHOLOGICAL PATTERNS

Seldom, if ever, will you play a role which parallels your own psychological patterns exactly. More often, Stanislavski's comment that "every role is a character role" will apply. One character's personality will have its conditioned rejection experience; another will feel compulsions and obsessions with status and recognition which you don't fully share; another will be intensely involved with revenge-seeking and be unlike you. While all these personalities are a *part* of your life's previous experience, your socialization balance is in most instances different, and the achieving of the differences with ease in approaching all roles requires that you be a student and observer of other lifestyles and behavior patterns as well as your own.

Acting class work should encompass with some regularity the practicing of all kinds of psychological patterns—utilizing the preparation tools, of course, so that you have bases for quick and easy grasp of the bringing of excellent involvement and depth to those many different personalities' experiences.

The more practice you have in experiencing of psychological patterns other than your own, the more organic will be each such performance with which you involve in roles.

If you find yourself in an acting class environment where *no characterization work at all* is involved, I for one would recommend that you consider leaving quickly.

ERADICATING CLICHES AND PERFECTION GOALS AND EXPLORING MOMENTS FOR THEIR ADVENTURES

One of the biggest mistakes an actor can make, or be taught, is that there is *one single way* to do something because of a character's profession, personality, family or social role, etc. This violates the very essence of every character's individual life! Yet there are people who are destined to play long successions of tiny roles such as hotel desk clerks or elevator operators having only one line usually, hotel doormen seen twice and only briefly in scripts, second and third level business functionaries who say "Good morning, sir" as the star passes, etc., simply because they have been taught to play a profession rather than a human being.

241

Such teaching can develop a very limited actor, and usually a very false one.

It's probable that every acting coach of any worth has either his own or someone else's device for teaching actors and actresses to explore moments for their available *adventures* more than for any kind of perfect appropriateness. A good coach should help the actor fall in love with *the unusual, the inventive and unpredictable* ways of doing what he does, both in characters and in his everyday life in order to form the habit more securely.

Truly character-involved impulses are stifled under any standardized concepts. The surface becomes uninteresting and rather procedural for both the actor and the spectator. The legitimate subtext of the character has to be facially "mugged" or "indicated" whenever the body is doing some supposedly important job such as sitting or standing the "right way". Ridiculous as this misapprehension is, it is common in some actors.

Which attracts your attention when you're walking along a sidewalk or sitting in a park—the stiff, perfect effigy of civilization, marching to the drums of timeclocks, appointments and depersonalized social pursuits in general, or the other character who's tossing and catching something, perhaps playing hopscotch on the sidewalk blocks, perhaps weaving or dancing a little, or merely walking with hands doing something like snapping cracker crumbs and throwing them to a waiting pigeon, then waving to the pigeon with a big smile? Certainly one of those latter folks will be more apt to catch and hold your attention more surely. The former, you won't even have noticed. And you wouldn't hire the former to play a role in any form of entertainment which is expected to attract and hold the attention of an audience!

There are many different and fairly well known exercises which are used in classes to cultivate the habits of capturing impulsive moments. Among them is of course the *Private Moment* group of exercises, wherein the actor finds that when he is doing something in privacy he does so many more little parts of that something than would occur to him in its public version. He tends to find so many little impulsive things—non-objective things which are not part of the common understanding about such a moment but are nevertheless inspired by it—when it's expe-

242

rienced in a more private manner. Again, as mentioned earlier, this is one of the values of always working in a manner that includes a sense of "privacy in public".

In my own teaching I use a habit-forming exercise called, simply, *Find A Different Way*. Through improvising with the many different—rather than usual—ways of sitting, standing, walking, handling props, opening and closing doors, etc., actors are able to discover the little adventures available in separate moments. Once tried, this manner of working so appeals to actors that it can become habit very quickly.

The quotation attributed to Sir Laurence Olivier mentioned earlier, to the effect that one of the actor's prime responsibilities is to keep the audience awake, is an apt one. The actor whose every moment and position is predictable and dull, even though precisely "right" for a certain character type, isn't going to be able to do that. But the actor who brings something even just a little bit different or perhaps quite different to each moment will certainly hold the audience's delighted attention.

For the actor, every moment can become an adventure in some way. The picking up of a phone, the manner of holding it, the sitting to talk, the body use during the conversation and finally the putting down of the phone—each part of this simple moment offers its own adventure opportunity if the actor seeks it out.

There is no greater boon to *continuous relaxation*, by the way, than this manner of courting the different instead of the perfect as dictated by any accepted standards of behavior. It is impossible to apply any standards or limits on things that are simply different from the norms. There is no social judgment possible or even triggered in the mind of the observer when something is done in a manner that proclaims the character as its own social arbiter and indicates that the actor inside the character has the freedom to use himself in a self-determined and self-confident manner.

If a reader wonders how all this could apply to any of those characters which are determined by writers to be socially very precise, consider how much more interesting they could become, too, if their *efforts at being very precise* are used to constitute their "different ways". Here's an example:

One (dull) actor might simply lift his teacup in the right,

accepted manner for lifting teacups in a drawing room scene.

Another, conscious of the value of *Finding a Different Way*, looks down at the cup on the table; wipes an imaginary smudge off his hand; sneakily turns the cup around a little so it can be lifted in the "right, accepted" manner; prissily crooks his little finger just so; lifts the cup in an absolute straight line with great self-consciousness; adjusts his body a bit to be in the "idealized" tea-drinking position; sips ever so delicately; then makes sure that in setting the cup down it is tilted just a little askew in the saucer, so must be set carefully into its depression; then perhaps afterward even pats it for at last aiding his *efforts* at being precise. In other words, even for such a character some amount of "Finding a Different Way" can be a nice addition toward making the character far more interesting for the observer.

In my classes we occasionally devote an entire class session to practicing "finding a different way" to do all sorts of things for which there are standard, dull and boring manners of doing them.

In a first session I sometimes have individuals go into the workspace and follow commands to "Sit on the sofa", "Walk to the door", "Open the door", "Close the door", "Lie on the sofa", etc., while doing everything in a "different" way.

Later in the same session it's productive to have a male and a female go through a simple "Hi, honey, I'm home!" moment.... with different manners (for the homecomer) of opening the door, coming in, shutting the door, meeting the spouse and having some greeting contact in a very different way, and different manners (for the one who's home) of coming from a kitchen or other room, crossing the floor and eventually greeting the spouse in some way that is unique and different too.

The important product of this kind of exploration in acting classes is that actors quickly observe that the simplest physical moments can be removed from dull and ordinary "rightness" and, in the process of accomplishing this, can become small adventures of and by themselves to stimulate the actor's experiencing of their uniquely different and more personal-feeling moments.

Most actors enjoy the freedom and spontaneity which this kind of exploring brings, and after a session or two of finding those pleasures continue to "find a different way" after that!

THE USE OF DIFFERENT FEELINGS TO ENHANCE EMOTIONAL MOMENTS

Stanislavski, on that chart that he diagrammed and gave to Stella Adler in Paris, included another manner of eradicating cliches— the use of *other feelings* to portray emotion. It can be highly effective.

You might find, for example, that laughing actually helps you suffer something more deeply. You might discover that becoming suddenly quiet and gently sad helps you bring that moment that could be only *half* experienced in some cliche manner as your character says "I'm so happy."

You might look for the possibility of using this *different feeling* approach on occasion also.

STYLES OF ACTING

Coaches of the persuasion that a conscious technique such as ours can serve *all* areas of actors' needs occasionally hear remarks such as "The method isn't any good when *style* is involved." It's a not uncommon misapprehension. I've learned to ask "What method are you talking about?" It usually evolves that the speaker isn't even half aware of how the system elements taught by Stanislavski and the systematized approaches which have come along since can be used in all the many distinctly different styles.

Style is defined by Webster's Dictionary as "Characteristic manner of expression in any art, period, etc.". The problem with solely intuitive actors and actresses as they approach roles requiring specific styles is that they have mostly worked in *only their own* style, and their own "characteristic manners of expression" aren't all that elastic that they can bend toward any *different* styles. Further, even in their own specialized work, what they bring over and above or under or behind the surface is usually negligible at best, except for perhaps charismatic personality, if they are not also employing some methodology for the creating of a character.

The systems associated with "the Stanislavski Method" don't

pretend to teach how people moved in 1900 or 1488 or any other year; how costumes should be handled; the sentiments of the time; the characteristic pastimes; the modes of speech; etc. The actor should recognize that a role-preparation system is an approach to building roles which must be used *side by side with* a knowledge of periods, costumes, customs, characteristic movement and prop-handling, wigs, makeup, social relations and the sentiments of the languages used in periods which were different from our own contemporary phrases and contractions.

Also, some Method-derivative systems for preparing roles such as my own do include steps to remind the actor of the necessity of researching the many elements of style in the earlier phase of breaking down roles. The *"Six Questions"* step, embodying research and inspiration reminders as it does, should point the actor preparing a "style" role in the right direction and take him even more deeply into such research through its thoroughness than he might be able to go without those evocative questions to lead him.

In any event, the study of different periods, different peoples, different countries and their customs, different religions and their dogmas, etc., can never be considered complete. It should be continous *in addition to* preparing roles that have their personality cores.

It is regrettable that, since acting study isn't possible twenty-four hours a day, every day, not much classwork time is devoted to the study of style, periods, etc., except in some classes specifically devoted to the study of Shakespeare and the other classics. As a result, some actors are satisfied when they find ultimate clarity and depth of involvement in emotional characterization and fail to venture forward into a sufficient amount of research into the *styles* often required for their characters' fullest and truest experience.

There are actors I know who do continue their private research and careful observation of the "style" elements in both written and performed works. Some even gather private reference files of such research for its time-saving benefit at those future moments when such research is needed. Always in the mind of such an actor is the foreknowledge that such information and ability to

246

use it constructively may be asked and expected of him at some later time, perhaps on a few moments' notice. When such a moment comes unexpectedly there may not be enough time for a sufficient amount of "cramming" research.

Imagine the poor actor who suddenly gets a call to go to an interview the very next morning for the type of emotional role he is anxious to play, and is ready for otherwise, but is told in the call that the audition will require some knowledge of the style involved in that particular work. Of course he'll go to the audition, but the director and producer will look more closely at the qualifications of the actor who not only brings the emotional facets of the role but also has a knowledge of and proficiency with the style of the period.

We're discussing here not only the styles of Moliere farce or Greek tragedy or Shakespeare, however. There is style involved in the role of a Social Registerite, a nun, a priest, a ballerina, a bricklayer, a Nebraska farmer or any other contemporary calling, profession or lifestyle, and that style is often quite separate and apart from the analysis of the inner character and preparation of tools.

The Stanislavski System and most other systems possessing any definitive methodology can and do work with *all* styles. The actor must simply research any style appropriate or required for his character and study the use of that style *in addition to* his preparing of the inner character!

THE COMIC SENSE

Another *style* which can utilize systematic approach if desired but which requires some extracurricular work in other areas also is *comedy*. It's a very broad field, involving several types of public performances.

There is *Situation Comedy*; most television series are of this type, wherein there are certain basic comedy requirements for all characters, such as "*takes*"; comfort with *facing the audience or the camera lens* while delivering lines to other characters; *exaggerated attitudes* so that the comic collisions can occur between characters more often; and *timing*. Beyond these basics little more is required of situation comedy performers except, to begin with,

247

a personality which *can be* amusing if the writers supply the right material with which it can be amusing. Situation comedy basically depends upon comic situations.

There is *Character Comedy*, wherein the character is so amusingly prepared and brought, all by itself, that even if it should just walk into a room, without lines even, it's amusing. There are usually one or two fine character comedy performers in each television "sitcom". They help sustain the series when the writing falters.

Naturally the character comedy player must also know takes; the advantages (and requirements often) of facing the audience or the camera with many of his lines and reactions; exaggerated attitudes; and timing. Over and above those rudiments, the character comedy player also has to be able to *build the comic character*. Only occasionally can he simply clown his way through on his own unique talents to such a degree that he doesn't need anything else.

There is also *Farce*. Again, all the elements of the other "sitcom" approaches apply in this type of comedy. However, in addition, for ideal playing of farce the farce player must understand which end of the farcical situation he's on. It's the nature of farce, and its distinction from other comedy forms, that there must always be *one character in an impossible situation* and *other characters and conditions complicating his situation further* all the time. The farce player must recognize which category his character falls into of the aforementioned two, then employ all the usually oversize experiencing of that character's moments which are ideal for his category. This "one side of the fence" aspect is the prime characteristic of farce and the dilemnas and outrageous complications that are heaped upon the one in the impossible situation are what create its comedy for the spectator.

In addition to these styles of comedy most often seen in films, television and theatre there is the *Standup Comedy* style also. There is little definition possible for this, except that, whatever the comedian or comedienne does amusingly determines his or her own style, and probably no one else could duplicate its unique presentation.

The "Standup" has his own routines and his unique manners

248

of working, usually alone in a spotlight, before an audience. If they're good, these highly paid performers should be role models of sorts for comedy players who work mostly in the first three categories named. The "Standup" faces front with most of his lines; he does "takes"; he develops timing; and his material's success usually depends on a definite attitude being clearly exaggerated. The basics of the Sitcom Player, the Character Comedy Player and the Farceur must be consummately perfected by the Standup, simply because there is no one else with him and no writer's situation to carry the comic continuity in any moment if he falters!

Of course it's embarrassing to watch some fine dramatic actor attempt comedy if he doesn't possess any comic sense or perhaps doesn't realize that he has a perfectly good one that he hasn't learned how to bring with any assurance to a role. Some basically dramatic actors are so afraid to try comedy that they avoid it altogether, limiting themselves by avoiding it and missing out on professional opportunities they might carry off stunningly otherwise.

I've heard that Lucille Ball, in a discussion of comedy some years ago, stated that "Comedy is something that if you ain't got you ain't gonna get." While it's true that the comic sense can't be taught, still some of the ingredients can be extrapolated from the whole and worked on for possible development in classes.

Certainly, *takes* can be practiced if the primarily dramatic actor or actress isn't too embarrassed to "mug", which is part of any good take of the garden variety. There are the other takes, even simpler and closer to home, which are those such as comedian Jack Benny used to use and which Johnny Carson and Bob Hope have always used, which involve simply looking at the audience or camera with almost no expression but still just enough to indicate an attitude or reaction. It behooves any actor who would like comic role opportunities to become used to feeling a little silly and ridiculous, if they have to, in order to learn to do "takes" easily and effectively.

The *facing front* with lines or with thinking moments or reactions, also required for both film and theatre where comedy is concerned, is the hardest item for dramatic actors to even practice with any comfort, much less remember to use when reading for comic roles or performing them. The feeling of essentially "announcing" their thoughts or lines to other characters is usually quite foreign to them and they may resist it until that day when a director forces them to do it and they discover then, under duress at first, the silly pleasure sensations it brings.

I've often employed plain old *comic melodrama* style work to sneak the facing front into otherwise dramatic players' development toward doing comedy. In that style, usually comic to us in the present time but taken very seriously when it was popular, there are so many of those "aside" moments directed toward the audience when the character is truly itself—free to honestly show and share its colors, its thoughts, its explaining of what it's going through, etc. I point out to my people that the *other* moments in such melodrama, when the character is working directly with other characters, are generally the more false ones. It usually works, and it usually helps some of the exclusively dramatic actors overcome their fears of trying the "face front". They probably consider this *melodrama* requisite to be only a *style* (which it is) while they think and fear that all aspects of *comedy* are more a *gift* which they are sure they don't possess.

The *exaggerated attitudes* of comedy can either be brought by deciding them and "playing" them ridiculously without any character preparation tools of any sort, or in other cases the same attitudes in exaggerated levels can be achieved by the player who has some comic sense enabling him to form the tools of characterization into somewhat "petty" or in any event fairly extreme versions so they can appear quite ridiculous. If tools are to be used in preparation then that same ridiculousness, that pettiness, that outrageousness and silliness should be built into all the preparation items from the top down.

The actor who wants to develop comedy must explore and find which approach works best for him—preparing with or without the preparation tools.

Comedy timing is perhaps an unfortunate title for that other requisite for good comedy, since it implies some secret art or gift that one either does or doesn't possess.

Timing of a comic variety will occur all by itself if the actor

250

consistently *does takes* instead of jumping right back with dialogue or outgoing action of some kind. In fact, timing is not often the domain of the person who is speaking at the moment. It is the result of the next speaker's stopping to do a "take" (which may be amusing on its own) which tells the viewer that the other person who has just said something is crazy, absurd, disgusting, stupid, shocking or something else before he responds!

When actors can accept this easy relief from the responsibility implied by that word "timing" there is much less hesitation to take the moments to do "takes" on the other characters and, via those "take" moments, easily create good comedy timing!

The sum total of all the basic ingredients of good comedy mentioned in these paragraphs is that *an exaggerated attitude* will insure the comic collision with other equally definite attitudes and, even in advance, the audience is allowed to share the dynamic secret that those collisions will occur *because* of those attitudes…. The *takes* any good, ridiculously exaggerated attitude all by itself will produce will make not only the actor's own character amusing because of its offended sensibilities; they will also make the other character's last moment amusing as well (whether it was all that funny or not), simply because it caused a "take" on the other character's part…. And the *facing front* as often as possible can point up your own ridiculousness and what's behind it that the audience enjoys sharing; it also will often put your body in a position to become the secret foil for other characters' "takes" behind your back that will again make you more comic because of the unspoken comments being made about you!

It's a neat package—the result of combining these three main aspects of good comedy playing, and one which will enable you to do comedy whether you think you're a natural comedian or not. Work on these separate areas sufficiently and you may well surprise yourself with the discovering of a comic "gift" that you didn't think you had.

The *Character Comedy* player might profit from some suggested items on a *Comic Character Checklist* given me by the late Chico Marx, of the famous Marx Brothers, when we were preparing a production of "*The Fifth Season*" for a summer tour some years

251

ago. Thinking it over later, I realized that the Marx Brothers must have used most of these items to construct those zany characterizations which made them, and kept them, one of the most famous comedy groups in the entertainment world's history.

I'm happy to pass the list along to you in case part or all of it appeals to you:

A COMIC CHARACTER CHECKLIST
1. A ridiculously exaggerated attitude....
2. A special walk, either ridiculously right for your character or ridiculously out of place....
3. A special speech or dialect.... Try the one that's most appropriate, but don't overlook the comic possibilities of one that's out of place....
4. A special hairstyle....
5. One piece of special wardrobe.... Again, either to make your character more obvious or to be ridiculously out of place....
6. One recurring mannerism or habit.... to constitute an available "running gag" as it recurs without warning from time to time....
7. A special hand prop, or more than one.... if they don't get in the way or complicate moments that would be funnier without them.

That's the checklist. And if the aficionados of those old Marx Brothers films stop to consider each of the brothers' crazy characters they'll observe that this list may very well have been the inspiration for all the ridiculous items that made each of the Marxes so hilariously funny.

Having used this checklist on several occasions in my classes to help otherwise dramatic actors cross the bridge of fear into at least trying comedy characters with some hope of desirable result, I recall one class vividly.

Even though all class members had been warned that the next session would be Character Comedy, and all class members had been provided with the foregoing checklist, many did little or no preparation at home, hoping the checklist would in class at the last moment bring them all the inspiration they'd need.

One fellow—who was a fine dramatic actor who had always been afraid to try comedy, had done his homework.... and it paid off for him! He had used the checklist, item by item. He brought from home a pocketful of sunglasses, a toothpick, two different changes of shirts and pants from what he wore to the class, a number of other things which I've forgotten, and then proceeded to keep the rest of the class in stitches three times during the evening by having a complete plan for each of his three characters and providing all the checklist inspirations, obviously practiced ahead of time and ready, along with very close to professional level "routines" for each.

He hadn't known for sure it would all work, he said afterward, but he was so overjoyed with his success and the class members' responses during the evening that he remained in the studio for some time after the class ended, just sitting in a dazed state and musing at the reexperiencing of his moments of triumph over the demon Comedy. He wasn't sure he hadn't "cheated" by using the Comic Character Checklist because he'd been afraid of failing in an area he hadn't thought could ever work for him. I reminded him that that had been why I gave out the Checklist ahead of time. I'm sure he's used it since, because he began to be cast in comedy roles occasionally after that.

Do a little "cheating" yourself with the Checklist, and see the results!

Section VI

Adapting an Acting System to Your Individual Needs

Chapter Twelve

Variations And Adaptations of Individual Tools' Use

After this lengthy review of the manner in which I personally teach *The Method As A System*, you must still be aware that this system or any other system—and any of the parts, separately—can certainly be tailored a little here and there to fit the particular needs of different actors and actresses whose professional needs and psychological makeups vary and whose life study aptitudes and directions vary even more. This individual tailoring should not to any great degree reduce the over-all effectiveness of the whole or any individual item.

No two actors' responses are ideally triggered by the same stimuli. Different psychologies have their differing response triggers, as do the forms and manners of use of systems available for their use in evoking their uniquely personal forms of those desired responses. The thought and feeling spectrums of the many different psychologies are determined by the phenomenon mentioned often herein ... *conditioned response*. What works ideally for one actor in a certain manner may not achieve that same desired result for others with different responses.

Also, all actors and actresses who use any systematic approaches for preparing roles and performing them know that those systems

257

sometimes require special adaptations of certain of their parts to best serve the needs of many different kinds of characterizations, styles and particular entertainment fields.

What you *can* do with this system or any other system that works has little to do with what you *will* do with it, simply because your own life and career paths will take you in different directions and into different circumstances from others who are using the same system.

OBJECTS—HOW THEY WORK WITH OTHER APPROACHES

Certainly, if the actor has not previously worked with "Objects". *their* values should be tested *in addition to* whatever system or approach the actor has adopted and uses.

For the actor who feels that an *Action* or *Intention* serves ideally in whatever phase of preparation and use—the life personality or the current period concern (the unit) or the individual moment (the beat), the Object, if added as the cause for the action can supply so much more personal experience enriching for both the character and the actor. The Object can be formed to add the negatives which cause positive attempts at action; it can supply the experience behind the action; it can bring into sharp focus the problem and the conditioned response which determines its impact upon the character.

The Object need not be viewed by the Action or Intention actor as an entirely different approach. It can simply be added, and its addition—as Stanislavski observed so late in his own life—can supply what has preiously been felt by so many actors to be "the missing link".

For those who customarily opt for *"positive goal" objectives* the Object is almost imperative, and it should certainly be used in such cases to supply the negative force which makes the positive goal so urgently desirable. Since the "positive goal" in character-ization suggests action aimed at achieving that goal so inescapably, the Object's addition, in its negative force aspect, can supply those personal experiencing stimuli which may otherwise be missed on occasion by this actor.

Even for the actor who has gone through all that searching, trying, failing and occasionally succeeding with the finding of

Emotional Memory, Affective Memory or Emotional Recall moments which are at least moderately successful when evoked and which have encouraged the actor to depend on them for desired results, the Object has proved valuable. The "key" or "trigger" thought, as it is called by some who use this device, can be so much more dependably effective if it is turned into an "object" wording. While, as previously stated, I personally disapprove of the use of this approach especially, those who do depend upon it should test the turning of that "key" or "trigger" image or experience thought into an Object. It can be an important catalyst!

Even for the actor who *abjures the use of any and all technique*, preferring to work in a strictly "intuitive" manner at all times, there are those moments of roles which demand a more solid foundation in selected truths. At least in those moments, even if in no others, Objects can supply those far more solid foundations and bring more meaningful truths!

OTHER SEPARATE ITEMS CAN SIMPLY BE ADDED

There are few items described herein and adopted by me as important parts of the System as I personally teach it which can't simply be adopted as additional tools to add to whatever approach the actor may opt to use. The "Six Questions" applies to *all* roles with equal effectiveness. The "Obstacle", already used in some form, if not this, in other standard approaches, is available to work easily with any system approach. The "Neurosis-Provoking Moment" of my own devising is adaptable to whatever characterization base forming process the actor may be currently using. The "Character Image", "Motive Center" and "Imaginary Surroundings Characters" approaches can certainly be utilized on occasion by actors, regardless of the emotional preparation approach they're currently using. All the items described in the Early and Later Rehearsal Period work can be added to any approach, also.

Actors who have studied with me who have later become directors of theatre, film and television (as well as remaining fine actors) have told me that some of these items, individually, have been easy to convey to actors for the curing of problems, the bringing of extra colors or enriching characterization depths.

259

SHORTCUTS FOR LAST-MINUTE, RUSHED SITUATIONS

There are times when, hired for a role at a late moment just prior to commencing rehearsals for a theatre work or just before commencing shooting on a film, there simply isn't a lot of time for the use of everything this or any system provides for the preparation processes. It happens to all actors sooner or later.

There are many actors who, after years of developing instant call on deep feelings and quick perception of personality types and their behavior patterns, as well as quick grasp of the "tools" which help them personally to bring such personalities with all their colors and depth, can rapidly form a moving Life Object and its Vague Super Objective and immediately proceed to whatever other tools they feel they need for bringing their characters to life so rapidly.

In such rushed situations many actors might need only those two "top tools" to form their characters' personalities and the breaking down of the script into separate Beats.

In some cases, when the actor's personality and customary role category are the reason for such last-minute, hurried casting it is often sufficient for the actor to simply and quickly prepare the Beats with good Objects. (Some actors fall into this "single role type" mold after some period of professional work. They are in fact the ones usually brought in at the last minute, simply because they are "so right" for what is needed.)

PERSONALITY ACTING AS IN TELEVISION SERIES

The casting of dramatic television series roles is so drawn out and is "supervised" by so many people—all attempting to determine whether this or that actor is "exactly right" for each role—that, once cast in a television series role, the actor is wise to avoid any extreme characterization. His personality is "exactly right" as it is, without characterization. He must adopt the stance that he "is" the character. If the series is successful, and if it returns season after season, he will have successfully brought the character without "top tools" use of any kind.

Many of my people have been cast in series, and many of those series have returned year after year for sometimes eight or nine years. I've been told by some of these folks that the only thing they do in breaking down the episodes' scripts is to form the best Objects they can for the Beats; that it helps bring more concentrated and effective work and that it is invaluable in maintaining continuity when part of one Beat is shot on location and the remaining part of the Beat is shot on a studio sound stage sometime later.

Bottom line for them, however, remains that what is desired by their productions is basically "personality acting"—acting themselves, rather than bringing elaborately constructed character types of any kinds.

For them, the main gratifications obtained from any system tools are the depths and continuities available in just Objects.

THE CHARACTER ACTOR'S INSPIRATION GARDEN

Those who become recognized and sought after Character Actors will probably, like some others of the same category, want to keep a checklist in their pocket which includes not only the items listed in this book but all the items which they've tried and liked out of all the other books as well!

For this actor, each role offers the opportunity to use so many ideas, inspirations, preparation approaches, etc.! That there should always be that "core", or "spine of the character" as Stanislavski called it, is not debatable. It should always be there for a good, meaningful character role. But, beyond that personality core and meaningful preparation of the emotional aspects, there are so many, many other possibilities, and the actor who is a "Character Actor" primarily needs to explore as many of those devices and inspiration sources as he can discover. At some point in the future each or all can be valuable!

MANY ACTORS ALSO DIRECT!

Directors (which many actors become after observing that, in the end, the actor's work is subject to good or bad direction!) are in that position which requires them to direct actors who use many, many different acting approaches.

Regardless of his own preferred techniques and approaches, he must find the manners of communicating what he wants to actors who don't share his terminologies. The director needs to find, and keep handy for use in communicating with all those other actors, quick solutions to problems and quick and effective manners of suggesting changes and additions.

Most systems, including this one, can have their separate items adapted into "layman's language" so that the desired effect can be communicated to those actors who speak those "foreign languages" of acting study orientations of all kinds.

It's easy, for instance, for a director who appreciates the Object, to ask an actor to "Make your own problem worse," or "Keep thinking of what it's doing to you," or something of the sort, to guide the heavy-handed "action"-taker into a more personal experiencing moment.

It's equally easy to find phrases to remind actors of any character realities they've overlooked, or to suggest that they simply "agitate their feelings" a bit more.

The director's problem in adapting any system tools to his purposes, is simply the finding of the words that bridge those terminology gaps that methodologies do create.

CAREER-REQUIRED ADAPTATIONS

Some of you will have successful dramatic acting careers and perhaps still never play a role substantially different from your own psychological patterns. You will find that if starring roles come with some regularity they will seem to be of the same kind always. Type casting does set in very quickly, certainly more in film than in theatre but often in both.

If you fall into this category as your career develops, you won't have ideal time between roles that follow each other almost immediately, one after another, for elaborate breaking down of scripts, researching if and to the extent desired, lengthy role preparation or much exploration for added colors. Hopefully, in your case, the habits you've developed in acting classes will be firmly established and always ready on call; the quick and easy touching of your own emotional resources, developed in all those acting classes, will help you bring excitement to roles when time is too short for full preparation; and you'll grow through continuing and regular work.

You may use the system in an internalized form to at least afford you clarity and depth without being evident in a highly creative surface result—which is appropriate for many of the standard film roles you may be getting. Or you may use the system to be always creative and exciting within whatever range others in charge will allow you to be. In either event, you may still be substantially playing yourself, figuratively speaking, at all times, because you have certain unique qualities that are sought by producers and directors who would not think of casting you in other types of roles.

Form your creative habits well, before this single dimensioned career of self-playing starts rolling, so you'll be allowed freedom to be creative when you want to be, even if essentially playing yourself as well.

One of our leading actors, possessing all those personal qualities that often lead to this kind of career, spent years developing his talents, then found himself being cast in starring roles most often because of his personal appeal and charisma, eventually said in an interview "All they want is my blond hair and blue eyes!" It has so often come to that for many, so if you discover that you've been channeled into a career that is mostly the playing of yourself you should still try to bring the most interesting colors possible to your moments as you continue to deposit large salaries in the bank. The day will surely arrive, as it has for the aforementioned actor and others like him, when you will once more have the opportunity to work in the manner you planned from the beginning. It's a privilege which regrettably doesn't come for some actors until long established stardom buys them the right.

Also, there is a long list of stars in today's film, television and theatre worlds who essentially play themselves but who have from the start insisted on being allowed to be creative every step along the way and who win awards simply because they always use a system of approach to bring the most interesting work out of those places in themselves where Michael Chekhov said "the higher self" resides.

I want to point out that when this happens—this top magnitude stardom resulting from your using your creativity at the same time as basically playing yourself because it's demanded, you've established a new style all your own; a style which will always be allowed to function right alongside your playing of yourself. Otherwise you wouldn't have become a star that way in the first place!

A small consolation: This "playing yourself" area does often or at least occasionally offer some amount of variation in the types of characters, and the subtle variations will require at least a little preparation, perhaps, to bring a special facet of your own or a very similar personality. Be grateful when even these opportunities surface.

Of course there are some who will be trapped in the "playing themself" category who will, if they're not careful, find themselves reduced to being faces and bodies and having few opportunities to bring much of anything else. When this is allowed to happen— ususally as a result of the actors' own impressionable gullibility in the face of friends', agents', managers', producers' and directors' advice and counselling—or simply laziness and ego-polishing on the actors' part, those actors will have "made their own bed" and must lie in them forever, unfortunately. It's already too late then to ever dare creative work.

Such an actor could, if sufficiently caring by that time, at least employ a system, or part of a system, to plan the deepest possible involvements for characters and himself. He probably won't, though, since this kind of career usually leads to a lot of fan mail that demands a lot of signing (even though several secretaries write the letters); personal appearances demand even more time; the many meetings with business managers, personal managers, press agents, accountants, stock brokers, press interviewers and photographers consume still more; gym workouts to stay in shape (because that top shape is his career) and probably a continuous round of parties (while more dedicated actors are at home preparing roles conscientiously) consume what's left; and those by then "boring hours at the factory" (the time still spent on film sets) absolutely destroy any chances for a meaningful social life. All together, these activities offer a marvelous package of excuses for not doing any constructive work on roles!

Some of you will carve out *careers based on playing highly creative roles*, probably in theatre first, then in film, television and theatre combined. For you, the system you use is a tremendous help in preparing those always varied and always excitingly different roles which come your way because you've sought them from the start. *You* probably stand a better chance at eventual awards in all fields because your use of yourself will have freer rein and attract attention every time you work. Your fan mail will probably begin coming much later, if ever, but your starring billing will be in just as large letters, for brilliance rather than for sex appeal or charm.

You too can make large amounts of money in your profession, and you'll probably live a happier life in the long run than any of your "playing themself" friends because of the creative opportunities which loom around every corner once you establish your insistence on those kinds of roles as your only interest.

When you insist on time to prepare roles for added excitements you'll probably be given it, because you'll be recognized as making it count toward making your own roles and productions as well more effective. When you insist on reading all scripts and making all the decisions which others—agents and managers primarily—would like to make for you, you'll get what you want.

When your talents and the excitements you bring in roles are universally recognized everyone will want you to describe the approaches you use. Be circumspect enough to resist all those opportunities to discuss your homework. The public wants to believe that your excitements are pure "magic", not the hard work which has brought those colors for which you'll become known. To you in this far more self-determining category, the system you use can prove the greatest possible contributor to each creative result, as it has for so many others in your category.... but the less the public knows about your approaches and becomes distracted by trying to detect them in your roles, the better.

Some of you will do *many fine supporting roles* in film, television and theatre but perhaps never make it to top stardom in any of those fields. You have the opportunity to bring excitements to each and every role. You are free to become known for bringing *extra dimensions* to all of those mostly "character" roles through the systematic approach you use. Those extra dimensions will often depend upon your consciously seeking all the inspirations you can utilize to create them.

In your category it's regrettable, of course, that you'll often be cast

265

quite late along the casting treadmill, whether it's for major theatre productions or for films. If it's for theatre you may well be cast the day before rehearsals begin, because the production has held out for someone else who at the last moment has decided they can't accept the role. If it's a film role, the same applies. You'll be among some of the last cast, for the same reason.

Even so, the system you've learned can help you prepare at a pace that allows you time for line study afterward so you can bring, even sometimes overnight, not only the lines (which are all some people are prepared to bring under such rushed circumstances) but also a decent number of your usual "extras" to those first days on the film set or those first days of theatre rehearsals.

Those of you who choose *theatre* as your life careers, whether there may or may not be those occasional acceptings of film roles and then quick returns to Broadway or other large stages at some points, will of course have *much more time* for preparation, exploration and growth in roles. But sometimes, just because of that extra time, the theatre actor comes to take too much for granted and occasionally puts off preparation and exploration, feeling there will be more time than it turns out later there is.

In theatre you'll experience the system helping you project even subtle emotional shadings before large audiences through the psycho-physical processes of sensory and simile-involving tools (such as the Creative Psychological Objectives, perhaps). There need be no fear of being too large for the camera closeup— except that you especially will need to be conscious of this possibility in those few film roles you accept, since you'll be so accustomed to playing to those more distant balcony folks. You find much joy in the immediacy of your live audience's responses. When your work is especially excellent, that's a large part of theatre's excitement.

Also, you'll encounter less type-casting in theatre, since the distance between the actor and his audience allows makeup to convincingly alter appearance so that the potential range of character types, ages and physicalities for which a systematic approach can help in preparation is far wider.

An added pleasure available for theatre folk who use a systematic approach is that, even though they remain subject to the director's and others' approval in all respects, their wardrobe, makeup, hairstyle, props and other items involved for their characters are at least to a degree more open to the actors' suggestions and inspirations, and in the blocking of scenes the actors are allowed to contribute more than they can when there are the limits of film's "cameo" settings, camera angles and lighting to be considered.

The one major distinction which the actor accustomed to theatre work discovers in his first film role is that the subtle shadings which were necessarily sacrificed in theatre for the sake of projection and larger movement are more possible, and in fact demanded, in closeup and medium shots in film. Many actors who have chosen film careers over theatre roles are attracted by this always available "living presence" level of experiencing, appreciating the freedom to totally believe and simply "be" that it provides.

Any debate about which is more satisfying for the actor in career terms is pointless, however. Anyone who rises through their brilliance, whether they start in theatre or start in film, will certainly receive bids to play important roles in the other later. If it is indeed their brilliance which has attracted those later offers from the other field, then in all probability they will also have the quick observation and intelligence to know how to adapt their working style to the new arena.

On the other hand, if it is simply the *personality* of one who begins in film and becomes accustomed to the simpler, less projected level of performing which that medium allows, and there is a lack of knowledge of what theatre roles require of the instrument, chances are that the first outing on a large stage will be an unhappy education.

The examples of such crossover unhappinesses could fill a book. One of our finest actresses, after rapid rise on Broadway, was cast in a role opposite John Wayne. Those stylized mannerisms which had worked so stunningly for her on Broadway were not only too large for the camera but, when juxtaposed to John Wayne's earthy, so simple style, caused the actress an acutely embarrassing experience. When she dared return to films some time later she had learned to adapt her work more appropriately to the different medium.

Another actress, crossing the continent in the other direction to do her first Broadway role after years as a film star, was so criticized by the top critics that she has never considered trying again. (One critic wrote that, although I don't remember the exact words, her most impressive contribution to the performance was in looking down as she stepped offstage to make sure that she didn't trip!)

Another leading actress who in theatre habitually did much hand-fluttering in roles, after one major film role in which it was noted but not strongly criticized, later was brought back to Hollywood because of her brilliance in other respects to play a starring role under an English director who, in their first meeting to discuss the role, asked "Shall you try to be more conservative with your hands, or shall we try handcuffs?" She too has now learned the different manner of working and in a more recent role received an Academy Award nomination.

Some readers may wind up in *comedy* careers. A few will be able to alternate comic and dramatic roles, but those who do wind up in exclusively comedy need have no fear of being unemployed for too long periods at a time. There is apparently always a large number of diverting "sitcoms" and other theatre and film comedies of all kinds. For you there are those two choices as to how you work most effectively. Either you must work *solely with your own comic sense* or you must learn—even more securely than dramatic actors, by the way—how to *adapt the tools of your system* to create the desirable comic results. There are comedians who do use "tools" in creating their comic characters and who have won Academy Awards, Tony's, Emmy's and other awards through their consciously constructed comic roles, but there are also those comedy stars and supporting players who are thoroughly trained in system elements but who use systematic approaches only for dramatic roles and for comedy rely almost exclusively on their native comic sense and little else beside inspiration and invention. Some of those of the latter inclination have found that comic inspirations and extra colors simply cascade into their well prepared instruments because of all the serious work done in classes long ago.

I for one am convinced that this system, like many others,

applies excitingly for *all* actors and *all* roles, but it still requires the natural resources of the actor to learn it well first and then use it well in all situations later. If you have a good analytic mind and all the desirable aspects of talent, plus a good basis in systematic preparation of roles, you can be outstanding.

But there are still more things you will need. Ideally, they include a good and sensitized voice; speech that is intelligible and variable as emotions play on it; a developed knowledge of movement of all kinds and a body which will obey your commands in the use of it; an active imagination not limited by cultural restrictions; a craving for and intense love of meaningful involvement; a knowledge of history, styles, social forms, languages and dialects of different times and places; the ability to apply yourself with dedication and diligence; the will to go on when huge obstacles loom before you in the pursuit of the ever-changing horizons which stretch before you in your career; the ability to accept those things about yourself which can't be bettered; the wisdom to tailor even those things when possible into productive uniquenesses in your professional work; the ability to discern your own outstanding assets and their most productive application; and, in the end, the taste and judgment which, after all else, will be necessary to achieve success at each step along the way.

In this final moment of the book, a word about *talent*. It should come *first* in the actor, but it belongs *last*—right here in this final moment—in this kind of discussion.

Webster and other dictionaries define talent, variously, as "a particular, often creative or artistic, aptitude"; "the ability to apply oneself diligently", and many other quite different things. However, since aptitudes can be developed, and the ability to apply oneself diligently can be cultivated, the seeds of what is called talent are less important, I feel, than the manner of nursing them into life and growth until they burst forth into full bloom.

I recommend *The Method As A System* for that purpose. And.... good luck! I almost forgot, you'll need that too!

INDEX

270